THE MIDAS FLESH

VOLUME ONE

W9-CUH-174

BOOM! BOX™

THE MIDAS FLESH Volume One, December 2014. Published by
BOOM! Box, a division of Boom Entertainment, Inc. The Midas Flesh is ™
& © 2014 Boom Entertainment, Inc. Originally published in single magazine
form as THE MIDAS FLESH No. 1-4. ™ & © 2013, 2014 Boom
Entertainment, Inc. All rights reserved. BOOM! Box™ and the BOOM! Box
logo are trademarks of Boom Entertainment, Inc., registered in various
countries and categories. All characters, events, and institutions depicted
herein are fictional. Any similarity between any of the names, characters,
persons, events, and/or institutions in this publication to actual names,
characters, and persons, whether living or dead, events, and/or institutions
is unintended and purely coincidental. BOOM! Box does not read or accept
unsolicited submissions of ideas, stories, or artwork.

A catalog record of this book is available from OCLC and from the BOOM!
Studios website, www.boom-studios.com, on the Librarians Page.

BOOM! Studios, 5670 Wilshire Boulevard, Suite 450, Los Angeles, CA
90036-5679. Printed in China. First Printing.

ISBN: 978-1-60886-455-3, eISBN: 978-1-61398-309-6

BOOM! BOX™

ROSS RICHIE CEO & Founder
MARK SMYLIE Founder of Archaia
MATT GAGNON Editor-in-Chief
FILIP SABLIK President of Publishing & Marketing
STEPHEN CHRISTY President of Development
LANCE KREITER VP of Licensing & Merchandising
PHIL BARBARO VP of Finance
BRYCE CARLSON Managing Editor
MEL CAYLO Marketing Manager
SCOTT NEWMAN Production Design Manager
IRENE BRADISH Operations Manager
CHRISTINE DINH Brand Communications Manager
DAFNA PLEBAN Editor
SHANNON WATTERS Editor
ERIC HARBURN Editor
REBECCA TAYLOR Editor
IAN BRILL Editor
CHRIS ROSA Assistant Editor
ALEX GALER Assistant Editor
WHITNEY LEOPARD Assistant Editor
JASMINE AMIRI Assistant Editor
CAMERON CHITTOCK Assistant Editor
KELSEY DIETERICH Production Designer
JILLIAN CRAB Production Designer
DEVIN FUNCHES E-Commerce & Inventory Coordinator
ANDY LIEGL Event Coordinator
BRIANNA HART Administrative Coordinator
AARON FERRARA Operations Assistant
JOSÉ MEZA Sales Assistant
MICHELLE ANKLEY Sales Assistant
ELIZABETH LOUGHRIDGE Accounting Assistant
STEPHANIE HOCUTT PR Assistant

"I THINK I'D LIKE EVERYTHING I TOUCH TO TURN TO **GOLD.**"

CREATED & WRITTEN BY
RYAN NORTH

ILLUSTRATED BY
**SHELLI PAROLINE
& BRADEN LAMB**

LETTERED BY **STEVE WANDS**
COVER BY **EMILY PARTRIDGE**

DESIGNER **SCOTT NEWMAN**
ASSISTANT EDITOR **JASMINE AMIRI**
EDITOR **SHANNON WATTERS**

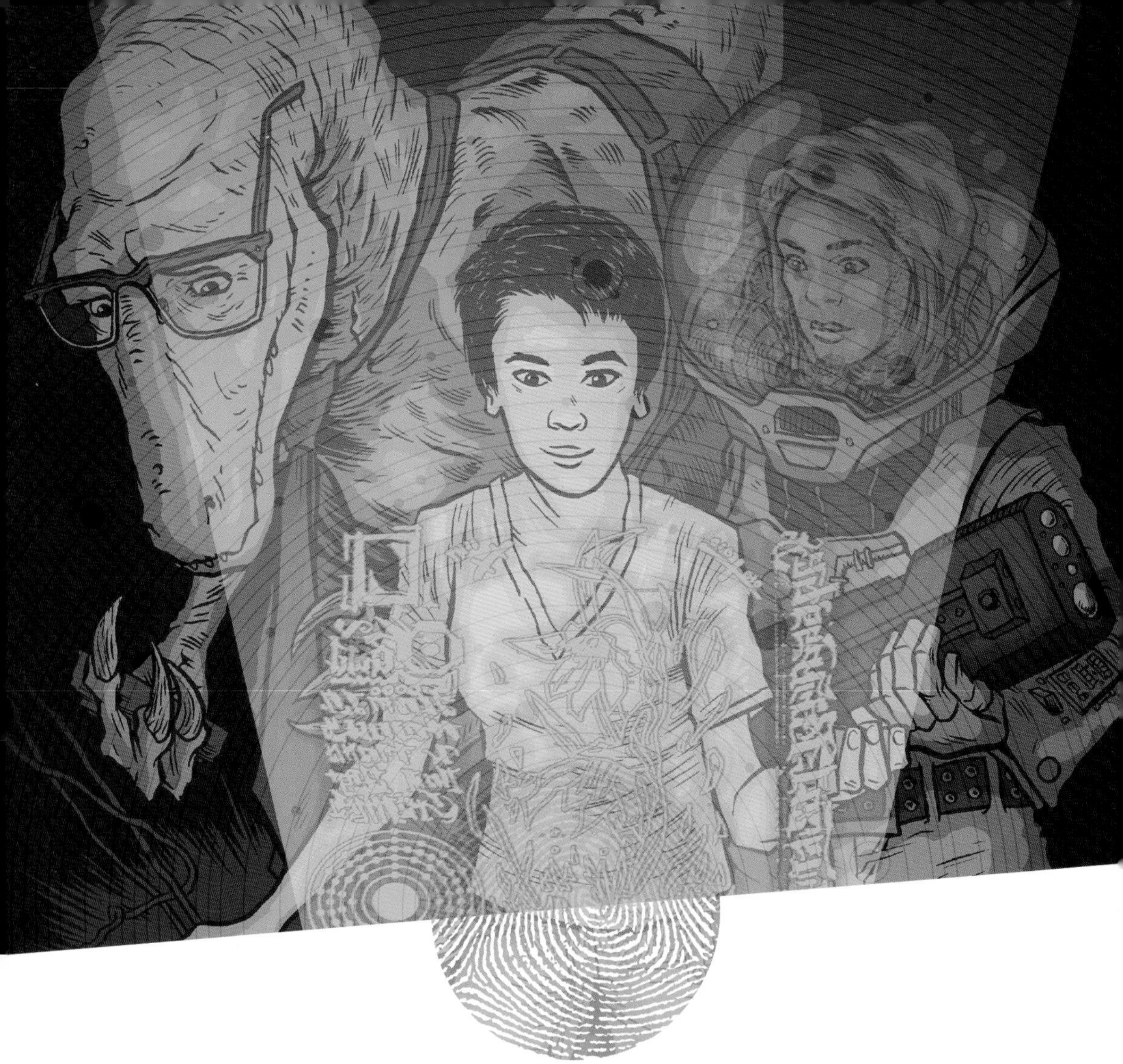

CHAPTER ONE

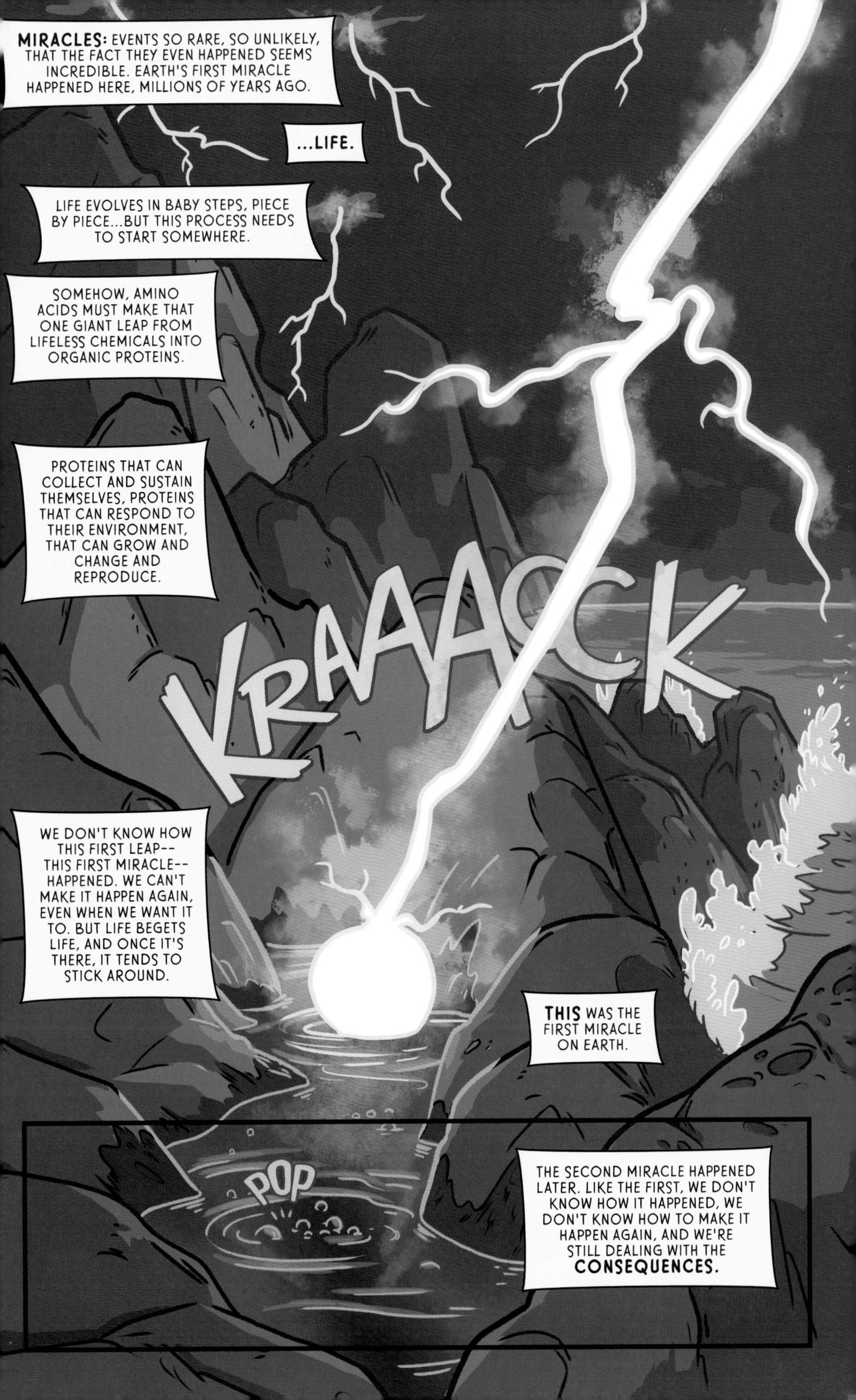
MIRACLES: EVENTS SO RARE, SO UNLIKELY, THAT THE FACT THEY EVEN HAPPENED SEEMS INCREDIBLE. EARTH'S FIRST MIRACLE HAPPENED HERE, MILLIONS OF YEARS AGO.
...LIFE.
LIFE EVOLVES IN BABY STEPS, PIECE BY PIECE...BUT THIS PROCESS NEEDS TO START SOMEWHERE.
SOMEHOW, AMINO ACIDS MUST MAKE THAT ONE GIANT LEAP FROM LIFELESS CHEMICALS INTO ORGANIC PROTEINS.
PROTEINS THAT CAN COLLECT AND SUSTAIN THEMSELVES, PROTEINS THAT CAN RESPOND TO THEIR ENVIRONMENT, THAT CAN GROW AND CHANGE AND REPRODUCE.
KRAAACK
WE DON'T KNOW HOW THIS FIRST LEAP-- THIS FIRST MIRACLE-- HAPPENED. WE CAN'T MAKE IT HAPPEN AGAIN, EVEN WHEN WE WANT IT TO. BUT LIFE BEGETS LIFE, AND ONCE IT'S THERE, IT TENDS TO STICK AROUND.
THIS WAS THE FIRST MIRACLE ON EARTH.
POP
THE SECOND MIRACLE HAPPENED LATER. LIKE THE FIRST, WE DON'T KNOW HOW IT HAPPENED, WE DON'T KNOW HOW TO MAKE IT HAPPEN AGAIN, AND WE'RE STILL DEALING WITH THE CONSEQUENCES.

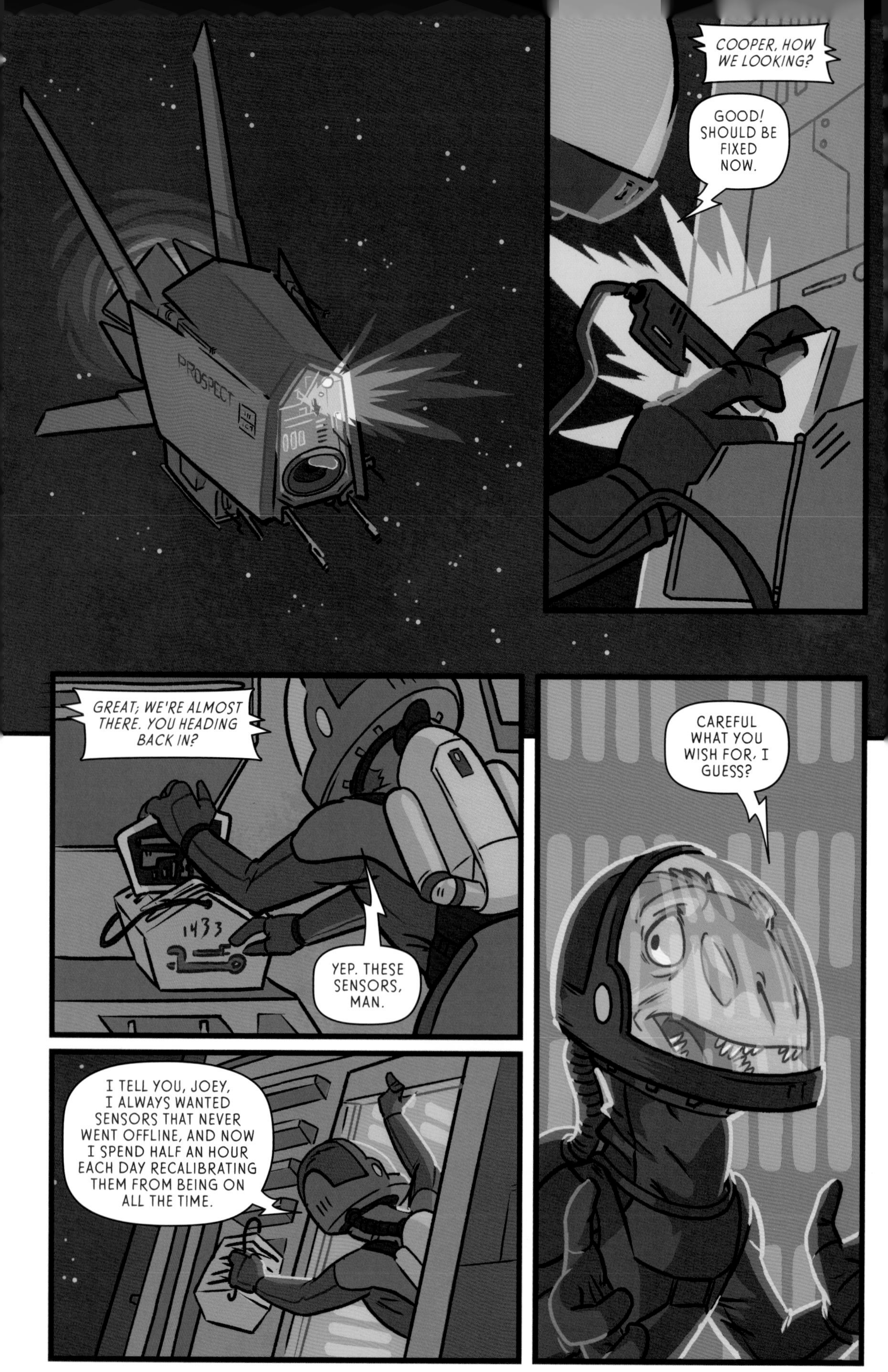
PROSPECT
COOPER, HOW WE LOOKING?
GOOD! SHOULD BE FIXED NOW.
GREAT; WE'RE ALMOST THERE. YOU HEADING BACK IN?
1433
YEP. THESE SENSORS, MAN.
I TELL YOU, JOEY, I ALWAYS WANTED SENSORS THAT NEVER WENT OFFLINE, AND NOW I SPEND HALF AN HOUR EACH DAY RECALIBRATING THEM FROM BEING ON ALL THE TIME.
CAREFUL WHAT YOU WISH FOR, I GUESS?

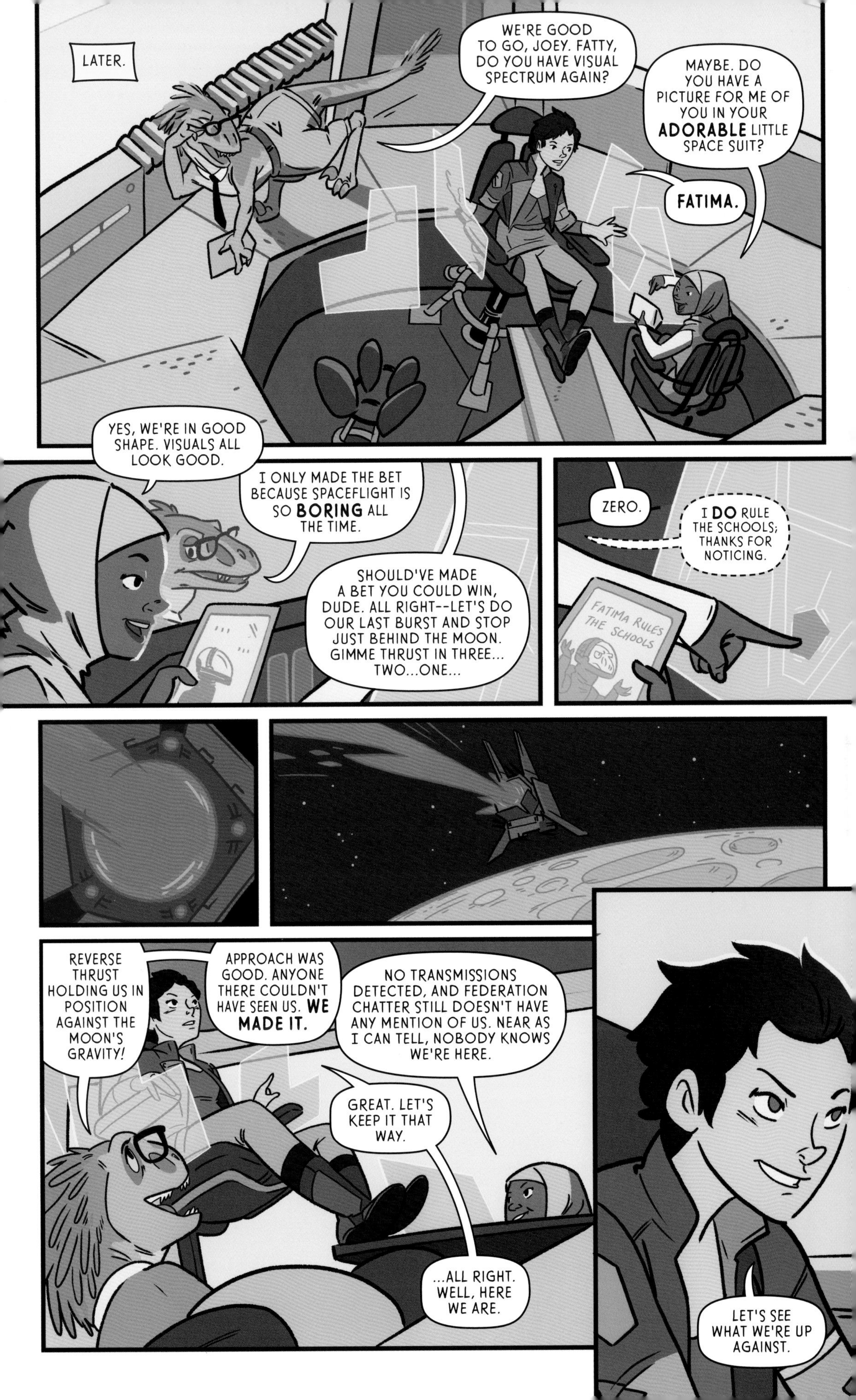
LATER.
WE'RE GOOD TO GO, JOEY. FATTY, DO YOU HAVE VISUAL SPECTRUM AGAIN?
MAYBE. DO YOU HAVE A PICTURE FOR ME OF YOU IN YOUR ADORABLE LITTLE SPACE SUIT?
FATIMA.
YES, WE'RE IN GOOD SHAPE. VISUALS ALL LOOK GOOD.
I ONLY MADE THE BET BECAUSE SPACEFLIGHT IS SO BORING ALL THE TIME.
SHOULD'VE MADE A BET YOU COULD WIN, DUDE. ALL RIGHT--LET'S DO OUR LAST BURST AND STOP JUST BEHIND THE MOON. GIMME THRUST IN THREE... TWO...ONE...
ZERO.
I DO RULE THE SCHOOLS; THANKS FOR NOTICING.
FATIMA RULES THE SCHOOLS
REVERSE THRUST HOLDING US IN POSITION AGAINST THE MOON'S GRAVITY!
APPROACH WAS GOOD. ANYONE THERE COULDN'T HAVE SEEN US. WE MADE IT.
NO TRANSMISSIONS DETECTED, AND FEDERATION CHATTER STILL DOESN'T HAVE ANY MENTION OF US. NEAR AS I CAN TELL, NOBODY KNOWS WE'RE HERE.
GREAT. LET'S KEEP IT THAT WAY.
...ALL RIGHT. WELL, HERE WE ARE.
LET'S SEE WHAT WE'RE UP AGAINST.

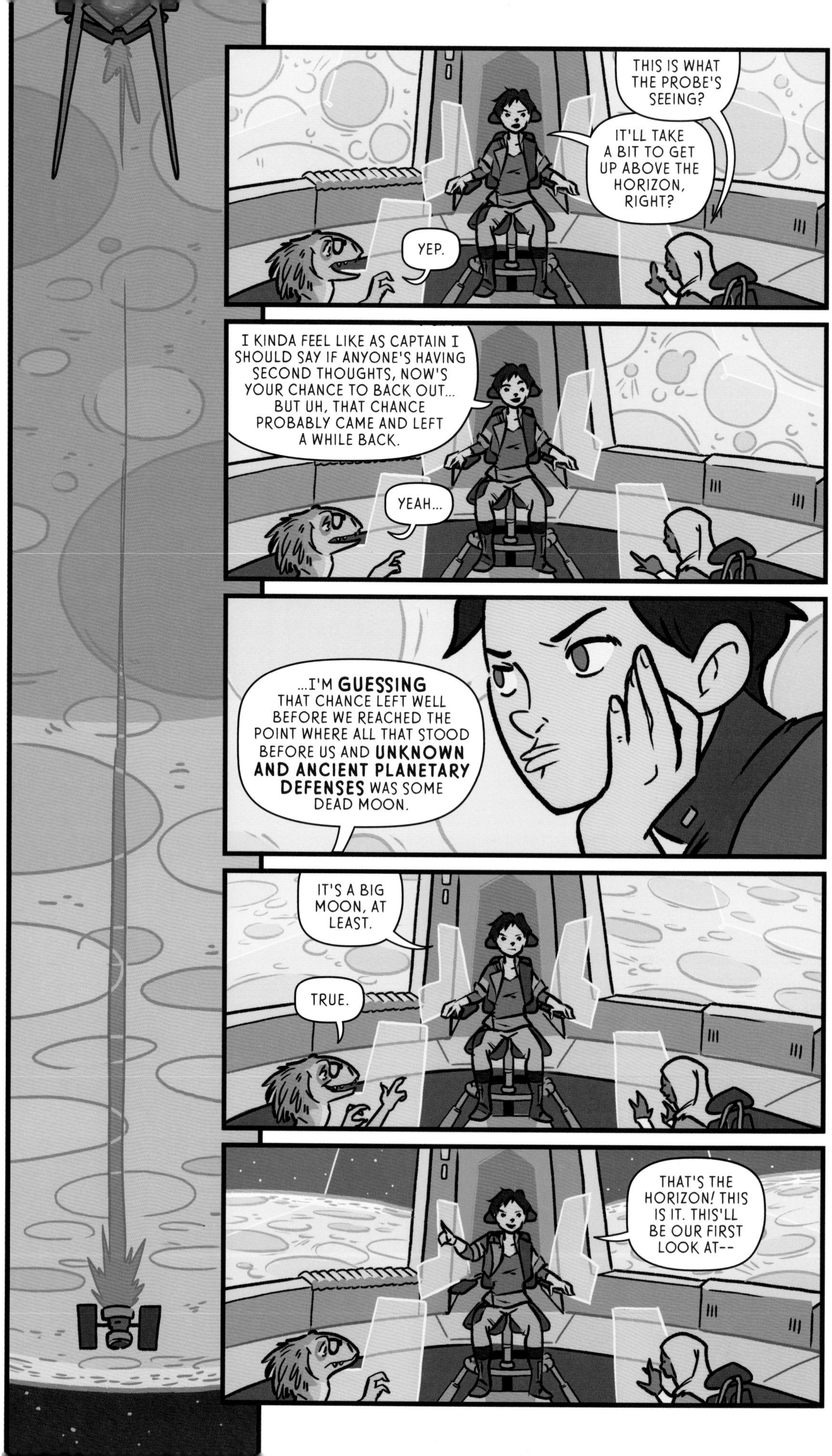
THIS IS WHAT THE PROBE'S SEEING?
IT'LL TAKE A BIT TO GET UP ABOVE THE HORIZON, RIGHT?
YEP.
I KINDA FEEL LIKE AS CAPTAIN I SHOULD SAY IF ANYONE'S HAVING SECOND THOUGHTS, NOW'S YOUR CHANCE TO BACK OUT... BUT UH, THAT CHANCE PROBABLY CAME AND LEFT A WHILE BACK.
YEAH...
...I'M GUESSING THAT CHANCE LEFT WELL BEFORE WE REACHED THE POINT WHERE ALL THAT STOOD BEFORE US AND UNKNOWN AND ANCIENT PLANETARY DEFENSES WAS SOME DEAD MOON.
IT'S A BIG MOON, AT LEAST.
TRUE.
THAT'S THE HORIZON! THIS IS IT. THIS'LL BE OUR FIRST LOOK AT--

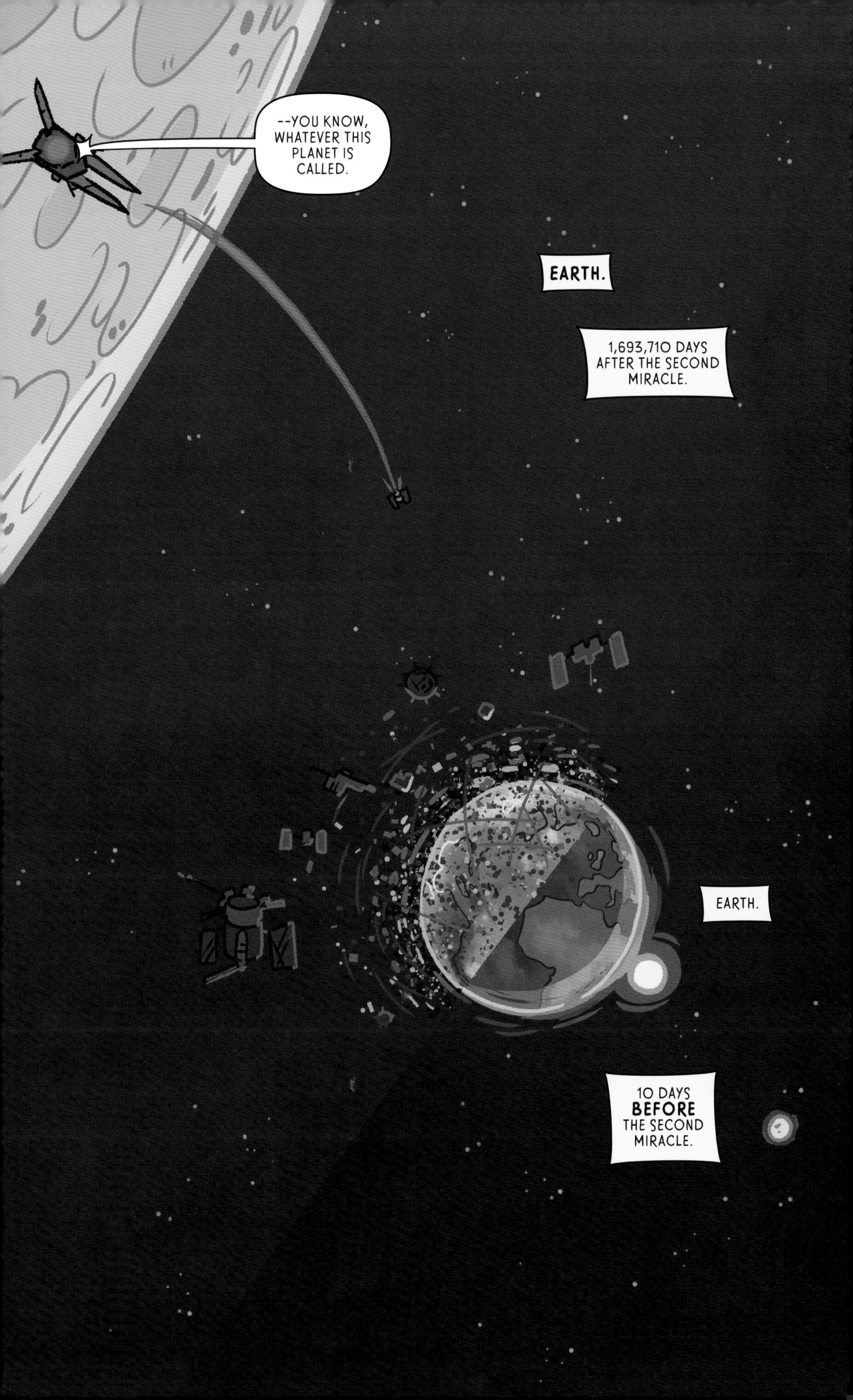
--YOU KNOW, WHATEVER THIS PLANET IS CALLED.
EARTH.
1,693,710 DAYS AFTER THE SECOND MIRACLE.
EARTH.
10 DAYS BEFORE THE SECOND MIRACLE.

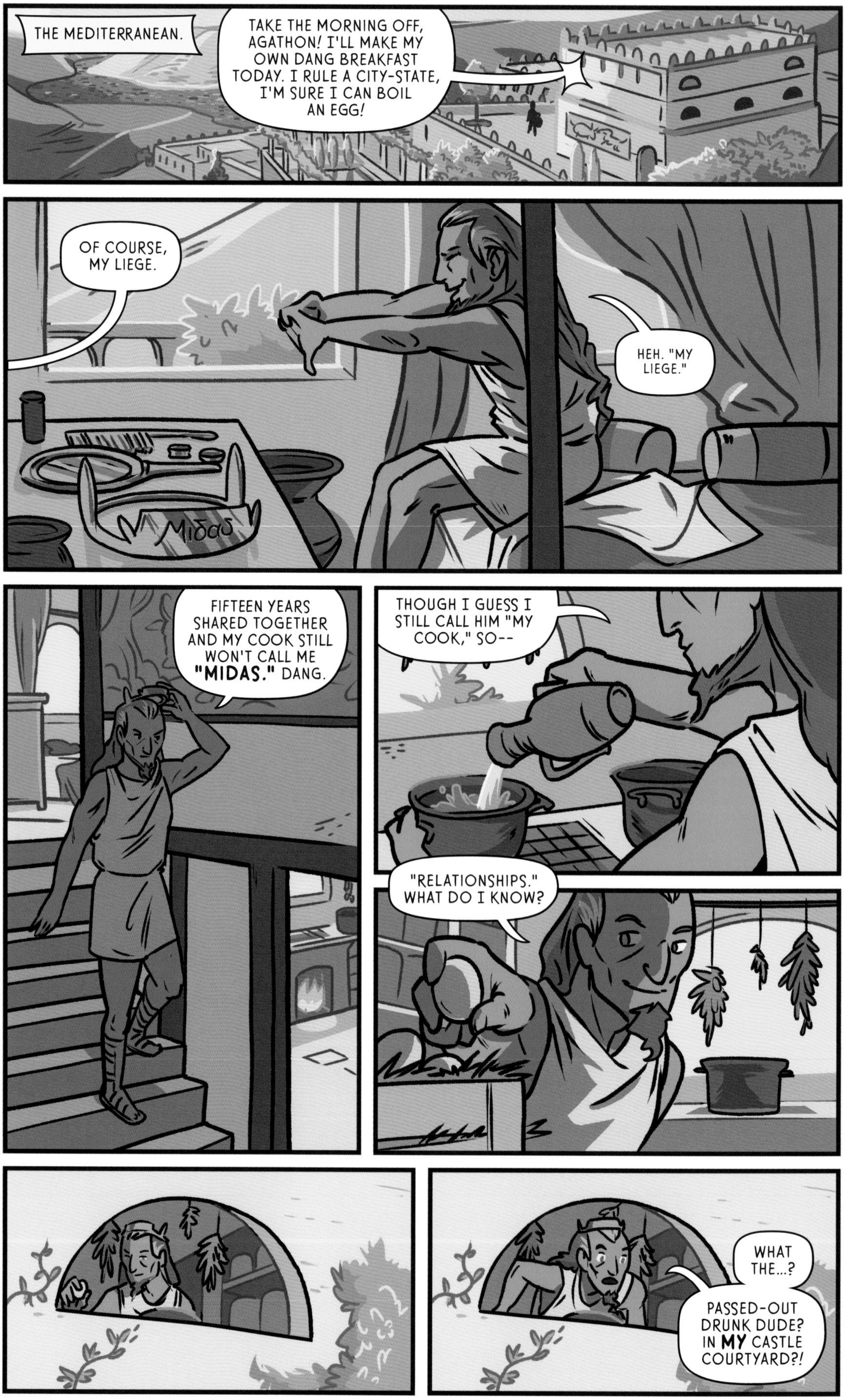
THE MEDITERRANEAN.
TAKE THE MORNING OFF, AGATHON! I'LL MAKE MY OWN DANG BREAKFAST TODAY. I RULE A CITY-STATE, I'M SURE I CAN BOIL AN EGG!
OF COURSE, MY LIEGE.
HEH. "MY LIEGE."
Μίδας
FIFTEEN YEARS SHARED TOGETHER AND MY COOK STILL WON'T CALL ME "MIDAS." DANG.
THOUGH I GUESS I STILL CALL HIM "MY COOK," SO--
"RELATIONSHIPS." WHAT DO I KNOW?
WHAT THE...?
PASSED-OUT DRUNK DUDE? IN MY CASTLE COURTYARD?!

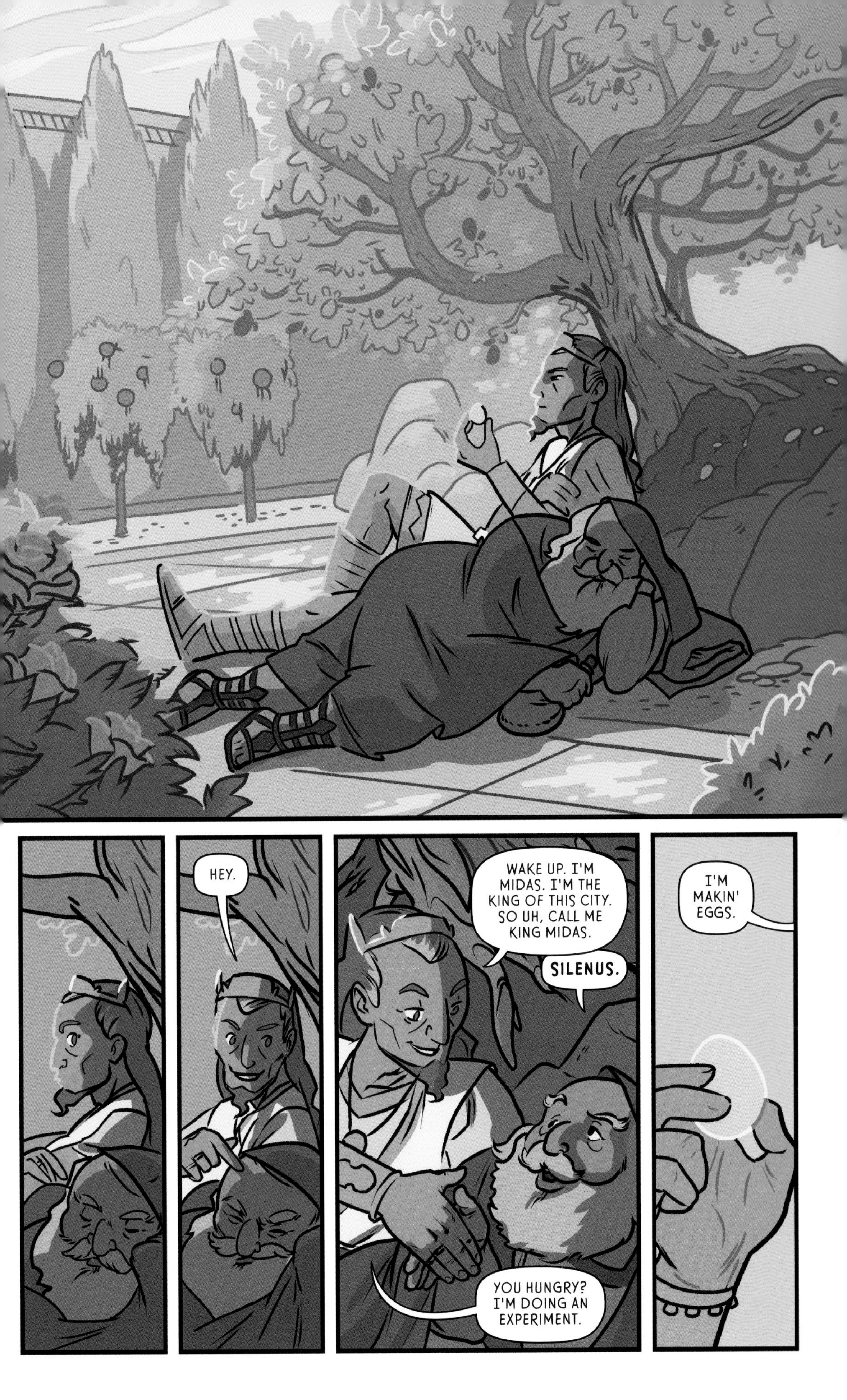
HEY.
WAKE UP. I'M MIDAS. I'M THE KING OF THIS CITY. SO UH, CALL ME KING MIDAS.
SILENUS.
YOU HUNGRY? I'M DOING AN EXPERIMENT.
I'M MAKIN' EGGS.

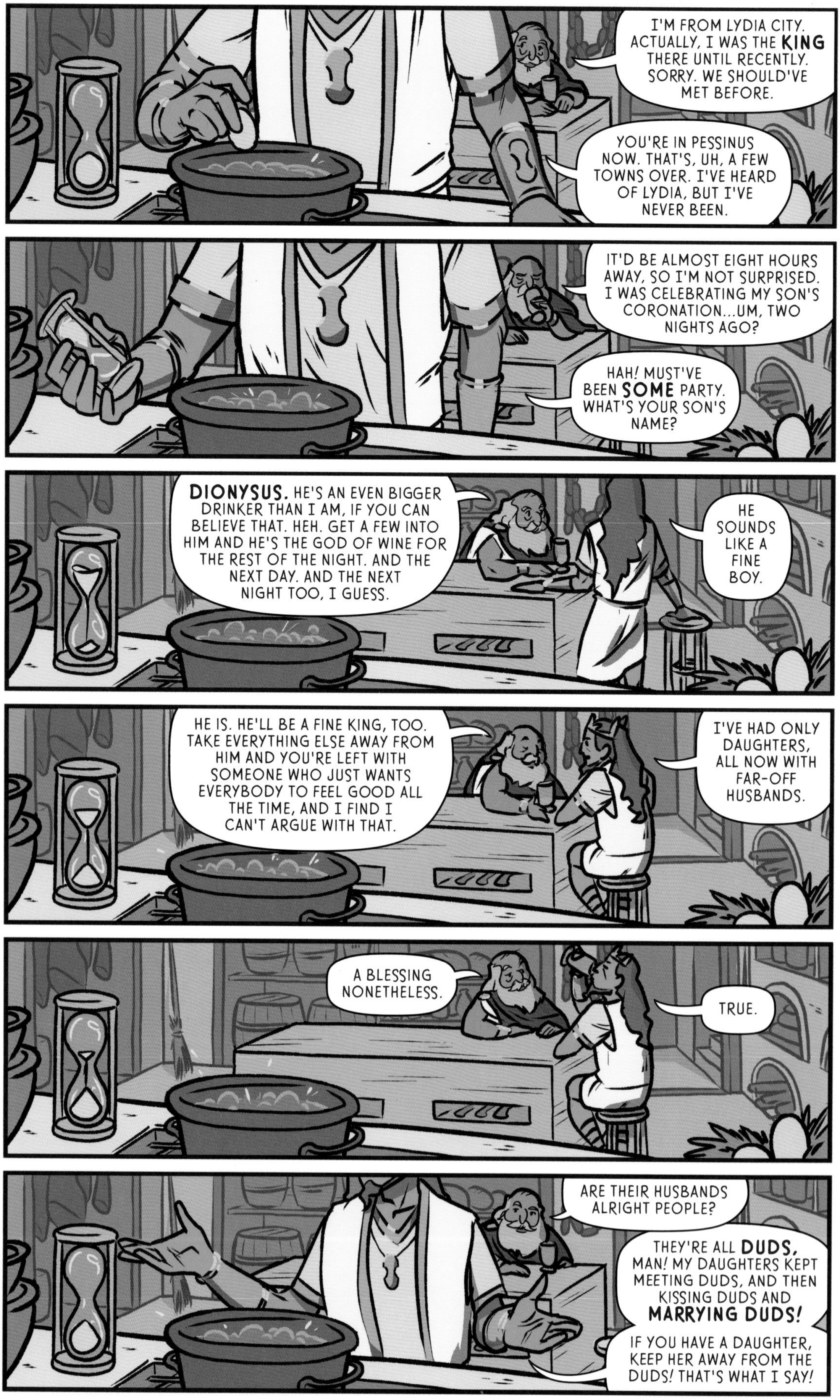
I'M FROM LYDIA CITY. ACTUALLY, I WAS THE **KING** THERE UNTIL RECENTLY. SORRY. WE SHOULD'VE MET BEFORE.
YOU'RE IN PESSINUS NOW. THAT'S, UH, A FEW TOWNS OVER. I'VE HEARD OF LYDIA, BUT I'VE NEVER BEEN.
IT'D BE ALMOST EIGHT HOURS AWAY, SO I'M NOT SURPRISED. I WAS CELEBRATING MY SON'S CORONATION...UM, TWO NIGHTS AGO?
HAH! MUST'VE BEEN **SOME** PARTY. WHAT'S YOUR SON'S NAME?
DIONYSUS. HE'S AN EVEN BIGGER DRINKER THAN I AM, IF YOU CAN BELIEVE THAT. HEH. GET A FEW INTO HIM AND HE'S THE GOD OF WINE FOR THE REST OF THE NIGHT. AND THE NEXT DAY. AND THE NEXT NIGHT TOO, I GUESS.
HE SOUNDS LIKE A FINE BOY.
HE IS. HE'LL BE A FINE KING, TOO. TAKE EVERYTHING ELSE AWAY FROM HIM AND YOU'RE LEFT WITH SOMEONE WHO JUST WANTS EVERYBODY TO FEEL GOOD ALL THE TIME, AND I FIND I CAN'T ARGUE WITH THAT.
I'VE HAD ONLY DAUGHTERS, ALL NOW WITH FAR-OFF HUSBANDS.
A BLESSING NONETHELESS.
TRUE.
ARE THEIR HUSBANDS ALRIGHT PEOPLE?
THEY'RE ALL **DUDS,** MAN! MY DAUGHTERS KEPT MEETING DUDS, AND THEN KISSING DUDS AND **MARRYING DUDS!**
IF YOU HAVE A DAUGHTER, KEEP HER AWAY FROM THE DUDS! THAT'S WHAT I SAY!

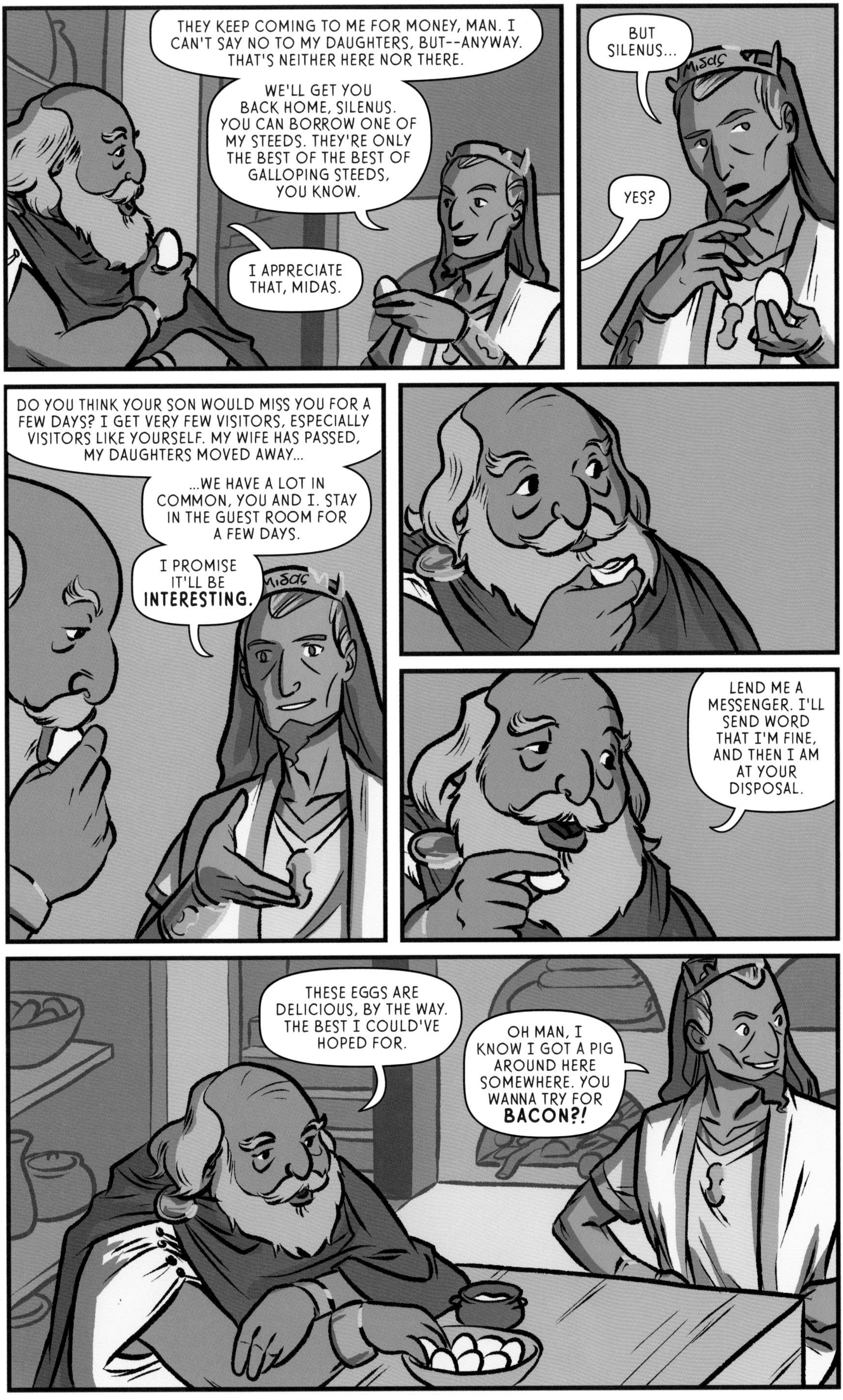
THEY KEEP COMING TO ME FOR MONEY, MAN. I CAN'T SAY NO TO MY DAUGHTERS, BUT--ANYWAY. THAT'S NEITHER HERE NOR THERE.
WE'LL GET YOU BACK HOME, SILENUS. YOU CAN BORROW ONE OF MY STEEDS. THEY'RE ONLY THE BEST OF THE BEST OF GALLOPING STEEDS, YOU KNOW.
I APPRECIATE THAT, MIDAS.
BUT SILENUS...
ΜΙΔΑΣ
YES?
DO YOU THINK YOUR SON WOULD MISS YOU FOR A FEW DAYS? I GET VERY FEW VISITORS, ESPECIALLY VISITORS LIKE YOURSELF. MY WIFE HAS PASSED, MY DAUGHTERS MOVED AWAY...
...WE HAVE A LOT IN COMMON, YOU AND I. STAY IN THE GUEST ROOM FOR A FEW DAYS.
I PROMISE IT'LL BE **INTERESTING.**
ΜΙΔΑΣ
LEND ME A MESSENGER. I'LL SEND WORD THAT I'M FINE, AND THEN I AM AT YOUR DISPOSAL.
THESE EGGS ARE DELICIOUS, BY THE WAY. THE BEST I COULD'VE HOPED FOR.
OH MAN, I KNOW I GOT A PIG AROUND HERE SOMEWHERE. YOU WANNA TRY FOR **BACON?!**

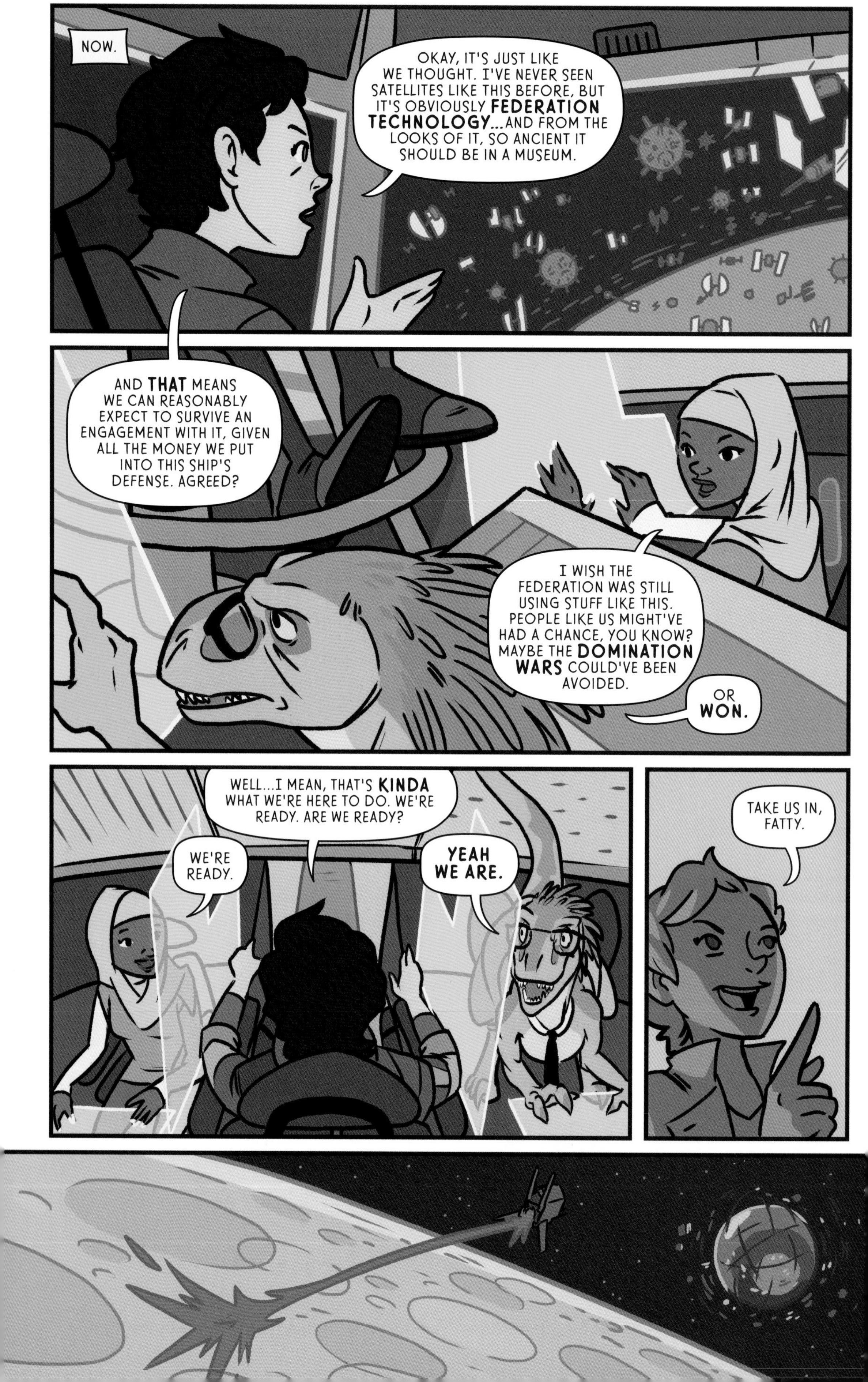
NOW.
OKAY, IT'S JUST LIKE WE THOUGHT. I'VE NEVER SEEN SATELLITES LIKE THIS BEFORE, BUT IT'S OBVIOUSLY FEDERATION TECHNOLOGY...AND FROM THE LOOKS OF IT, SO ANCIENT IT SHOULD BE IN A MUSEUM.
AND THAT MEANS WE CAN REASONABLY EXPECT TO SURVIVE AN ENGAGEMENT WITH IT, GIVEN ALL THE MONEY WE PUT INTO THIS SHIP'S DEFENSE. AGREED?
I WISH THE FEDERATION WAS STILL USING STUFF LIKE THIS. PEOPLE LIKE US MIGHT'VE HAD A CHANCE, YOU KNOW? MAYBE THE DOMINATION WARS COULD'VE BEEN AVOIDED.
OR WON.
WELL...I MEAN, THAT'S KINDA WHAT WE'RE HERE TO DO. WE'RE READY. ARE WE READY?
WE'RE READY.
YEAH WE ARE.
TAKE US IN, FATTY.

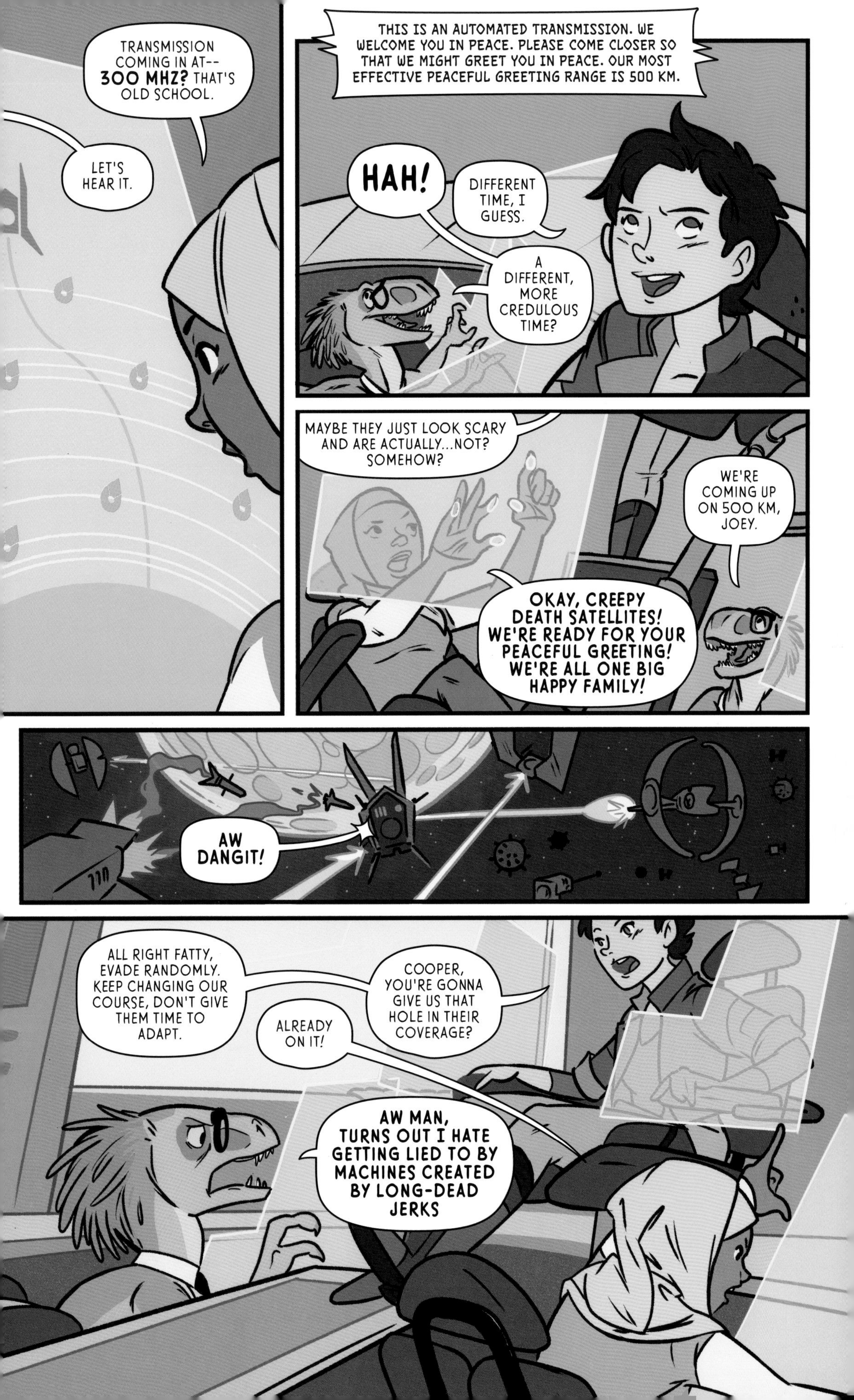
TRANSMISSION COMING IN AT-- 300 MHZ? THAT'S OLD SCHOOL.
LET'S HEAR IT.
THIS IS AN AUTOMATED TRANSMISSION. WE WELCOME YOU IN PEACE. PLEASE COME CLOSER SO THAT WE MIGHT GREET YOU IN PEACE. OUR MOST EFFECTIVE PEACEFUL GREETING RANGE IS 500 KM.
HAH!
DIFFERENT TIME, I GUESS.
A DIFFERENT, MORE CREDULOUS TIME?
MAYBE THEY JUST LOOK SCARY AND ARE ACTUALLY...NOT? SOMEHOW?
WE'RE COMING UP ON 500 KM, JOEY.
OKAY, CREEPY DEATH SATELLITES! WE'RE READY FOR YOUR PEACEFUL GREETING! WE'RE ALL ONE BIG HAPPY FAMILY!
AW DANGIT!
ALL RIGHT FATTY, EVADE RANDOMLY. KEEP CHANGING OUR COURSE, DON'T GIVE THEM TIME TO ADAPT.
COOPER, YOU'RE GONNA GIVE US THAT HOLE IN THEIR COVERAGE?
ALREADY ON IT!
AW MAN, TURNS OUT I HATE GETTING LIED TO BY MACHINES CREATED BY LONG-DEAD JERKS

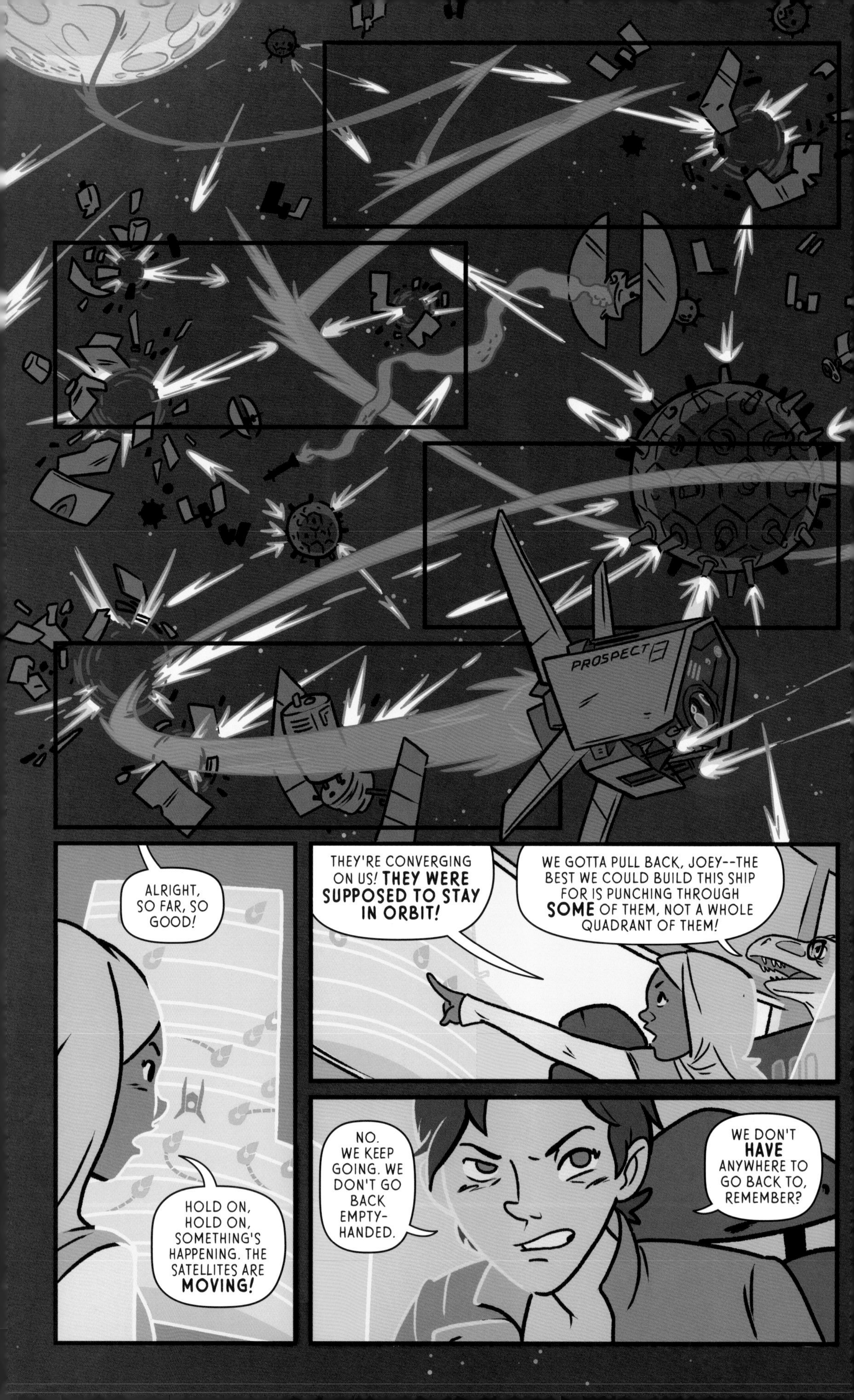
PROSPECT
ALRIGHT, SO FAR, SO GOOD!
HOLD ON, HOLD ON, SOMETHING'S HAPPENING. THE SATELLITES ARE **MOVING!**
THEY'RE CONVERGING ON US! **THEY WERE SUPPOSED TO STAY IN ORBIT!**
WE GOTTA PULL BACK, JOEY--THE BEST WE COULD BUILD THIS SHIP FOR IS PUNCHING THROUGH **SOME** OF THEM, NOT A WHOLE QUADRANT OF THEM!
NO. WE KEEP GOING. WE DON'T GO BACK EMPTY-HANDED.
WE DON'T **HAVE** ANYWHERE TO GO BACK TO, REMEMBER?

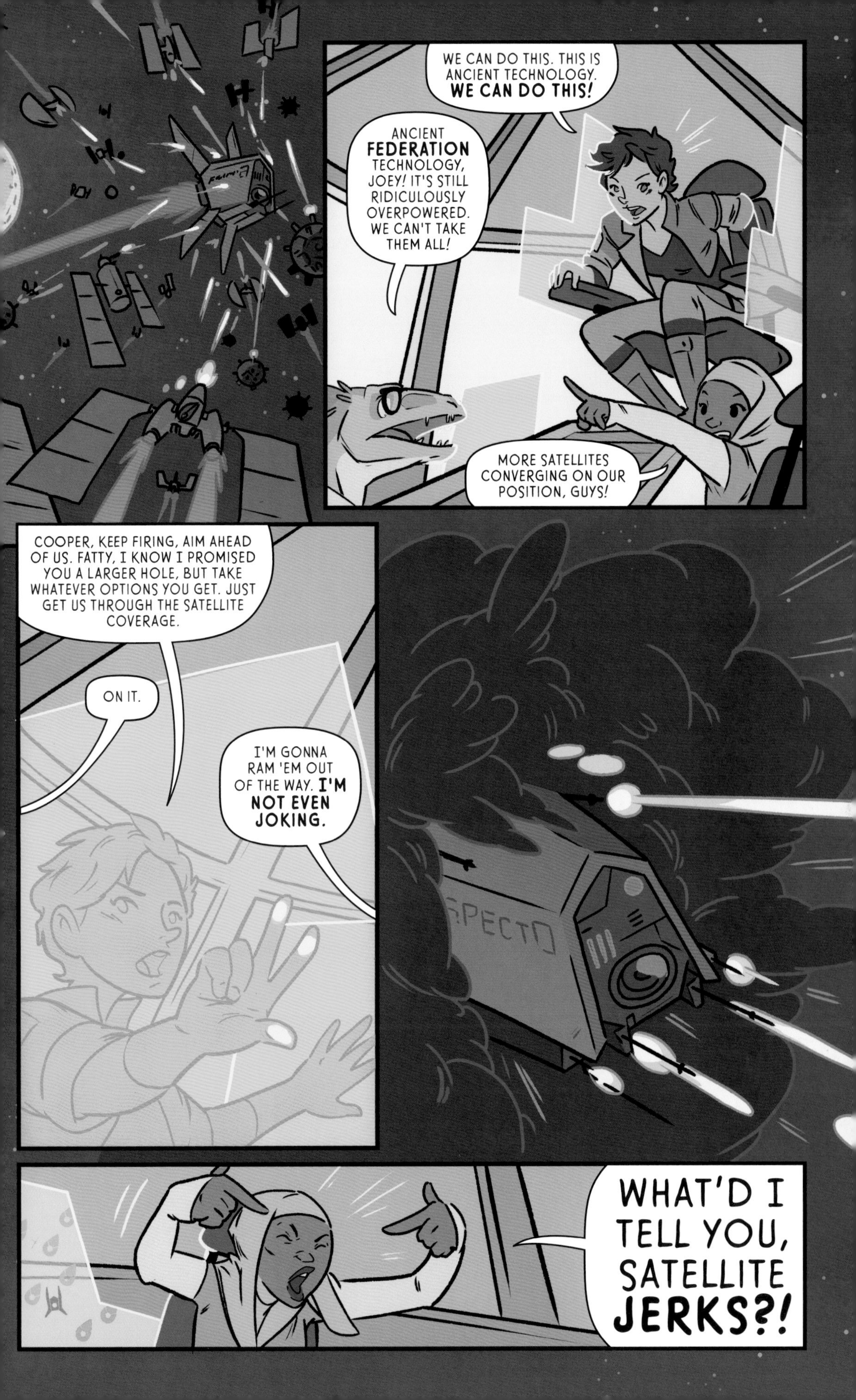
WE CAN DO THIS. THIS IS ANCIENT TECHNOLOGY. **WE CAN DO THIS!**
ANCIENT **FEDERATION** TECHNOLOGY, JOEY! IT'S STILL RIDICULOUSLY OVERPOWERED. WE CAN'T TAKE THEM ALL!
MORE SATELLITES CONVERGING ON OUR POSITION, GUYS!
COOPER, KEEP FIRING, AIM AHEAD OF US. FATTY, I KNOW I PROMISED YOU A LARGER HOLE, BUT TAKE WHATEVER OPTIONS YOU GET. JUST GET US THROUGH THE SATELLITE COVERAGE.
ON IT.
I'M GONNA RAM 'EM OUT OF THE WAY. **I'M NOT EVEN JOKING.**
SPECTO
WHAT'D I TELL YOU, SATELLITE **JERKS?!**

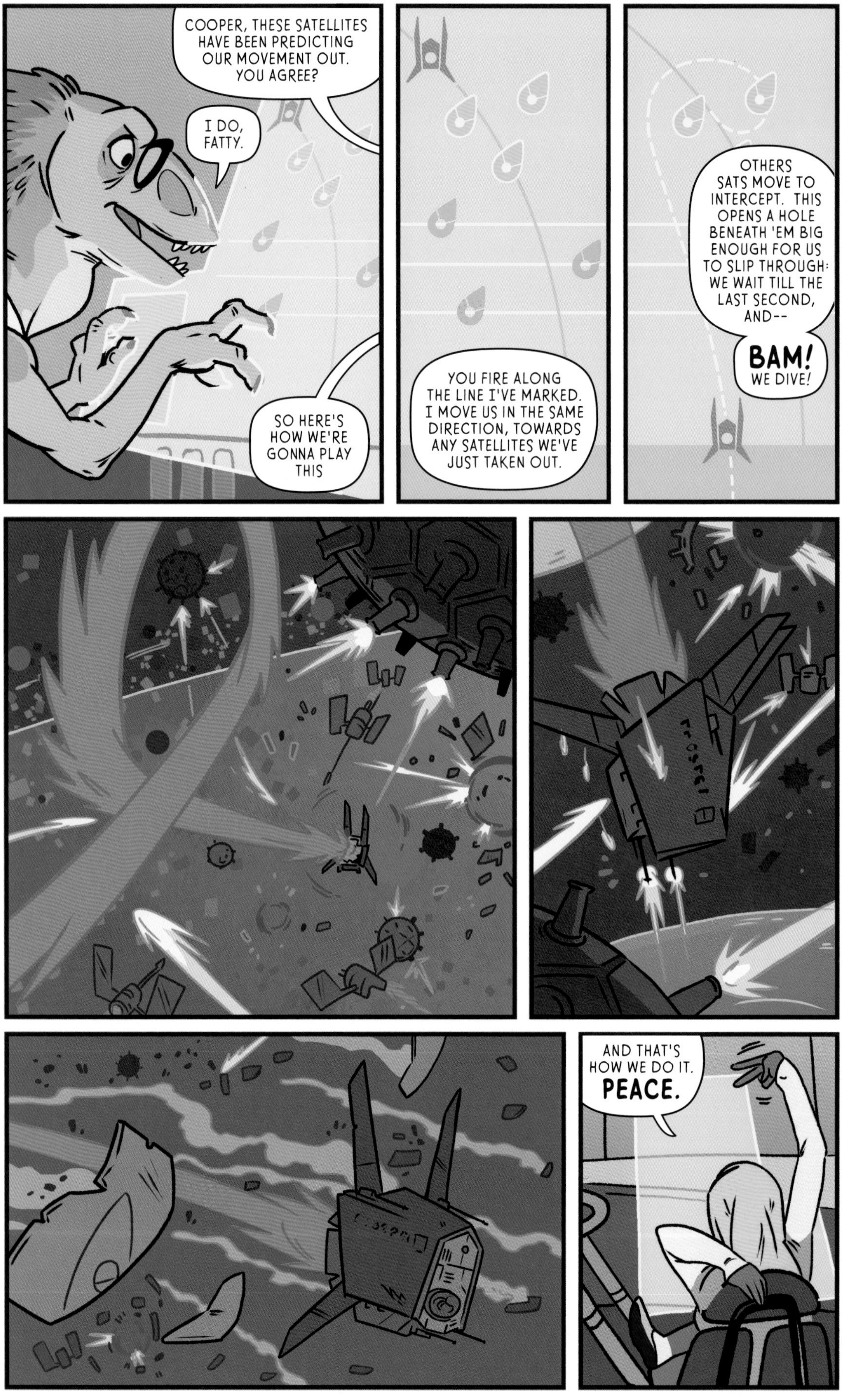
COOPER, THESE SATELLITES HAVE BEEN PREDICTING OUR MOVEMENT OUT. YOU AGREE?
I DO, FATTY.
SO HERE'S HOW WE'RE GONNA PLAY THIS
YOU FIRE ALONG THE LINE I'VE MARKED. I MOVE US IN THE SAME DIRECTION, TOWARDS ANY SATELLITES WE'VE JUST TAKEN OUT.
OTHERS SATS MOVE TO INTERCEPT. THIS OPENS A HOLE BENEATH 'EM BIG ENOUGH FOR US TO SLIP THROUGH: WE WAIT TILL THE LAST SECOND, AND--
BAM! WE DIVE!
AND THAT'S HOW WE DO IT. PEACE.

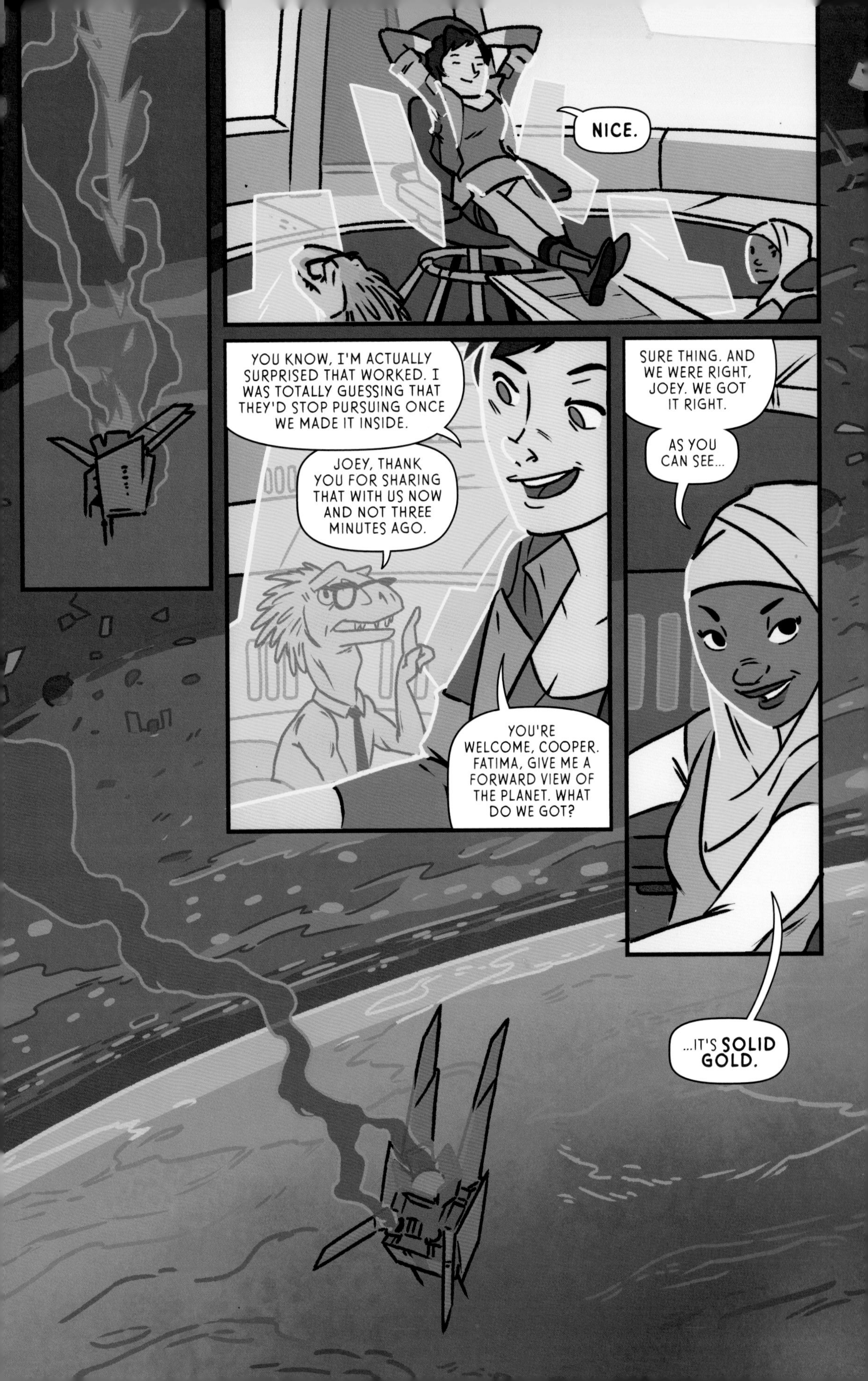
NICE.
YOU KNOW, I'M ACTUALLY SURPRISED THAT WORKED. I WAS TOTALLY GUESSING THAT THEY'D STOP PURSUING ONCE WE MADE IT INSIDE.
JOEY, THANK YOU FOR SHARING THAT WITH US NOW AND NOT THREE MINUTES AGO.
YOU'RE WELCOME, COOPER. FATIMA, GIVE ME A FORWARD VIEW OF THE PLANET. WHAT DO WE GOT?
SURE THING. AND WE WERE RIGHT, JOEY. WE GOT IT RIGHT.
AS YOU CAN SEE...
...IT'S SOLID GOLD.

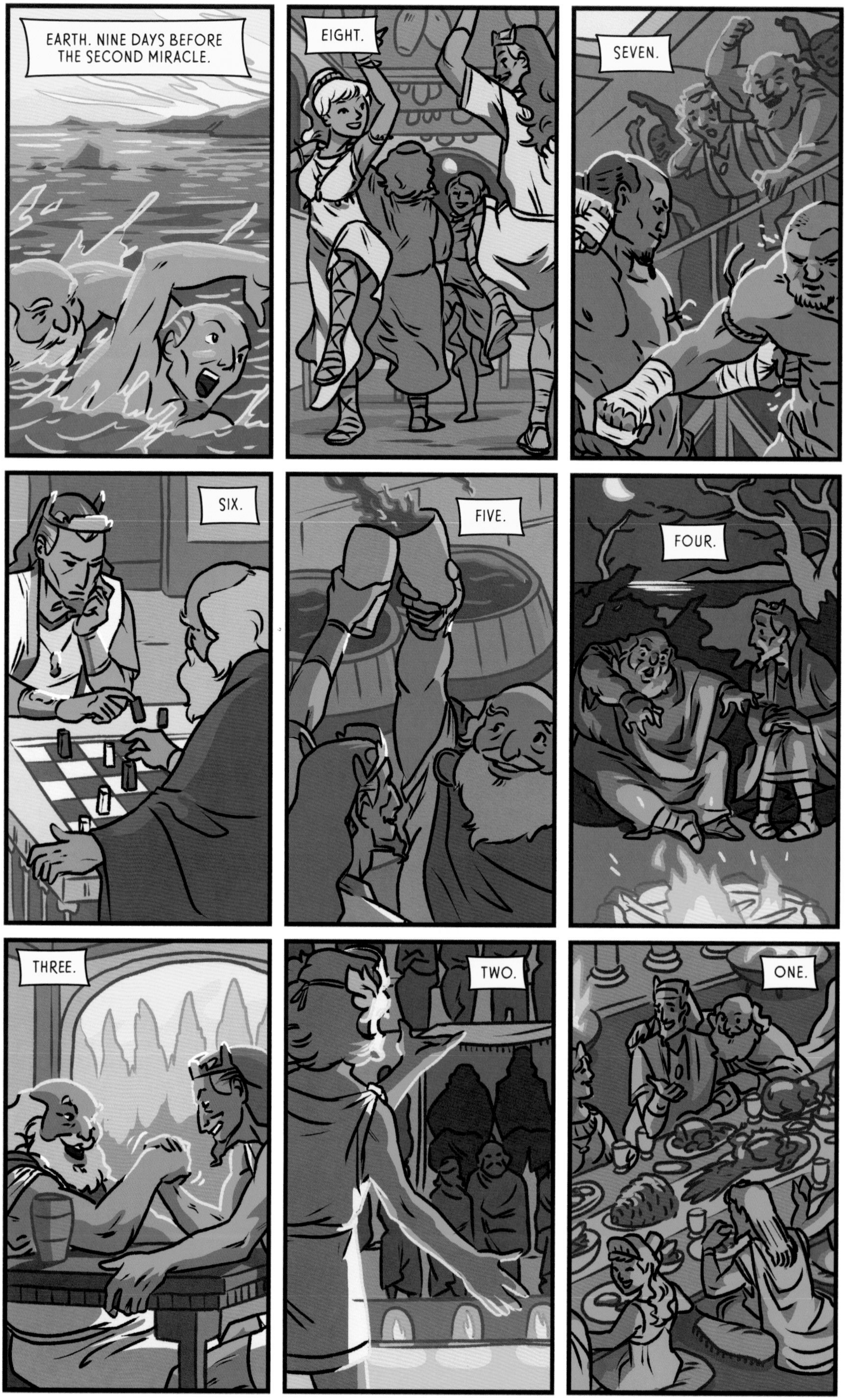
EARTH. NINE DAYS BEFORE THE SECOND MIRACLE.
EIGHT.
SEVEN.
SIX.
FIVE.
FOUR.
THREE.
TWO.
ONE.

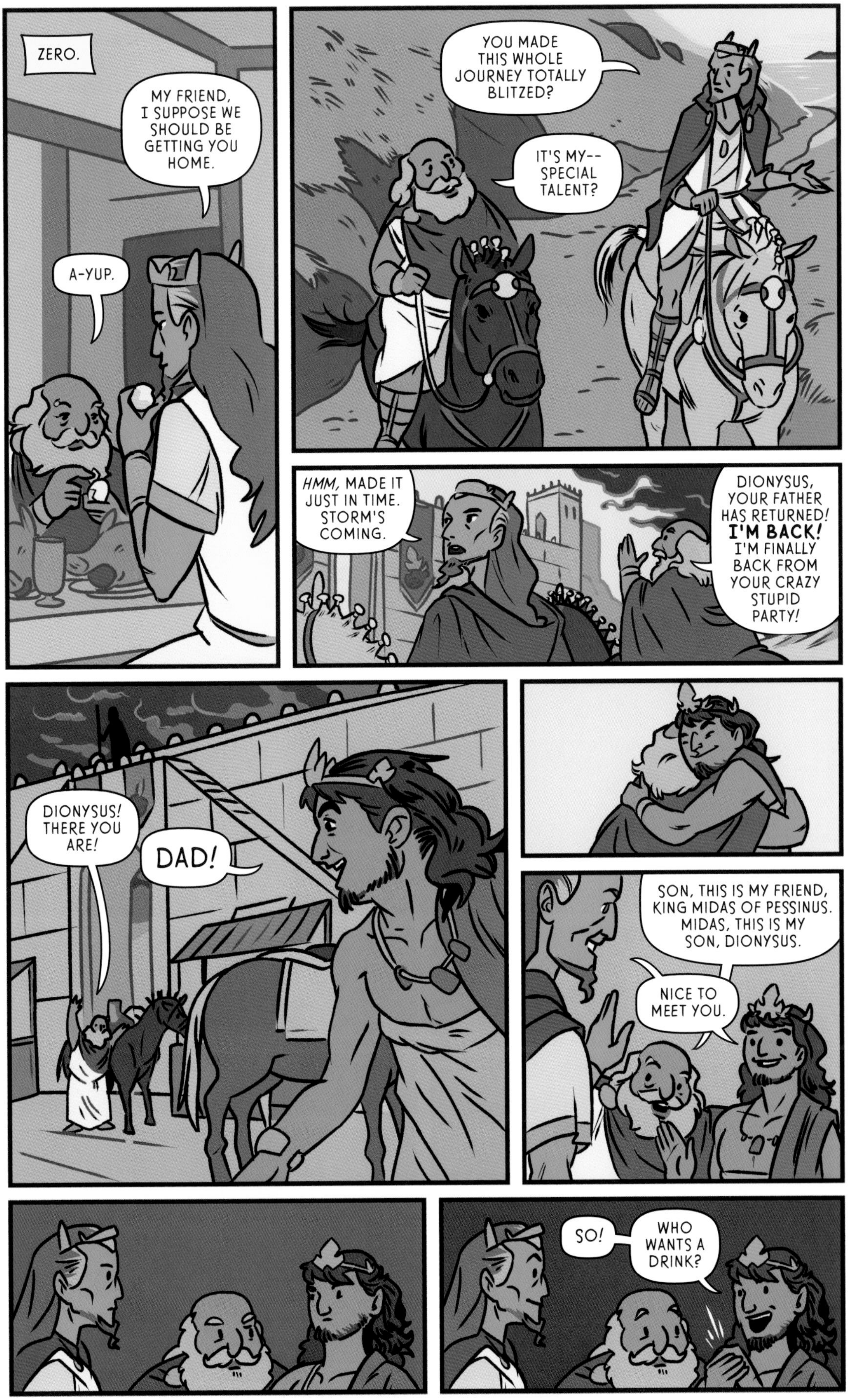
ZERO.
MY FRIEND, I SUPPOSE WE SHOULD BE GETTING YOU HOME.
A-YUP.
YOU MADE THIS WHOLE JOURNEY TOTALLY BLITZED?
IT'S MY-- SPECIAL TALENT?
HMM, MADE IT JUST IN TIME. STORM'S COMING.
DIONYSUS, YOUR FATHER HAS RETURNED! **I'M BACK!** I'M FINALLY BACK FROM YOUR CRAZY STUPID PARTY!
DIONYSUS! THERE YOU ARE!
DAD!
SON, THIS IS MY FRIEND, KING MIDAS OF PESSINUS. MIDAS, THIS IS MY SON, DIONYSUS.
NICE TO MEET YOU.
SO!
WHO WANTS A DRINK?

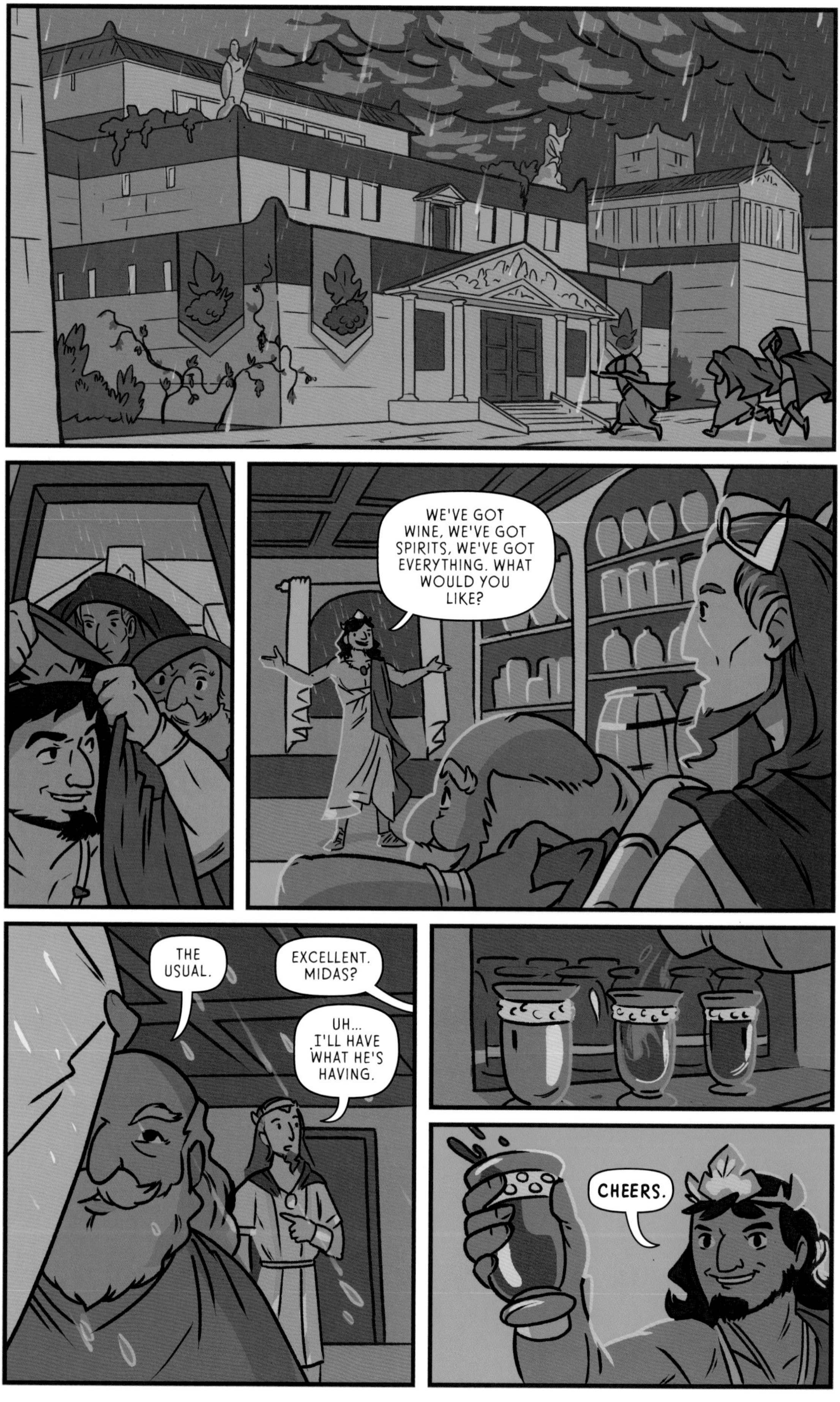

WE'VE GOT WINE, WE'VE GOT SPIRITS, WE'VE GOT EVERYTHING. WHAT WOULD YOU LIKE?
THE USUAL.
EXCELLENT. MIDAS?
UH... I'LL HAVE WHAT HE'S HAVING.
CHEERS.

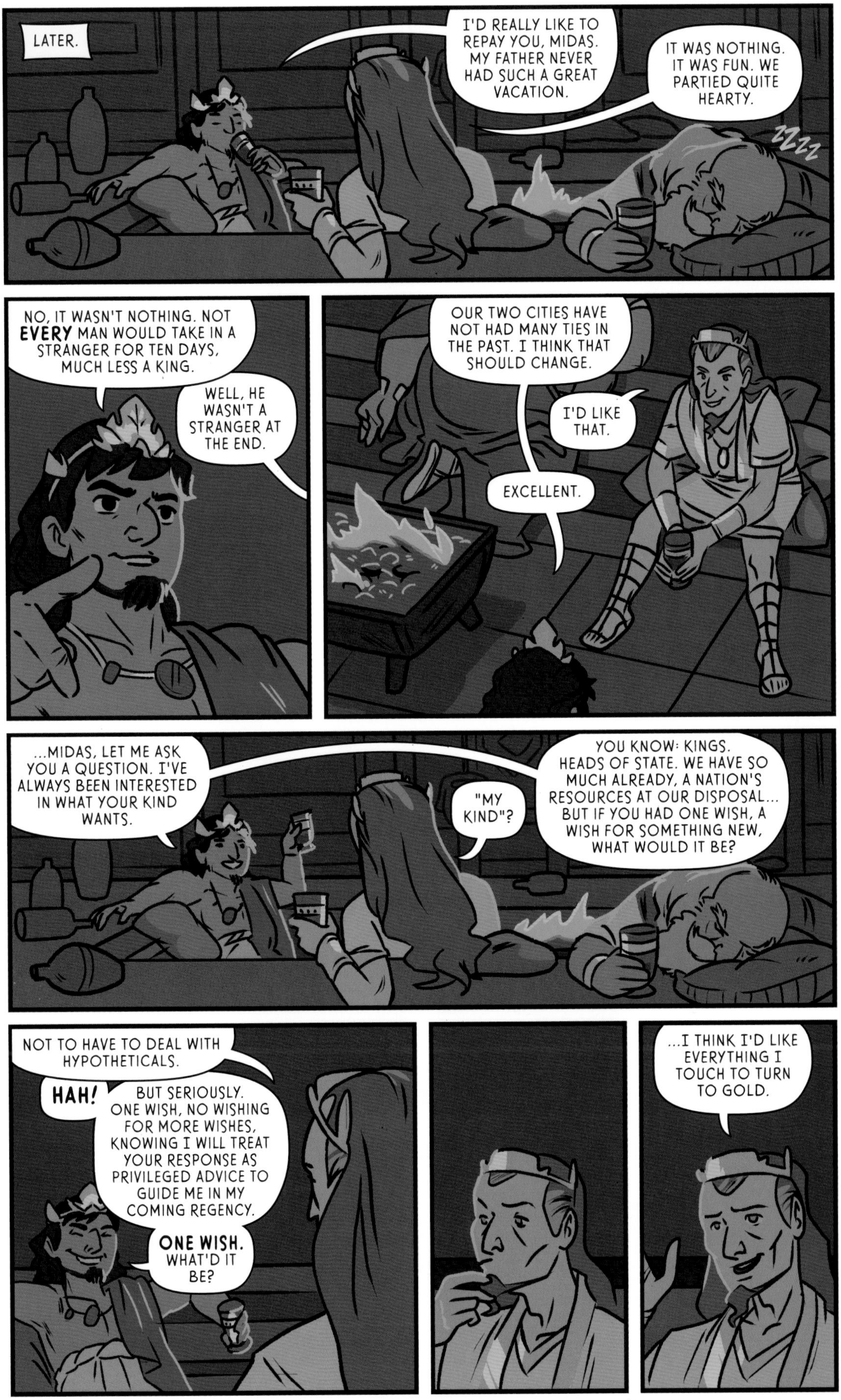
LATER.
I'D REALLY LIKE TO REPAY YOU, MIDAS. MY FATHER NEVER HAD SUCH A GREAT VACATION.
IT WAS NOTHING. IT WAS FUN. WE PARTIED QUITE HEARTY.
ZZZZ
NO, IT WASN'T NOTHING. NOT **EVERY** MAN WOULD TAKE IN A STRANGER FOR TEN DAYS, MUCH LESS A KING.
WELL, HE WASN'T A STRANGER AT THE END.
OUR TWO CITIES HAVE NOT HAD MANY TIES IN THE PAST. I THINK THAT SHOULD CHANGE.
I'D LIKE THAT.
EXCELLENT.
...MIDAS, LET ME ASK YOU A QUESTION. I'VE ALWAYS BEEN INTERESTED IN WHAT YOUR KIND WANTS.
"MY KIND"?
YOU KNOW: KINGS. HEADS OF STATE. WE HAVE SO MUCH ALREADY, A NATION'S RESOURCES AT OUR DISPOSAL... BUT IF YOU HAD ONE WISH, A WISH FOR SOMETHING NEW, WHAT WOULD IT BE?
NOT TO HAVE TO DEAL WITH HYPOTHETICALS.
HAH!
BUT SERIOUSLY. ONE WISH, NO WISHING FOR MORE WISHES, KNOWING I WILL TREAT YOUR RESPONSE AS PRIVILEGED ADVICE TO GUIDE ME IN MY COMING REGENCY.
ONE WISH. WHAT'D IT BE?
...I THINK I'D LIKE EVERYTHING I TOUCH TO TURN TO GOLD.

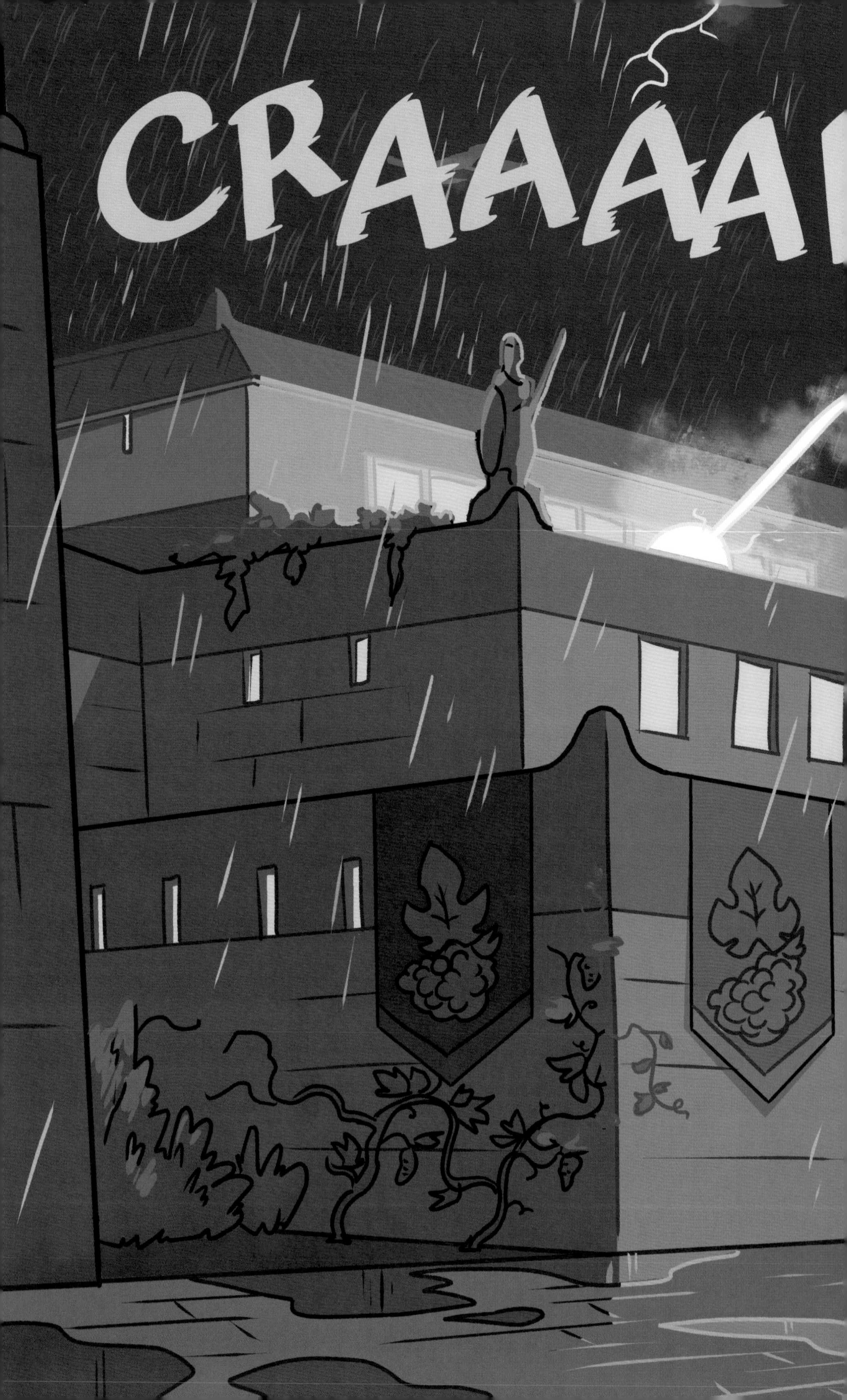
CRAAAA

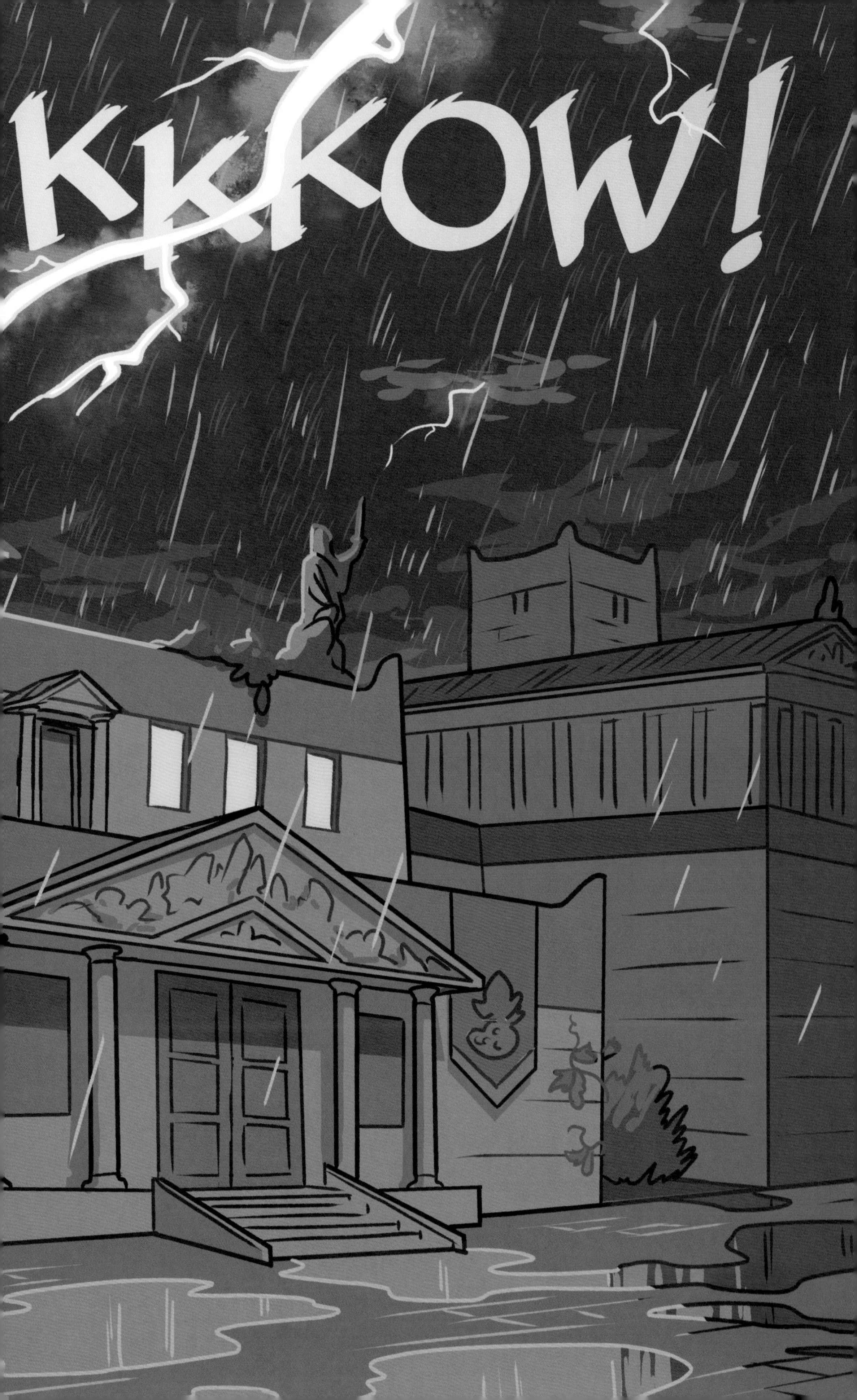
KKKOW!

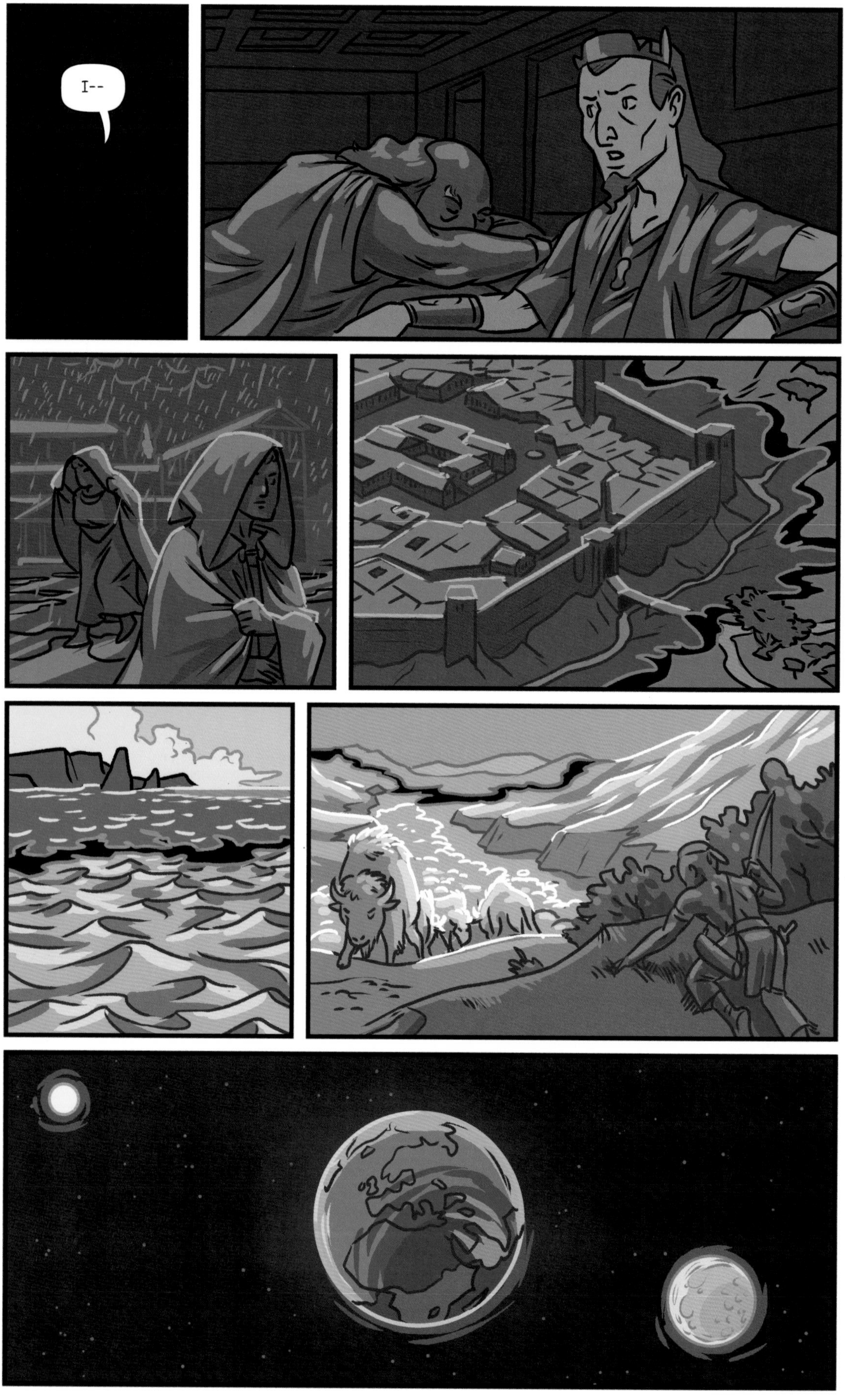
I--

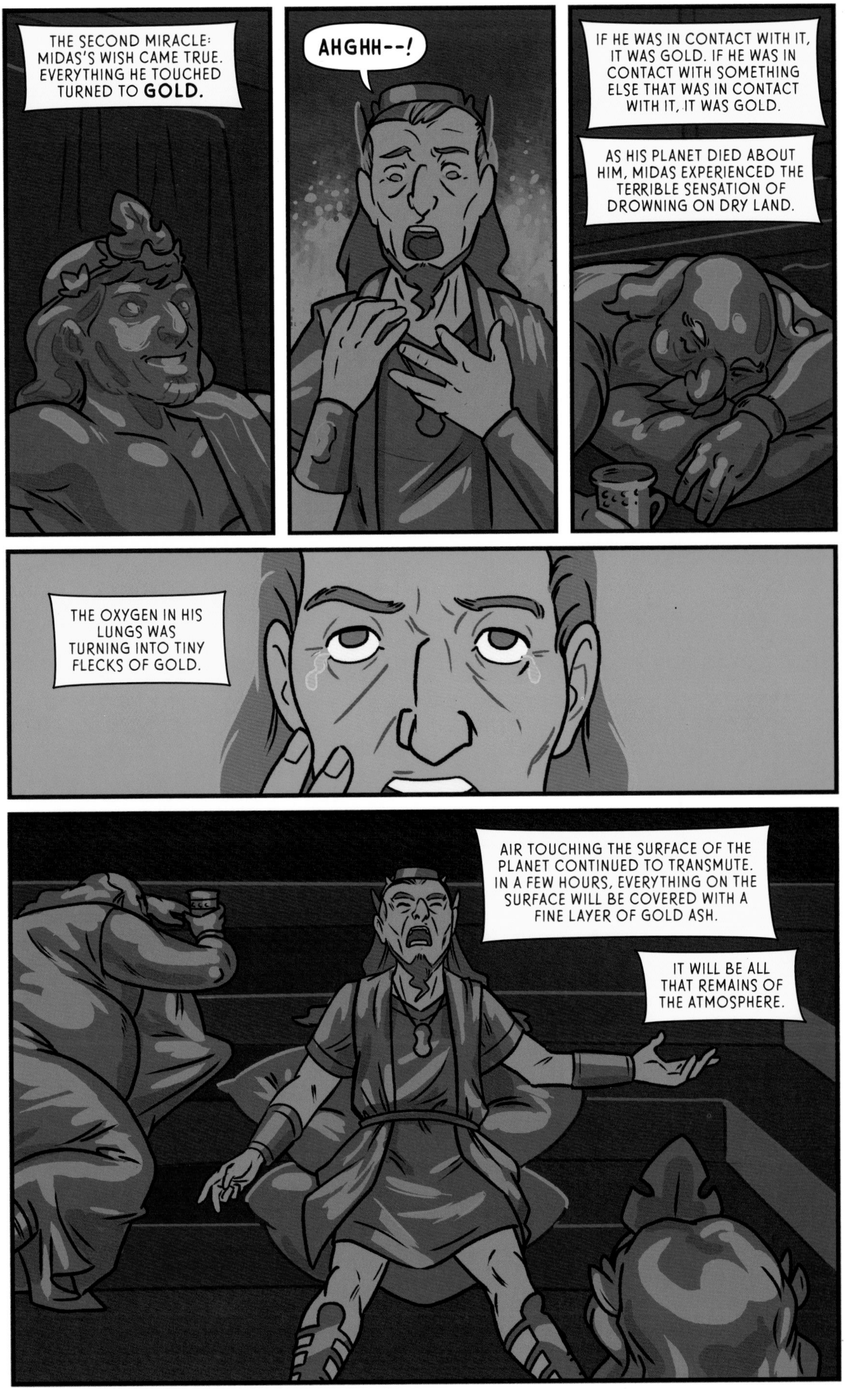
THE SECOND MIRACLE: MIDAS'S WISH CAME TRUE. EVERYTHING HE TOUCHED TURNED TO **GOLD.**
AHGHH--!
IF HE WAS IN CONTACT WITH IT, IT WAS GOLD. IF HE WAS IN CONTACT WITH SOMETHING ELSE THAT WAS IN CONTACT WITH IT, IT WAS GOLD.
AS HIS PLANET DIED ABOUT HIM, MIDAS EXPERIENCED THE TERRIBLE SENSATION OF DROWNING ON DRY LAND.
THE OXYGEN IN HIS LUNGS WAS TURNING INTO TINY FLECKS OF GOLD.
AIR TOUCHING THE SURFACE OF THE PLANET CONTINUED TO TRANSMUTE. IN A FEW HOURS, EVERYTHING ON THE SURFACE WILL BE COVERED WITH A FINE LAYER OF GOLD ASH.
IT WILL BE ALL THAT REMAINS OF THE ATMOSPHERE.

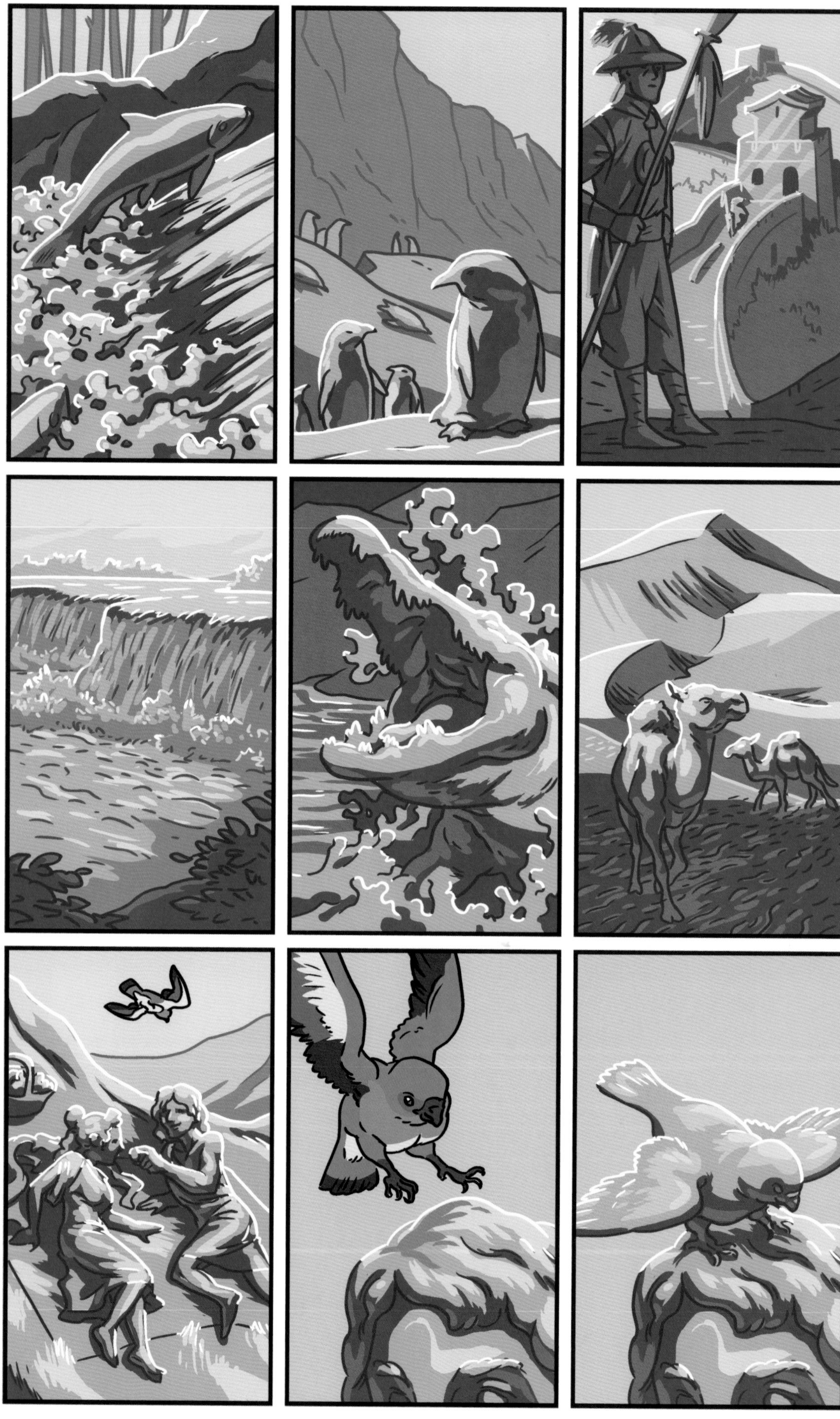

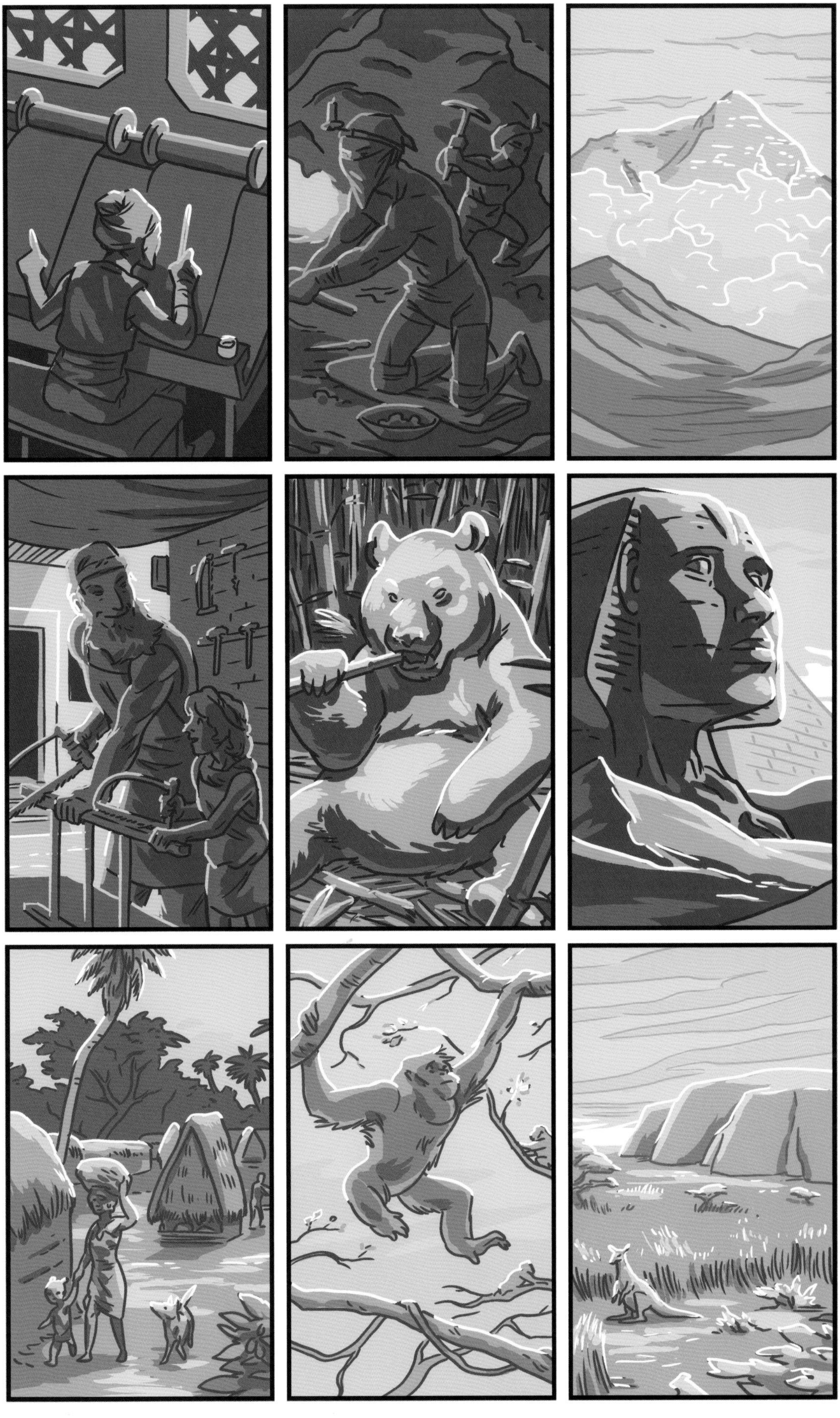

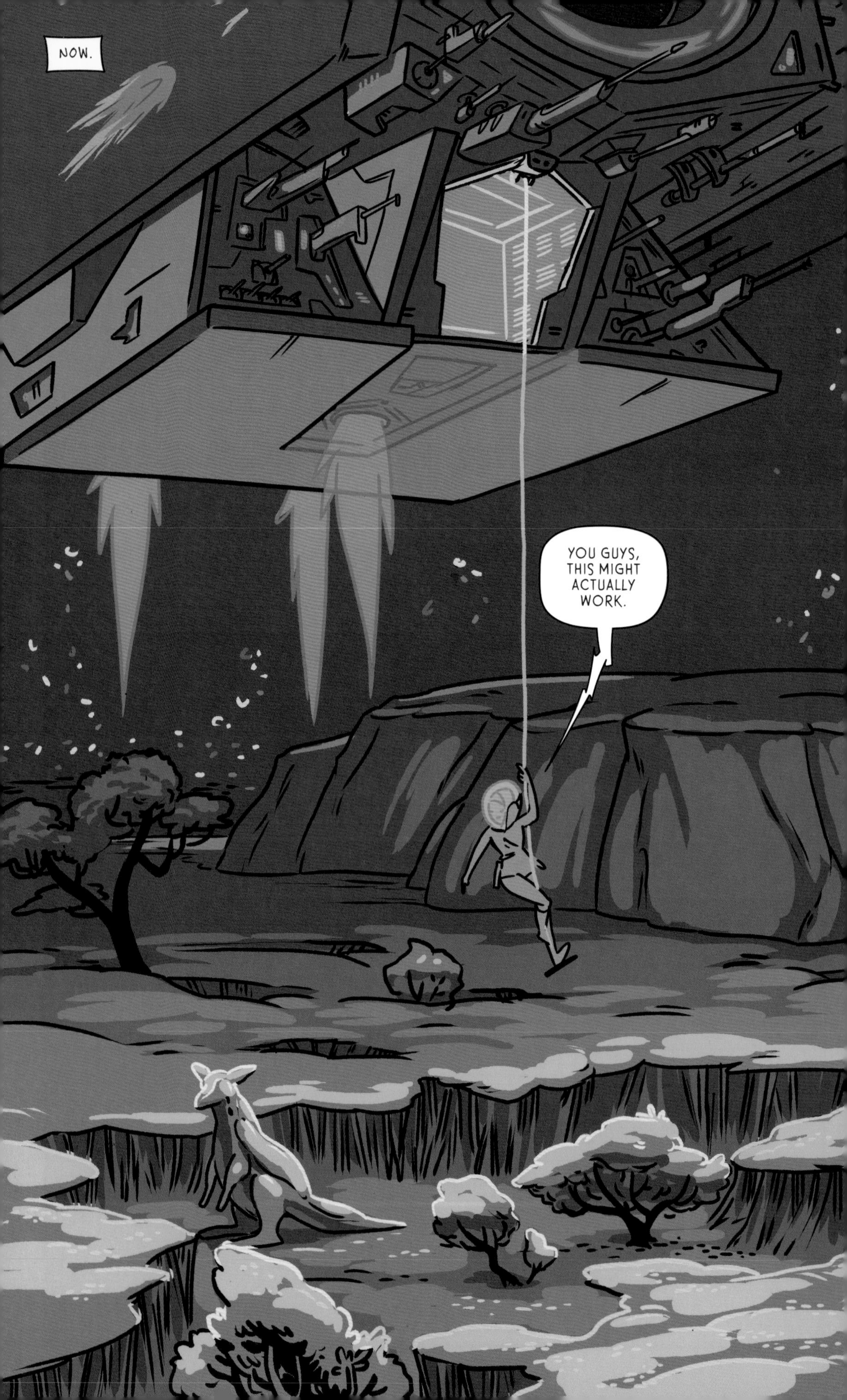
NOW.
YOU GUYS, THIS MIGHT ACTUALLY WORK.

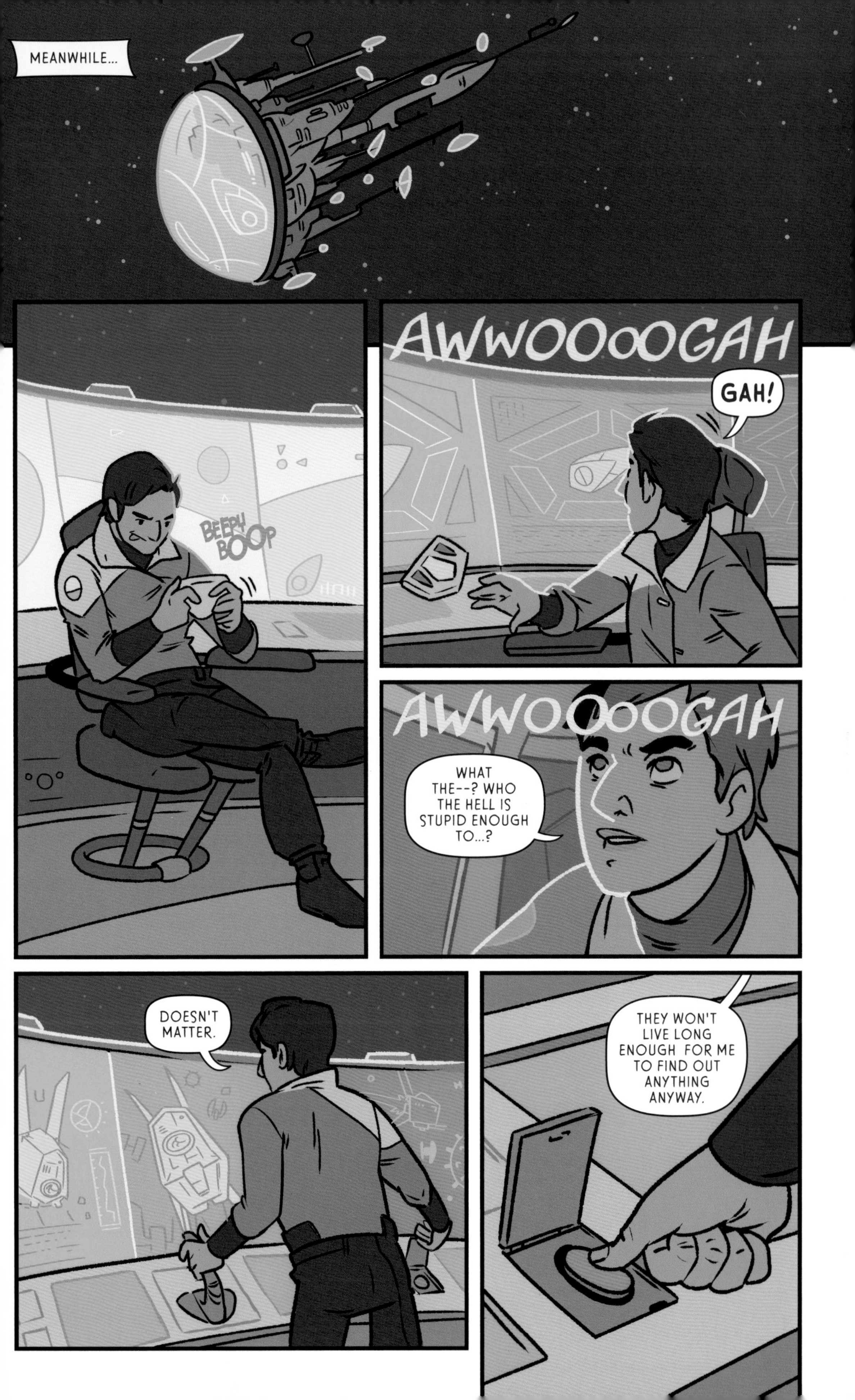
MEANWHILE...
BEEPH BOOP
AWWOOOOGAH
GAH!
AWWOOOOGAH
WHAT THE--? WHO THE HELL IS STUPID ENOUGH TO...?
DOESN'T MATTER.
THEY WON'T LIVE LONG ENOUGH FOR ME TO FIND OUT ANYTHING ANYWAY.

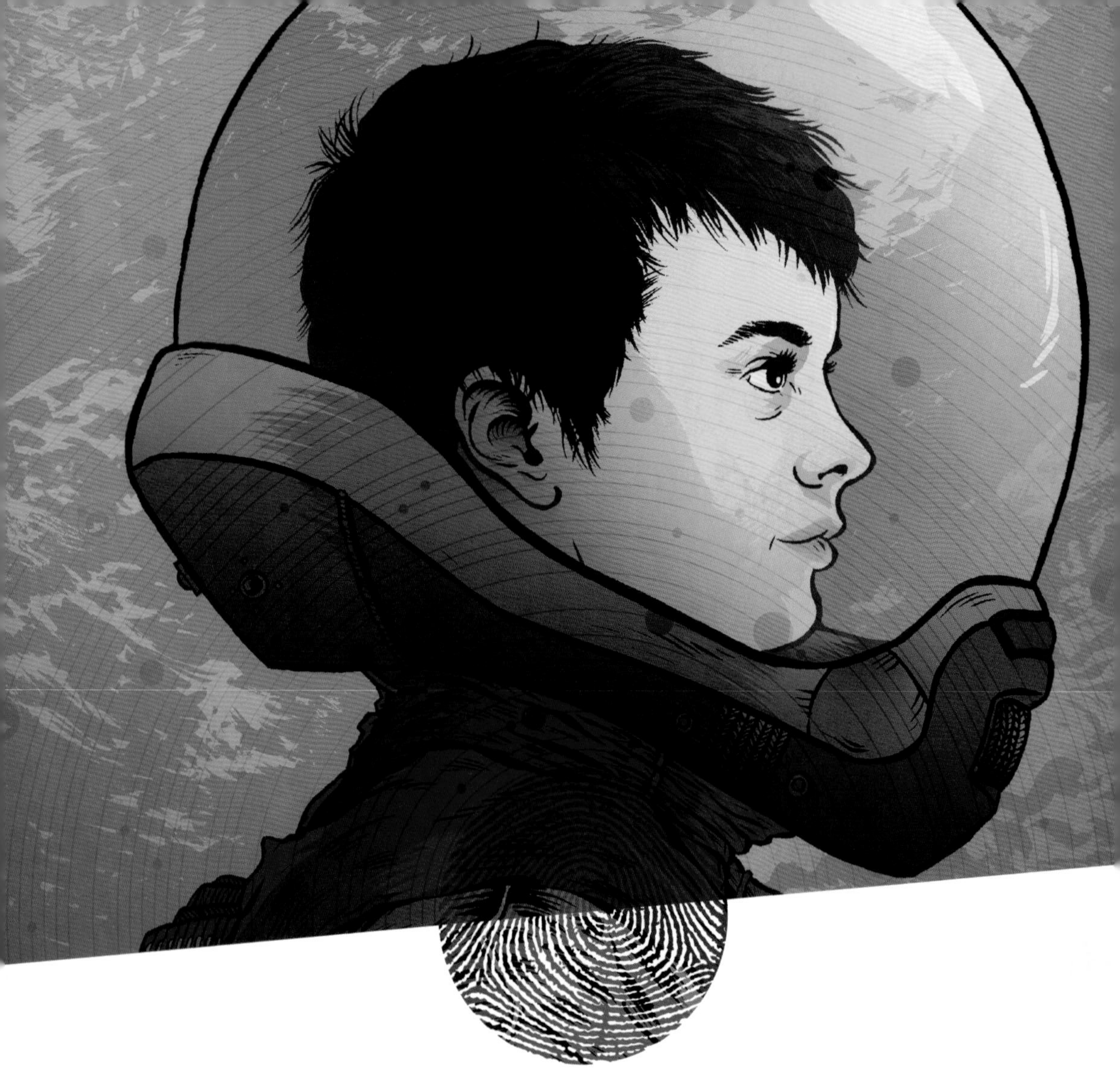

CHAPTER TWO

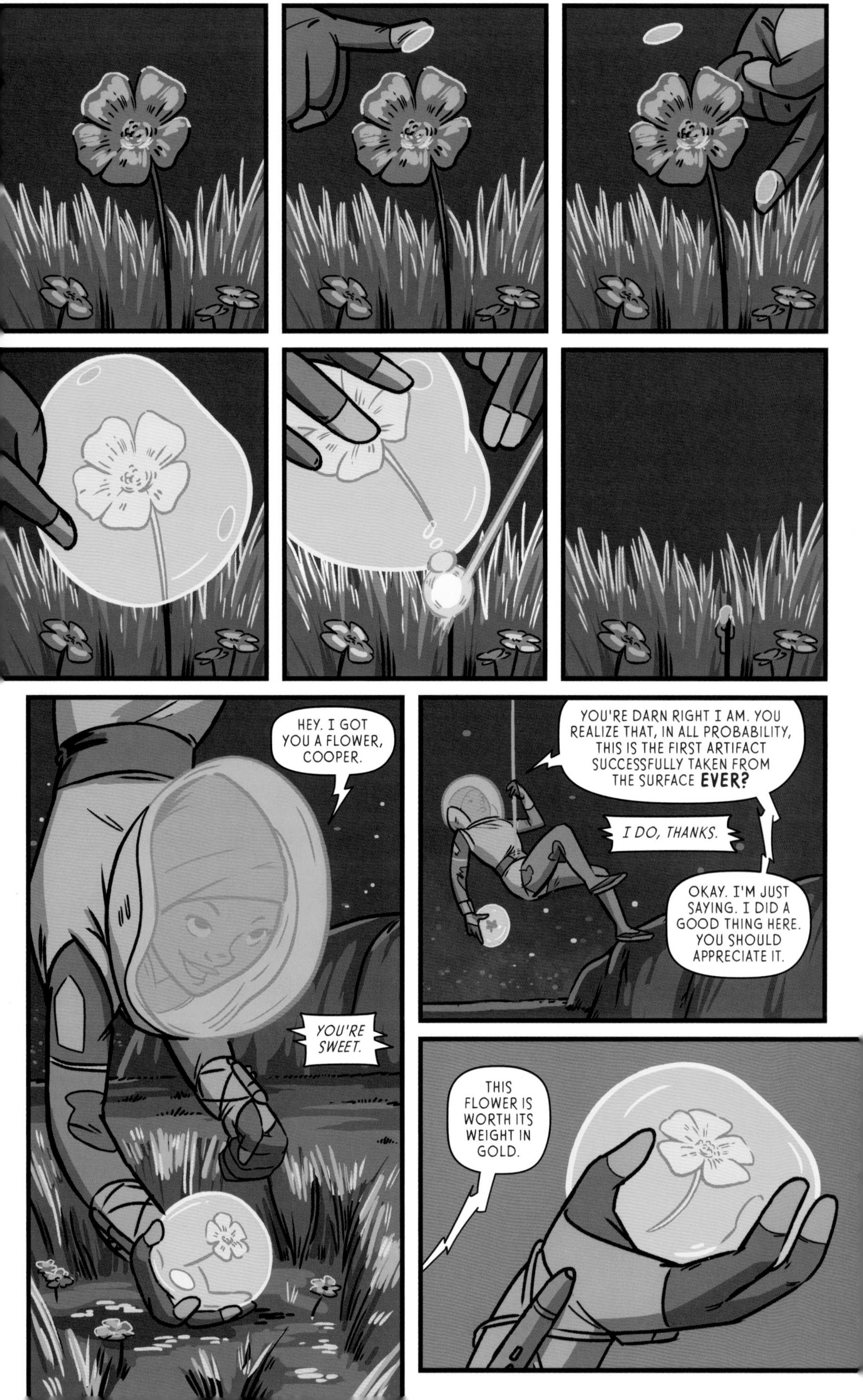
HEY. I GOT YOU A FLOWER, COOPER.
YOU'RE SWEET.
YOU'RE DARN RIGHT I AM. YOU REALIZE THAT, IN ALL PROBABILITY, THIS IS THE FIRST ARTIFACT SUCCESSFULLY TAKEN FROM THE SURFACE **EVER?**
I DO, THANKS.
OKAY. I'M JUST SAYING. I DID A GOOD THING HERE. YOU SHOULD APPRECIATE IT.
THIS FLOWER IS WORTH ITS WEIGHT IN GOLD.

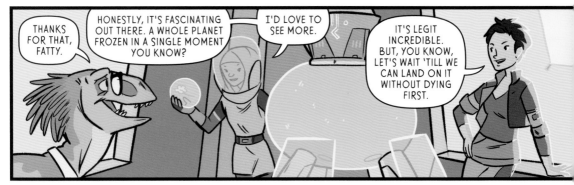

THANKS FOR THAT, FATTY.

HONESTLY, IT'S FASCINATING OUT THERE. A WHOLE PLANET FROZEN IN A SINGLE MOMENT YOU KNOW?

I'D LOVE TO SEE MORE.

IT'S LEGIT INCREDIBLE. BUT, YOU KNOW, LET'S WAIT 'TILL WE CAN LAND ON IT WITHOUT DYING FIRST.

ALRIGHT, WE'VE GOT ALL FOUR STASIS FIELD EMITTERS RUNNING IN REDUNDANT PARALLEL, AND IF THOSE SOMEHOW ALL FAIL, THE ADAPTIVE COMPRESSED AIR IS ON A SEPARATE POWER SYSTEM...THAT'LL KEEP WHATEVER'S INSIDE THE CHAMBER AIRBORNE FOR ABOUT 30 MINUTES.

UM, GIVE OR TAKE.

PUT 'ER IN.

THRUMMMM

WE'RE STABLE.

HEY. YOU WERE RAD OUT THERE.

AND MOM SAID MY DEGREE IN MUSEUM STUDIES WOULD NEVER COME IN USEFUL.

IT... BARELY WAS?

LISTEN, ARE WE READY?

AS WE'LL EVER BE.

LET'S DO IT, COOPER. **ENGAGE.**

CHOOM

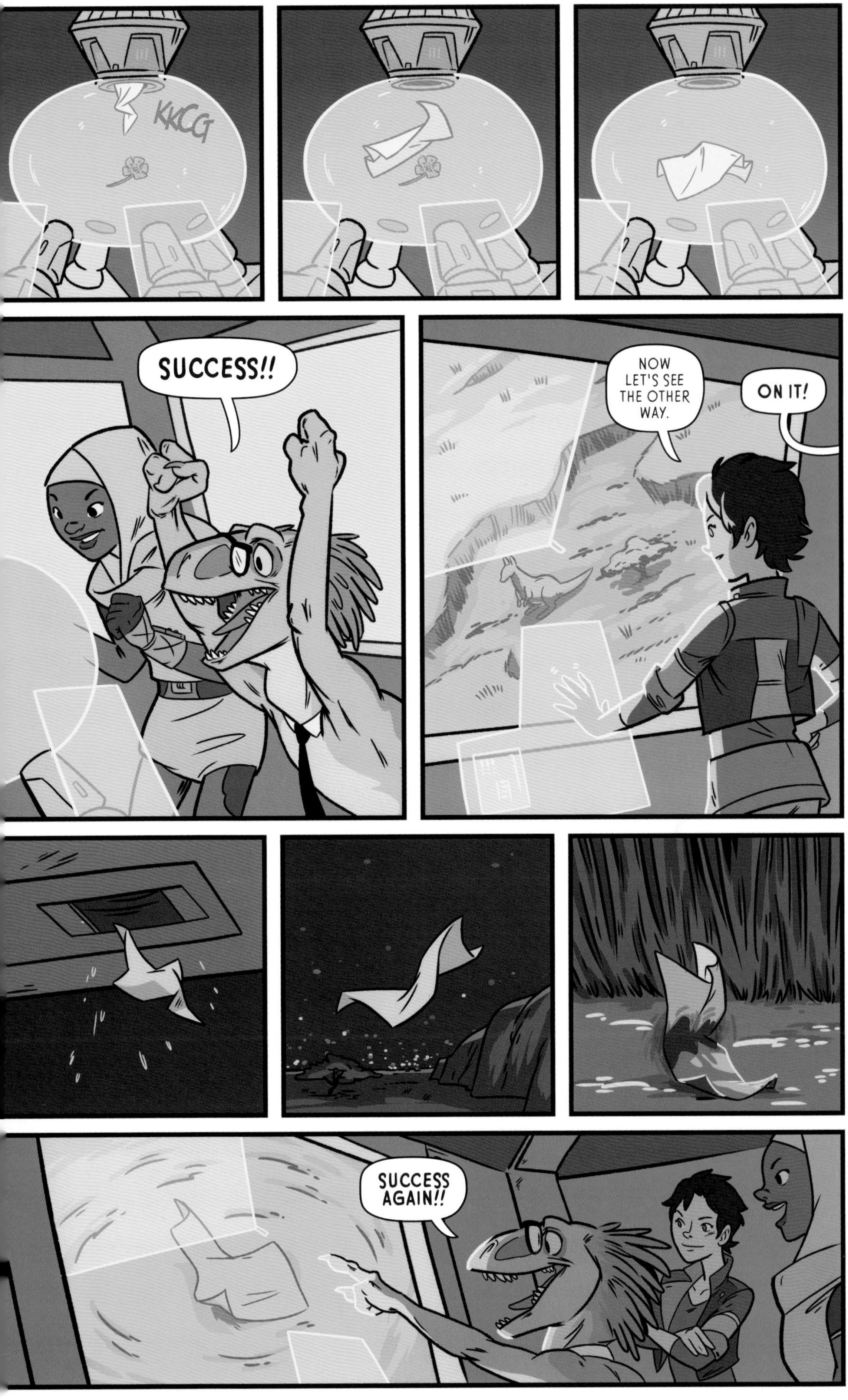
KKCG
SUCCESS!!
NOW LET'S SEE THE OTHER WAY.
ON IT!
SUCCESS AGAIN!!

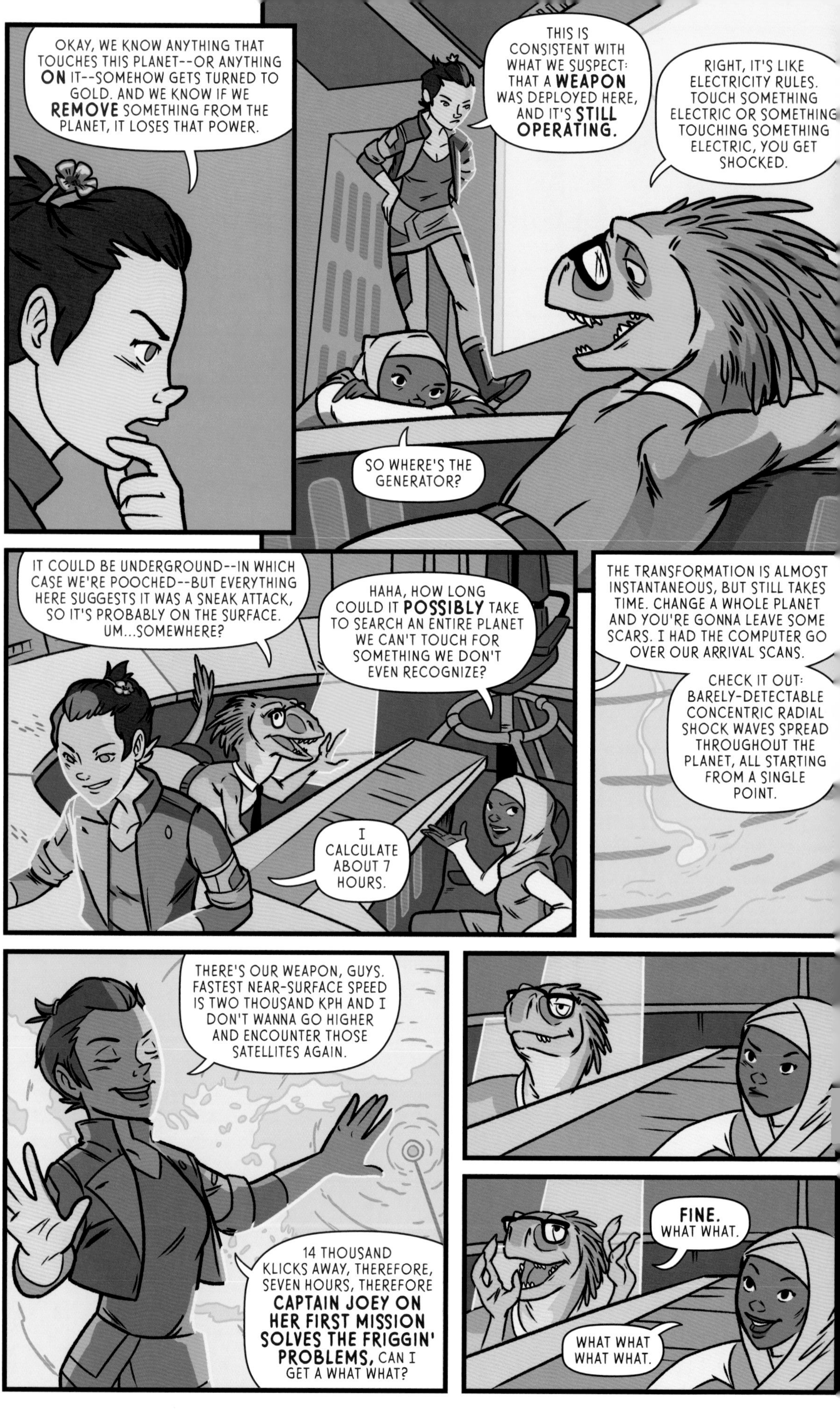
OKAY, WE KNOW ANYTHING THAT TOUCHES THIS PLANET--OR ANYTHING **ON** IT--SOMEHOW GETS TURNED TO GOLD. AND WE KNOW IF WE **REMOVE** SOMETHING FROM THE PLANET, IT LOSES THAT POWER.
THIS IS CONSISTENT WITH WHAT WE SUSPECT: THAT A **WEAPON** WAS DEPLOYED HERE, AND IT'S **STILL OPERATING.**
RIGHT, IT'S LIKE ELECTRICITY RULES. TOUCH SOMETHING ELECTRIC OR SOMETHING TOUCHING SOMETHING ELECTRIC, YOU GET SHOCKED.
SO WHERE'S THE GENERATOR?
IT COULD BE UNDERGROUND--IN WHICH CASE WE'RE POOCHED--BUT EVERYTHING HERE SUGGESTS IT WAS A SNEAK ATTACK, SO IT'S PROBABLY ON THE SURFACE. UM...SOMEWHERE?
HAHA, HOW LONG COULD IT **POSSIBLY** TAKE TO SEARCH AN ENTIRE PLANET WE CAN'T TOUCH FOR SOMETHING WE DON'T EVEN RECOGNIZE?
I CALCULATE ABOUT 7 HOURS.
THE TRANSFORMATION IS ALMOST INSTANTANEOUS, BUT STILL TAKES TIME. CHANGE A WHOLE PLANET AND YOU'RE GONNA LEAVE SOME SCARS. I HAD THE COMPUTER GO OVER OUR ARRIVAL SCANS.
CHECK IT OUT: BARELY-DETECTABLE CONCENTRIC RADIAL SHOCK WAVES SPREAD THROUGHOUT THE PLANET, ALL STARTING FROM A SINGLE POINT.
THERE'S OUR WEAPON, GUYS. FASTEST NEAR-SURFACE SPEED IS TWO THOUSAND KPH AND I DON'T WANNA GO HIGHER AND ENCOUNTER THOSE SATELLITES AGAIN.
14 THOUSAND KLICKS AWAY, THEREFORE, SEVEN HOURS, THEREFORE **CAPTAIN JOEY ON HER FIRST MISSION SOLVES THE FRIGGIN' PROBLEMS,** CAN I GET A WHAT WHAT?
FINE. WHAT WHAT.
WHAT WHAT WHAT WHAT.

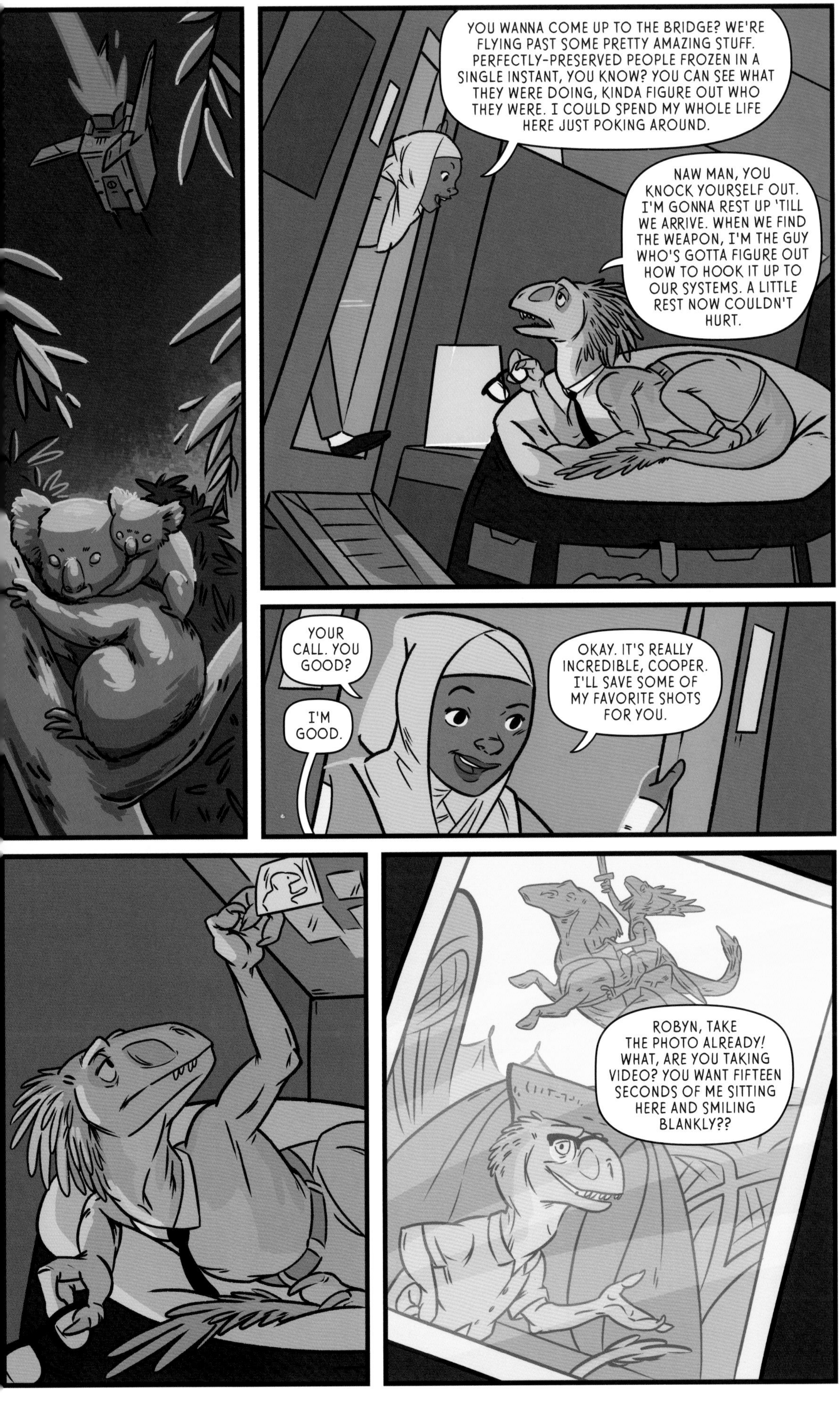
YOU WANNA COME UP TO THE BRIDGE? WE'RE FLYING PAST SOME PRETTY AMAZING STUFF. PERFECTLY-PRESERVED PEOPLE FROZEN IN A SINGLE INSTANT, YOU KNOW? YOU CAN SEE WHAT THEY WERE DOING, KINDA FIGURE OUT WHO THEY WERE. I COULD SPEND MY WHOLE LIFE HERE JUST POKING AROUND.
NAW MAN, YOU KNOCK YOURSELF OUT. I'M GONNA REST UP 'TILL WE ARRIVE. WHEN WE FIND THE WEAPON, I'M THE GUY WHO'S GOTTA FIGURE OUT HOW TO HOOK IT UP TO OUR SYSTEMS. A LITTLE REST NOW COULDN'T HURT.
YOUR CALL. YOU GOOD?
I'M GOOD.
OKAY. IT'S REALLY INCREDIBLE, COOPER. I'LL SAVE SOME OF MY FAVORITE SHOTS FOR YOU.
ROBYN, TAKE THE PHOTO ALREADY! WHAT, ARE YOU TAKING VIDEO? YOU WANT FIFTEEN SECONDS OF ME SITTING HERE AND SMILING BLANKLY??

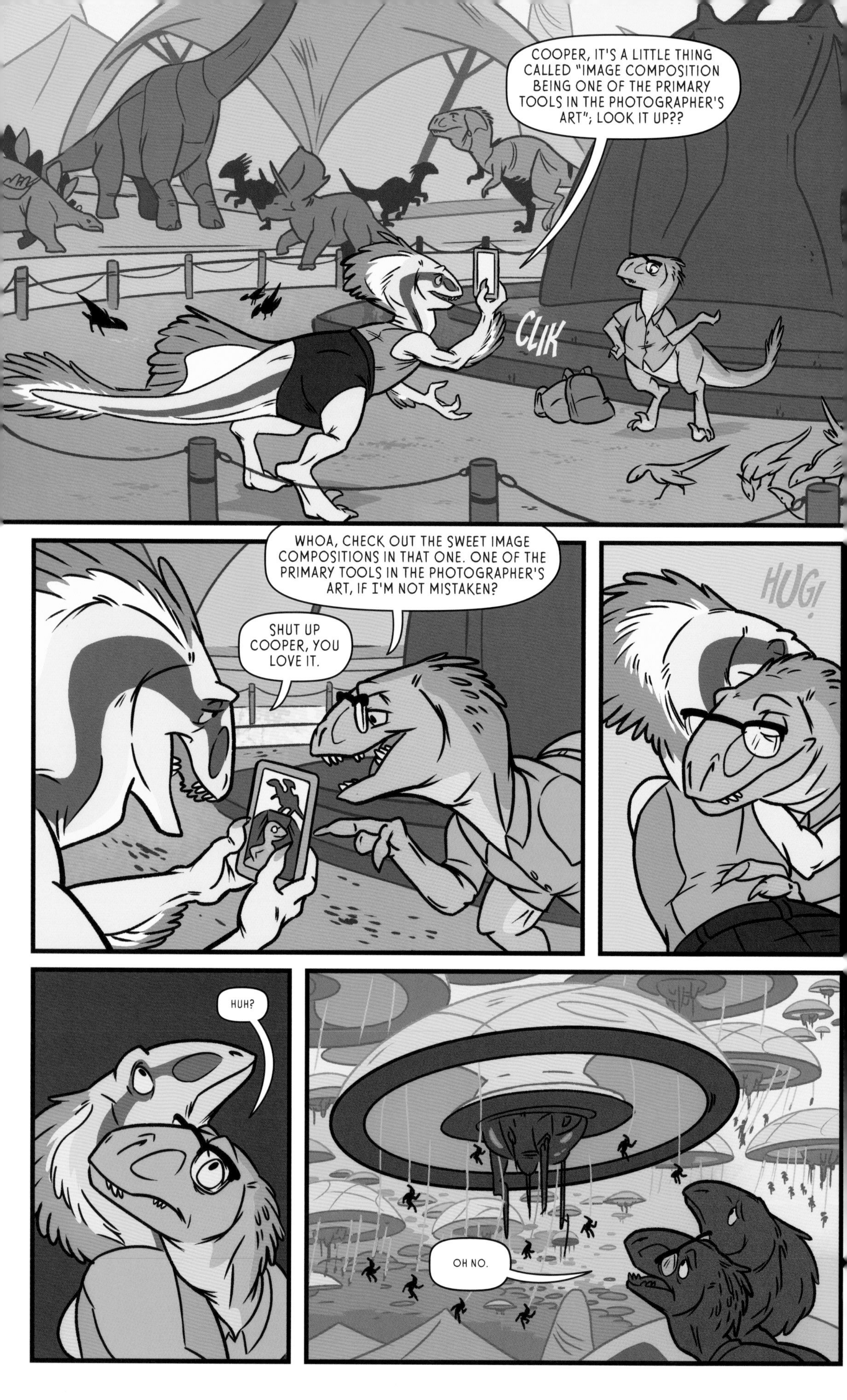
COOPER, IT'S A LITTLE THING CALLED "IMAGE COMPOSITION BEING ONE OF THE PRIMARY TOOLS IN THE PHOTOGRAPHER'S ART"; LOOK IT UP??
CLIK
WHOA, CHECK OUT THE SWEET IMAGE COMPOSITIONS IN THAT ONE. ONE OF THE PRIMARY TOOLS IN THE PHOTOGRAPHER'S ART, IF I'M NOT MISTAKEN?
SHUT UP COOPER, YOU LOVE IT.
HUG!
HUH?
OH NO.

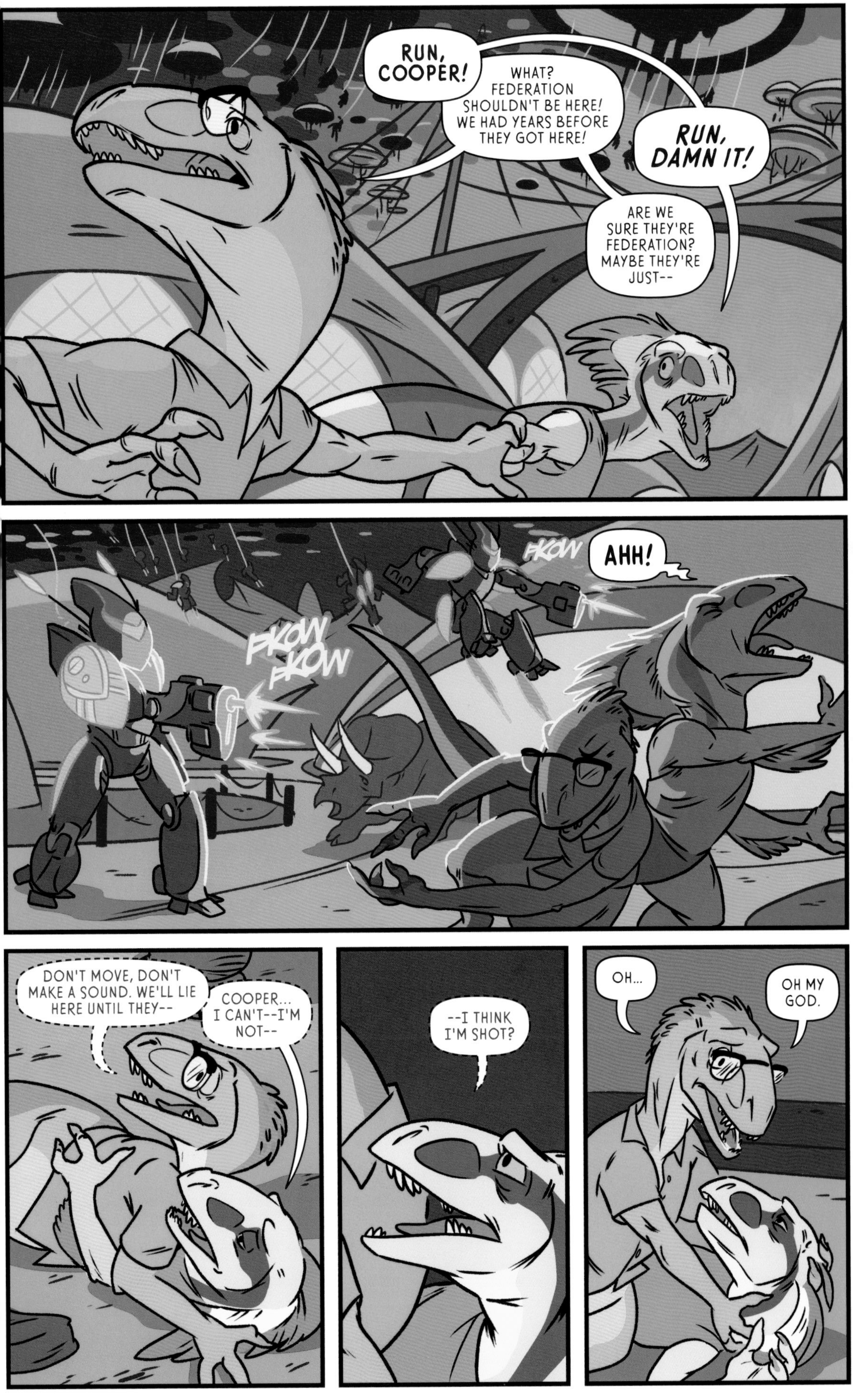
RUN, COOPER!
WHAT? FEDERATION SHOULDN'T BE HERE! WE HAD YEARS BEFORE THEY GOT HERE!
RUN, DAMN IT!
ARE WE SURE THEY'RE FEDERATION? MAYBE THEY'RE JUST--
PKOW
AHH!
PKOW PKOW
DON'T MOVE, DON'T MAKE A SOUND. WE'LL LIE HERE UNTIL THEY--
COOPER... I CAN'T--I'M NOT--
--I THINK I'M SHOT?
OH...
OH MY GOD.

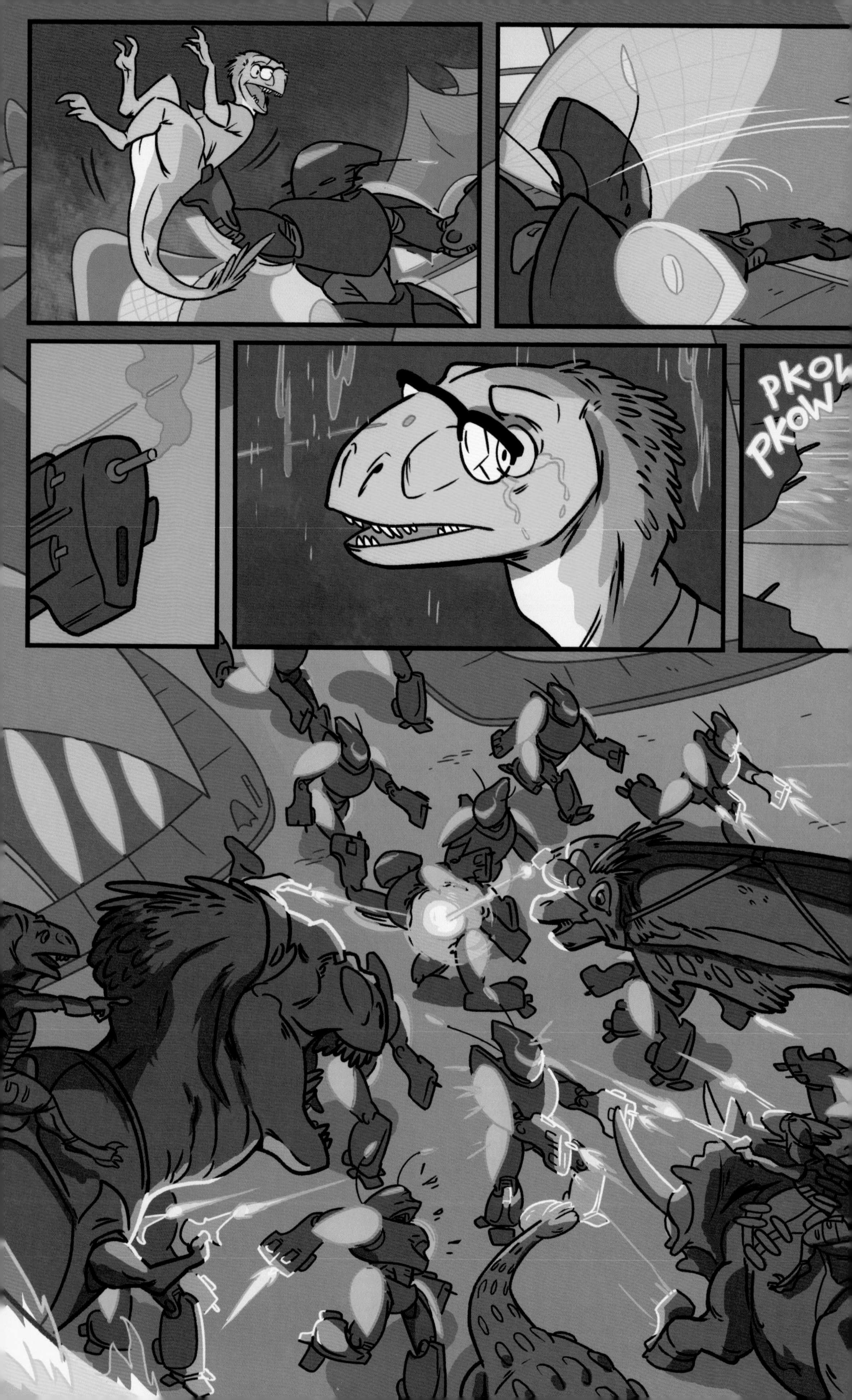
PKOW
PKOW

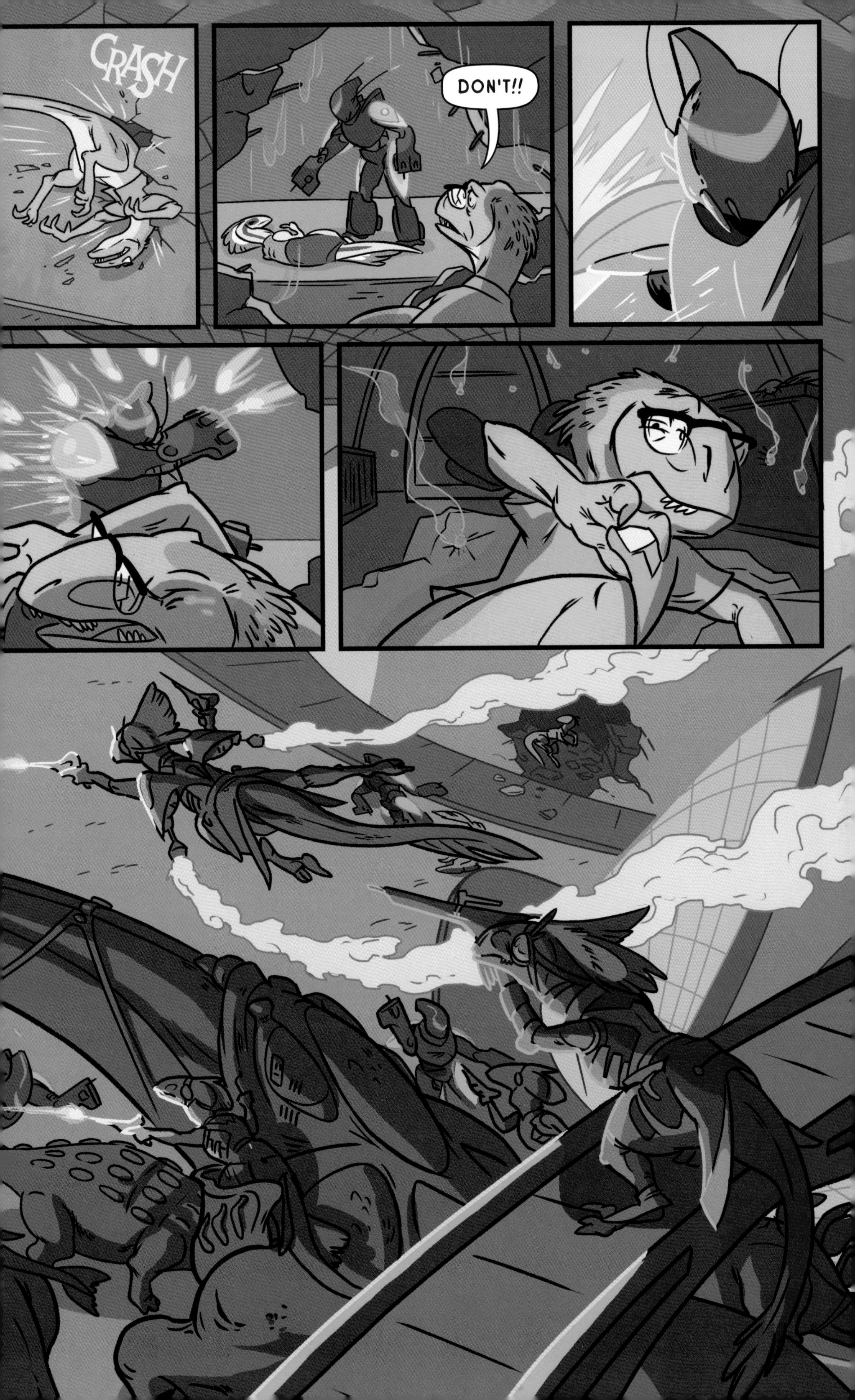
CRASH
DON'T!!

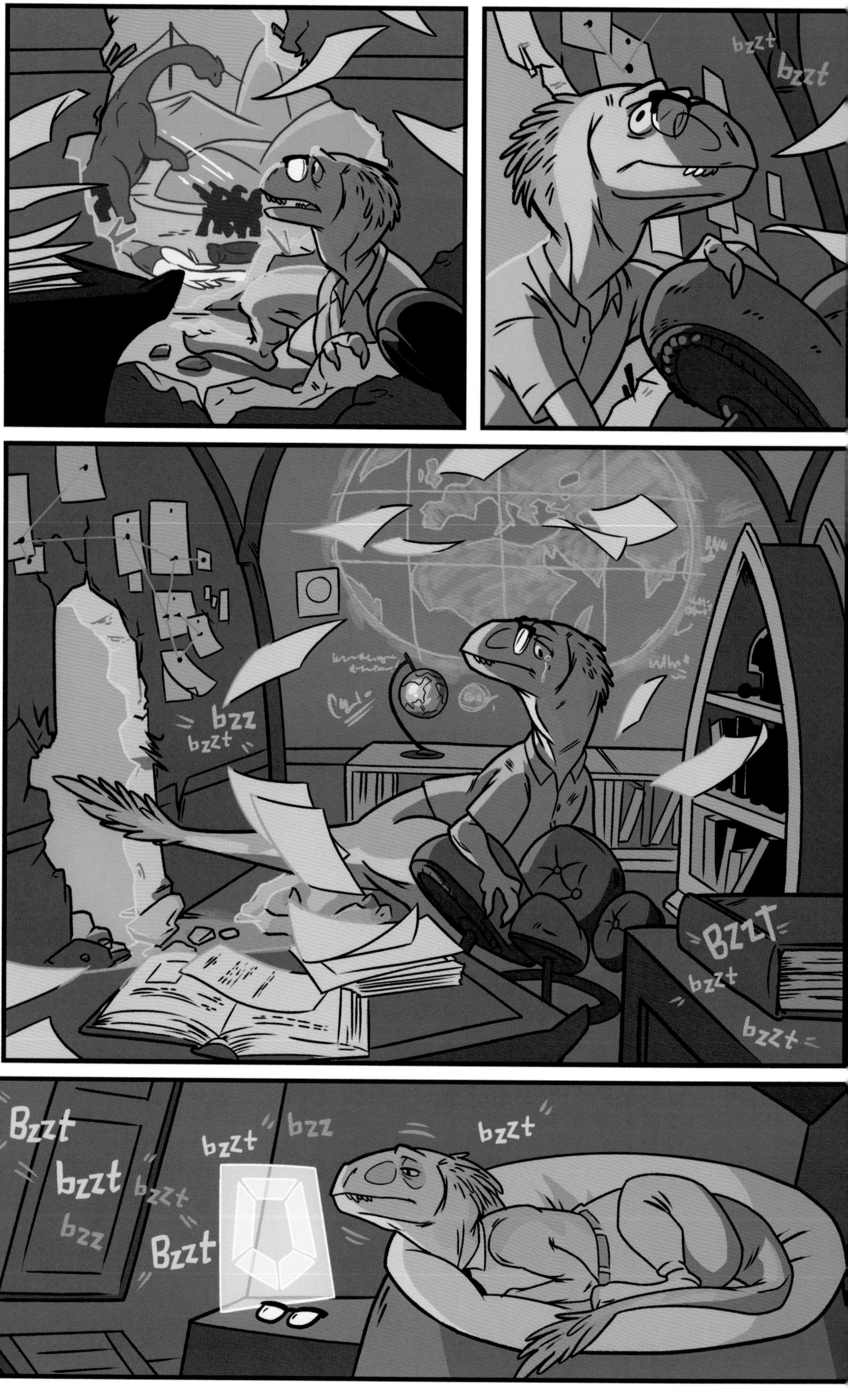
bzzt
bzzt
bzz
bzzt
BZZT
bzzt
bzzt
Bzzt
bzzt
bzzt
bzz
Bzzt
bzzt
bzz
bzzt

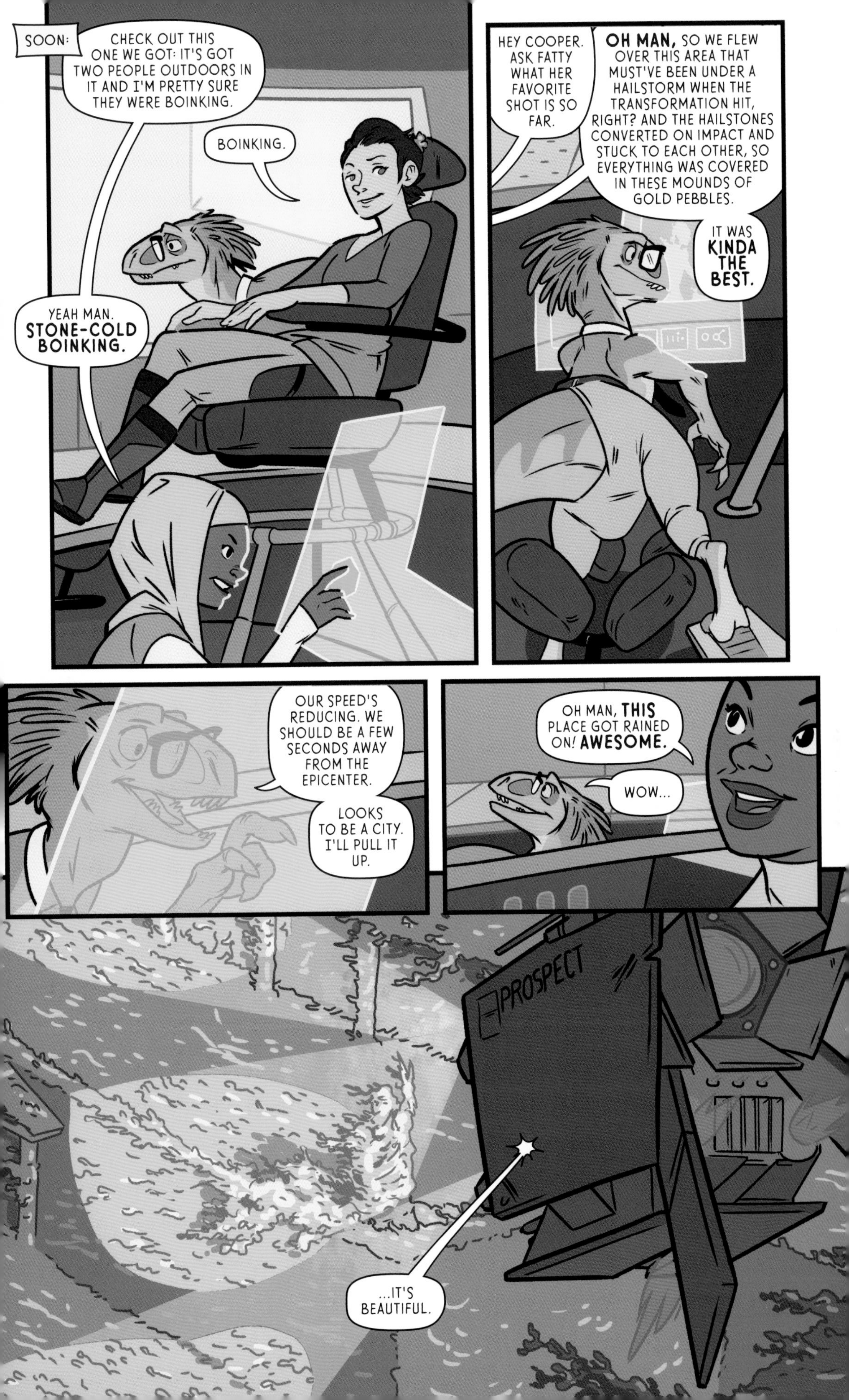
SOON:
CHECK OUT THIS ONE WE GOT: IT'S GOT TWO PEOPLE OUTDOORS IN IT AND I'M PRETTY SURE THEY WERE BOINKING.
BOINKING.
YEAH MAN. STONE-COLD BOINKING.
HEY COOPER. ASK FATTY WHAT HER FAVORITE SHOT IS SO FAR.
OH MAN, SO WE FLEW OVER THIS AREA THAT MUST'VE BEEN UNDER A HAILSTORM WHEN THE TRANSFORMATION HIT, RIGHT? AND THE HAILSTONES CONVERTED ON IMPACT AND STUCK TO EACH OTHER, SO EVERYTHING WAS COVERED IN THESE MOUNDS OF GOLD PEBBLES.
IT WAS KINDA THE BEST.
OUR SPEED'S REDUCING. WE SHOULD BE A FEW SECONDS AWAY FROM THE EPICENTER.
LOOKS TO BE A CITY. I'LL PULL IT UP.
OH MAN, THIS PLACE GOT RAINED ON! AWESOME.
WOW...
PROSPECT
...IT'S BEAUTIFUL.

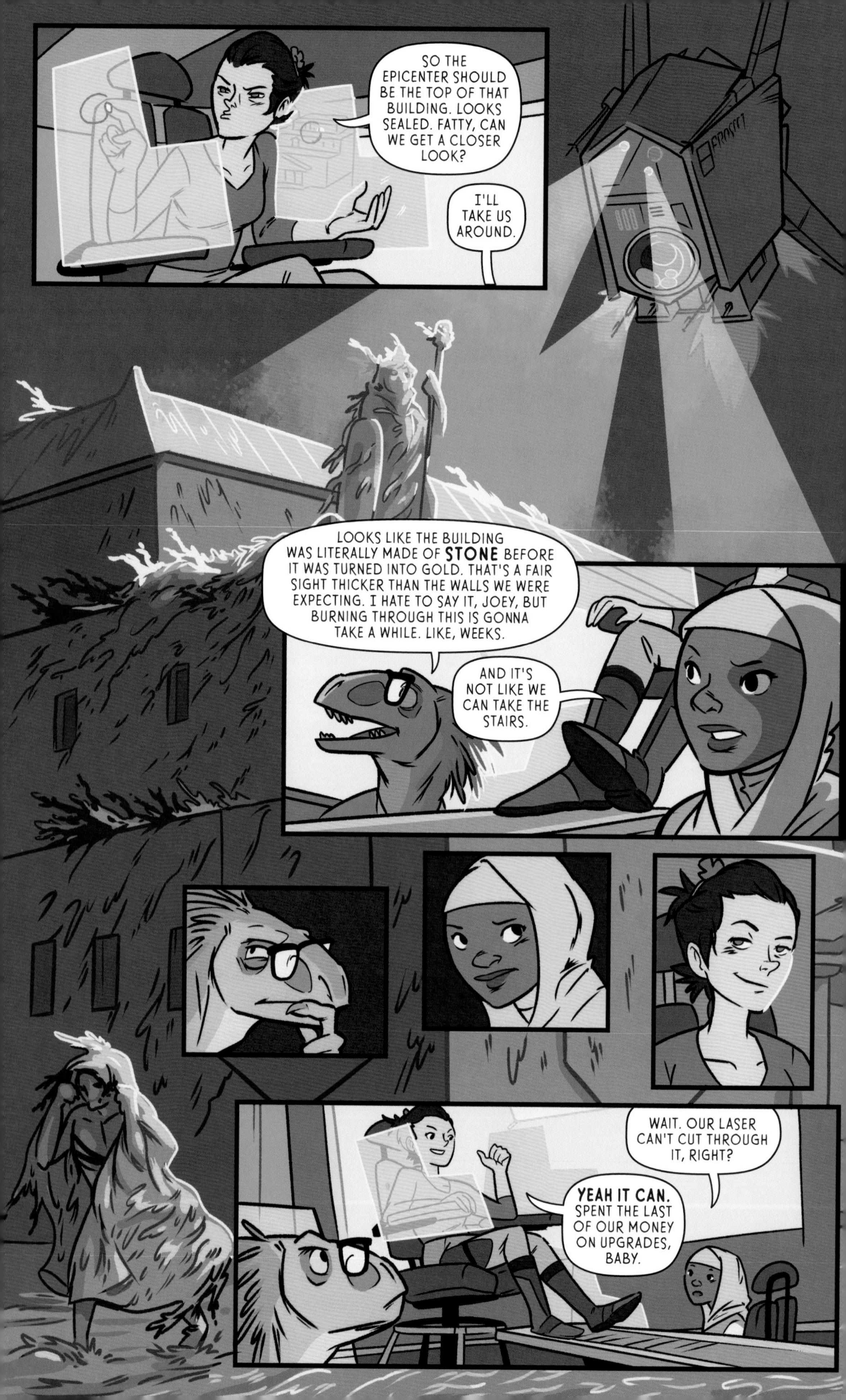
SO THE EPICENTER SHOULD BE THE TOP OF THAT BUILDING. LOOKS SEALED. FATTY, CAN WE GET A CLOSER LOOK?
I'LL TAKE US AROUND.
LOOKS LIKE THE BUILDING WAS LITERALLY MADE OF **STONE** BEFORE IT WAS TURNED INTO GOLD. THAT'S A FAIR SIGHT THICKER THAN THE WALLS WE WERE EXPECTING. I HATE TO SAY IT, JOEY, BUT BURNING THROUGH THIS IS GONNA TAKE A WHILE. LIKE, WEEKS.
AND IT'S NOT LIKE WE CAN TAKE THE STAIRS.
WAIT. OUR LASER CAN'T CUT THROUGH IT, RIGHT?
YEAH IT CAN. SPENT THE LAST OF OUR MONEY ON UPGRADES, BABY.

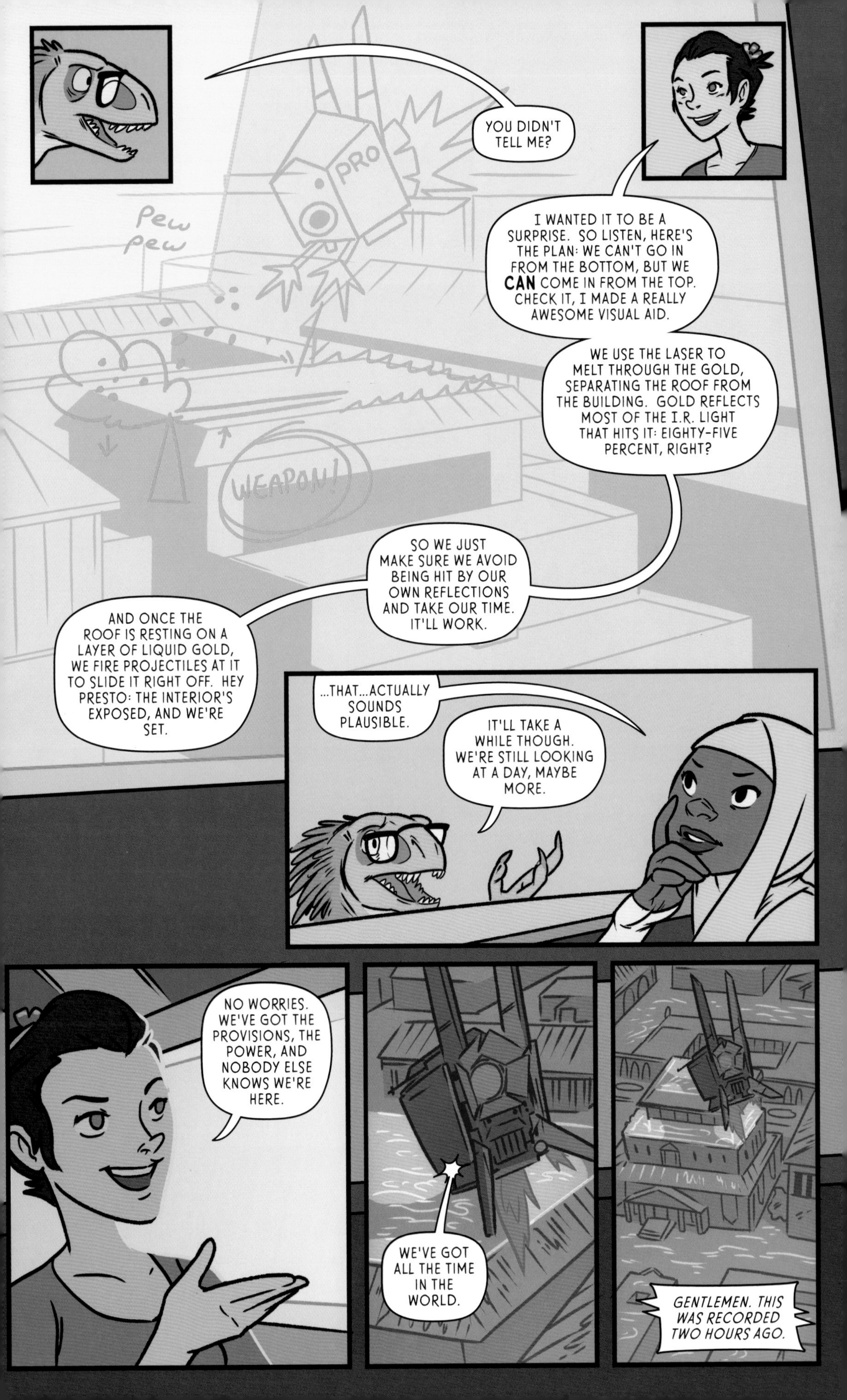

YOU DIDN'T TELL ME?
PRO
Pew pew
WEAPON!
I WANTED IT TO BE A SURPRISE. SO LISTEN, HERE'S THE PLAN: WE CAN'T GO IN FROM THE BOTTOM, BUT WE **CAN** COME IN FROM THE TOP. CHECK IT, I MADE A REALLY AWESOME VISUAL AID.
WE USE THE LASER TO MELT THROUGH THE GOLD, SEPARATING THE ROOF FROM THE BUILDING. GOLD REFLECTS MOST OF THE I.R. LIGHT THAT HITS IT: EIGHTY-FIVE PERCENT, RIGHT?
SO WE JUST MAKE SURE WE AVOID BEING HIT BY OUR OWN REFLECTIONS AND TAKE OUR TIME. IT'LL WORK.
AND ONCE THE ROOF IS RESTING ON A LAYER OF LIQUID GOLD, WE FIRE PROJECTILES AT IT TO SLIDE IT RIGHT OFF. HEY PRESTO: THE INTERIOR'S EXPOSED, AND WE'RE SET.
...THAT...ACTUALLY SOUNDS PLAUSIBLE.
IT'LL TAKE A WHILE THOUGH. WE'RE STILL LOOKING AT A DAY, MAYBE MORE.
NO WORRIES. WE'VE GOT THE PROVISIONS, THE POWER, AND NOBODY ELSE KNOWS WE'RE HERE.
WE'VE GOT ALL THE TIME IN THE WORLD.
GENTLEMEN. THIS WAS RECORDED TWO HOURS AGO.

ELEVEN HOURS BEFORE THAT, WE RECEIVED AN ALARM FROM AN AUTOMATED SYSTEM SO OLD WE COULDN'T UNDERSTAND IT AT FIRST.

TOOK US SIX HOURS JUST TO DECODE WHAT THE ALERT WAS ABOUT--OBSOLETE PROTOCOL WITHOUT ANY EXTANT DOCUMENTATION--AND SEVERAL MORE TO VERIFY WHAT IT WAS SAYING. THAT LED US TO SOME FORGOTTEN AND ENCRYPTED ARCHIVES, WHERE WE HAD TO BREAK INTO OUR OWN DAMN FILES.

WHAT YOU ARE ABOUT TO BRIEFED ON ARE THE FRUITS OF THAT EFFORT. I REMIND YOU THIS COMMUNICATION IS CLASSIFIED.

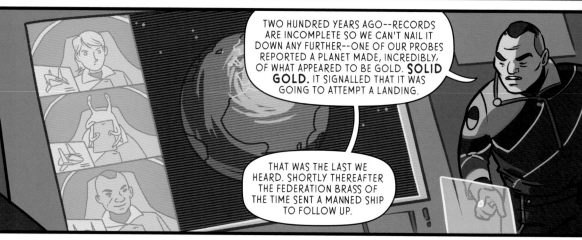

TWO HUNDRED YEARS AGO--RECORDS ARE INCOMPLETE SO WE CAN'T NAIL IT DOWN ANY FURTHER--ONE OF OUR PROBES REPORTED A PLANET MADE, INCREDIBLY, OF WHAT APPEARED TO BE GOLD. **SOLID GOLD.** IT SIGNALLED THAT IT WAS GOING TO ATTEMPT A LANDING.

THAT WAS THE LAST WE HEARD. SHORTLY THEREAFTER THE FEDERATION BRASS OF THE TIME SENT A MANNED SHIP TO FOLLOW UP.

THEY NEVER MADE IT OUT THE DOOR.

CAM 02

THAT GOT OUR ATTENTION. THIS TIME THE FEDERATION SENT FIVE MORE SHIPS WITH EXPLICIT ORDERS: TEST IT, OBSERVE IT, REPORT BACK. NO LANDINGS TO BE ATTEMPTED.

THESE SHIPS DISCOVERED FOUR THINGS. ONE: THE PLANET WAS AS IT APPEARED: SOLID GOLD. TWO: THE PLANET HAD BEEN UNREMARKABLE UNTIL THIS TRANSFORMATION TOOK PLACE, WHICH APPEARED TO HAVE CAUGHT THE WORLD OFF-GUARD.

02

CAM 03

THREE: ANY CONTACT WITH THE PLANET WOULD TURN THAT CONTACTING ENTITY, WHETHER ANIMAL, VEGETABLE, OR MINERAL, INTO GOLD ITSELF.

AND FOUR: THERE WAS NO WAY TO CONTROL THAT INTERACTION.

CAM 02

THE FEDERATION HAD STUMBLED UPON A WORLD LEFT PERMANENTLY UNINHABITABLE BY AN UNKNOWN WEAPON--LIKELY AN EXTREMELY STABLE POLYMORPH. IT OUTCLASSED OUR TECHNOLOGY IN EVERY WAY. WE DIDN'T EVEN KNOW HOW TO BEGIN PULLING OFF SOMETHING LIKE THIS. HELL, WE **STILL** DON'T.

BUT SOMEONE OUT THERE DID, AND THEY'D ALREADY DEPLOYED IT AT LEAST ONCE. MAYBE THEY'D LEFT OUR GALAXY AND MAYBE THEY'D STUCK AROUND, BUT THERE WAS NO REASON TO ASSUME THEY WEREN'T HOSTILE.

WE NEEDED TO BE STRONGER.

AND WE **BECAME** STRONGER. BUT IN THE BEGINNING, WHEN THE FEDERATION DETERMINED WE COULDN'T CONTROL, DUPLICATE--OR EVEN LOCATE--THE WEAPON, WE DID THE NEXT BEST THING. WE ENSURED THAT NOBODY ELSE COULD EITHER. **WE ERASED THE PLANET.**

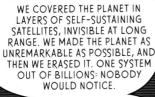

WE COVERED THE PLANET IN LAYERS OF SELF-SUSTAINING SATELLITES, INVISIBLE AT LONG RANGE. WE MADE THE PLANET AS UNREMARKABLE AS POSSIBLE, AND THEN WE ERASED IT. ONE SYSTEM OUT OF BILLIONS: NOBODY WOULD NOTICE.

NOBODY DID. THOSE WHO COULD'VE HAD ALREADY BEEN EXECUTED.

THE FEW WHO SURVIVED--THOSE WHO GAVE THE EXECUTION ORDER--UNDERSTOOD AND AGREED THAT THEIR NON-DISCLOSURE WAS UNDER PAIN OF DEATH FOR THEMSELVES, THE FAMILIES, AND WHOEVER THEY CONTACTED. AND WHEN THOSE GENERALS DIED...

...THE SECRET WAS FORGOTTEN. WE'D ERASED IT TOO WELL. THE AUTOMATIC SYSTEMS AROUND THE PLANET RAN THEMSELVES WITHOUT INCIDENT UNTIL YESTERDAY, WHEN FOR THE FIRST TIME IN CENTURIES, THEY WERE ENCOUNTERED. THEY WERE ENGAGED.

AND THEY WERE **BREACHED.**

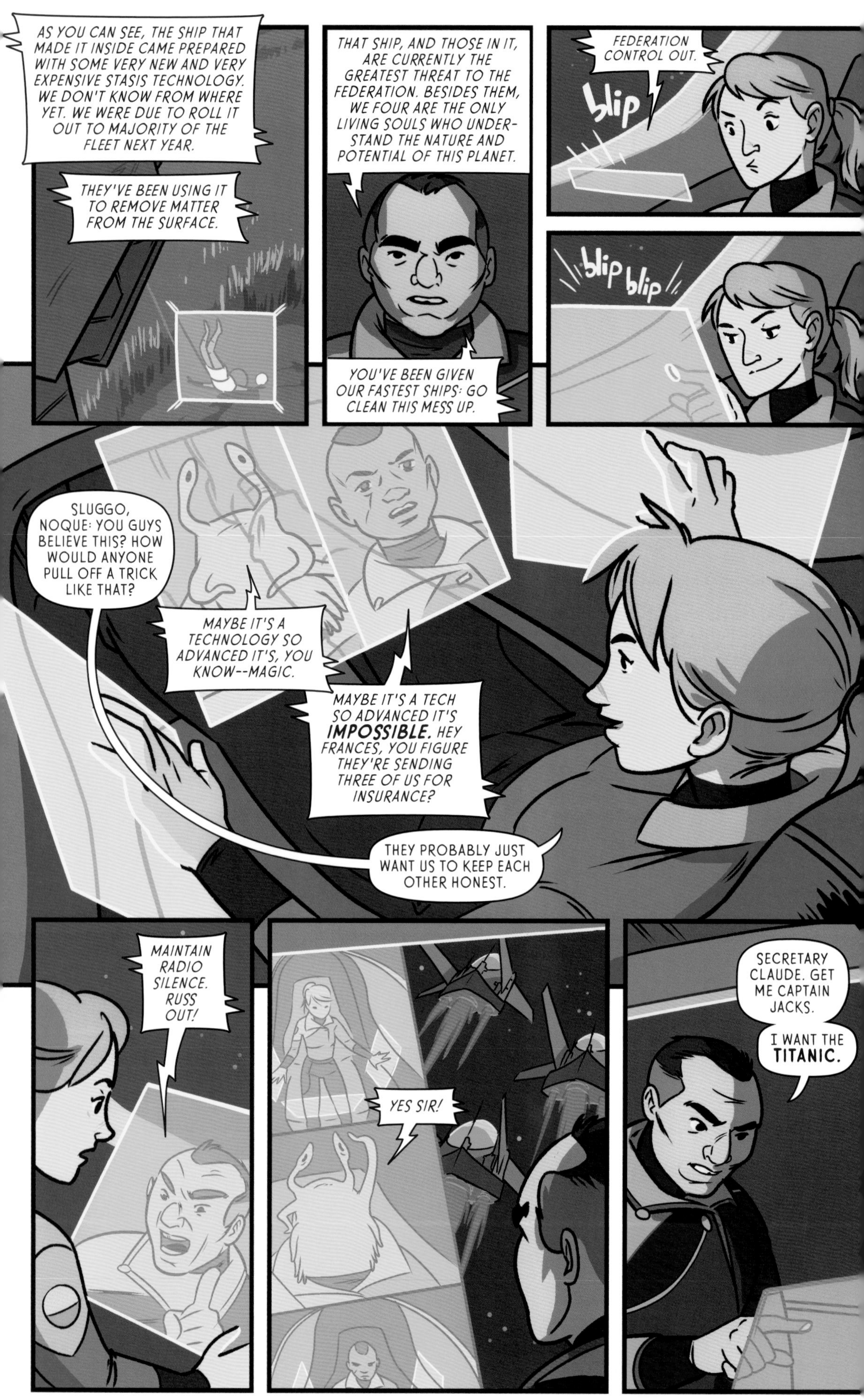
AS YOU CAN SEE, THE SHIP THAT MADE IT INSIDE CAME PREPARED WITH SOME VERY NEW AND VERY EXPENSIVE STASIS TECHNOLOGY. WE DON'T KNOW FROM WHERE YET. WE WERE DUE TO ROLL IT OUT TO MAJORITY OF THE FLEET NEXT YEAR.
THEY'VE BEEN USING IT TO REMOVE MATTER FROM THE SURFACE.
THAT SHIP, AND THOSE IN IT, ARE CURRENTLY THE GREATEST THREAT TO THE FEDERATION. BESIDES THEM, WE FOUR ARE THE ONLY LIVING SOULS WHO UNDERSTAND THE NATURE AND POTENTIAL OF THIS PLANET.
YOU'VE BEEN GIVEN OUR FASTEST SHIPS: GO CLEAN THIS MESS UP.
FEDERATION CONTROL OUT.
blip
blip blip
SLUGGO, NOQUE: YOU GUYS BELIEVE THIS? HOW WOULD ANYONE PULL OFF A TRICK LIKE THAT?
MAYBE IT'S A TECHNOLOGY SO ADVANCED IT'S, YOU KNOW--MAGIC.
MAYBE IT'S A TECH SO ADVANCED IT'S **IMPOSSIBLE.** HEY FRANCES, YOU FIGURE THEY'RE SENDING THREE OF US FOR INSURANCE?
THEY PROBABLY JUST WANT US TO KEEP EACH OTHER HONEST.
MAINTAIN RADIO SILENCE. RUSS OUT!
YES SIR!
SECRETARY CLAUDE. GET ME CAPTAIN JACKS.
I WANT THE **TITANIC.**

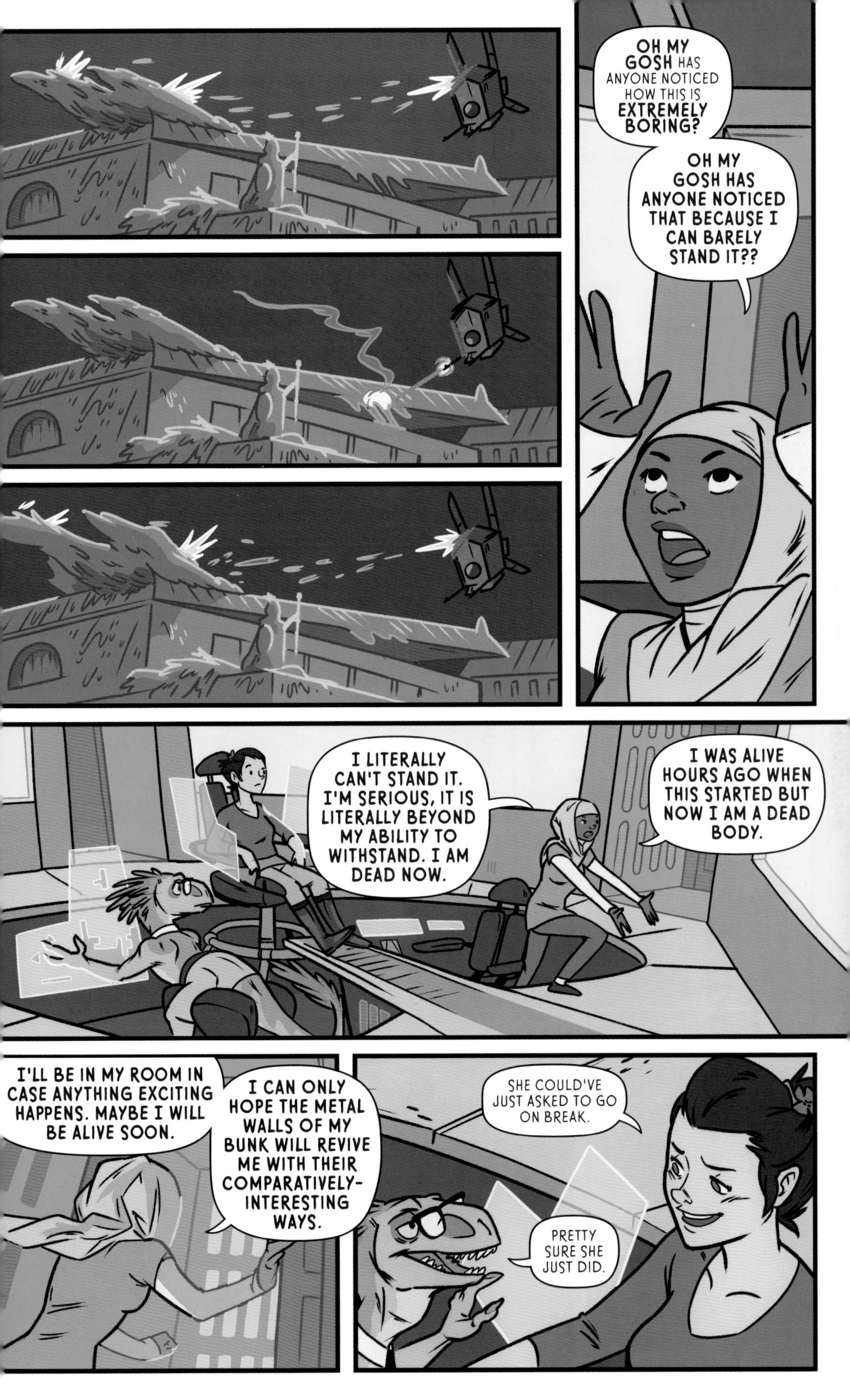
OH MY GOSH HAS ANYONE NOTICED HOW THIS IS EXTREMELY BORING?
OH MY GOSH HAS ANYONE NOTICED THAT BECAUSE I CAN BARELY STAND IT??
I LITERALLY CAN'T STAND IT. I'M SERIOUS, IT IS LITERALLY BEYOND MY ABILITY TO WITHSTAND. I AM DEAD NOW.
I WAS ALIVE HOURS AGO WHEN THIS STARTED BUT NOW I AM A DEAD BODY.
I'LL BE IN MY ROOM IN CASE ANYTHING EXCITING HAPPENS. MAYBE I WILL BE ALIVE SOON.
I CAN ONLY HOPE THE METAL WALLS OF MY BUNK WILL REVIVE ME WITH THEIR COMPARATIVELY-INTERESTING WAYS.
SHE COULD'VE JUST ASKED TO GO ON BREAK.
PRETTY SURE SHE JUST DID.

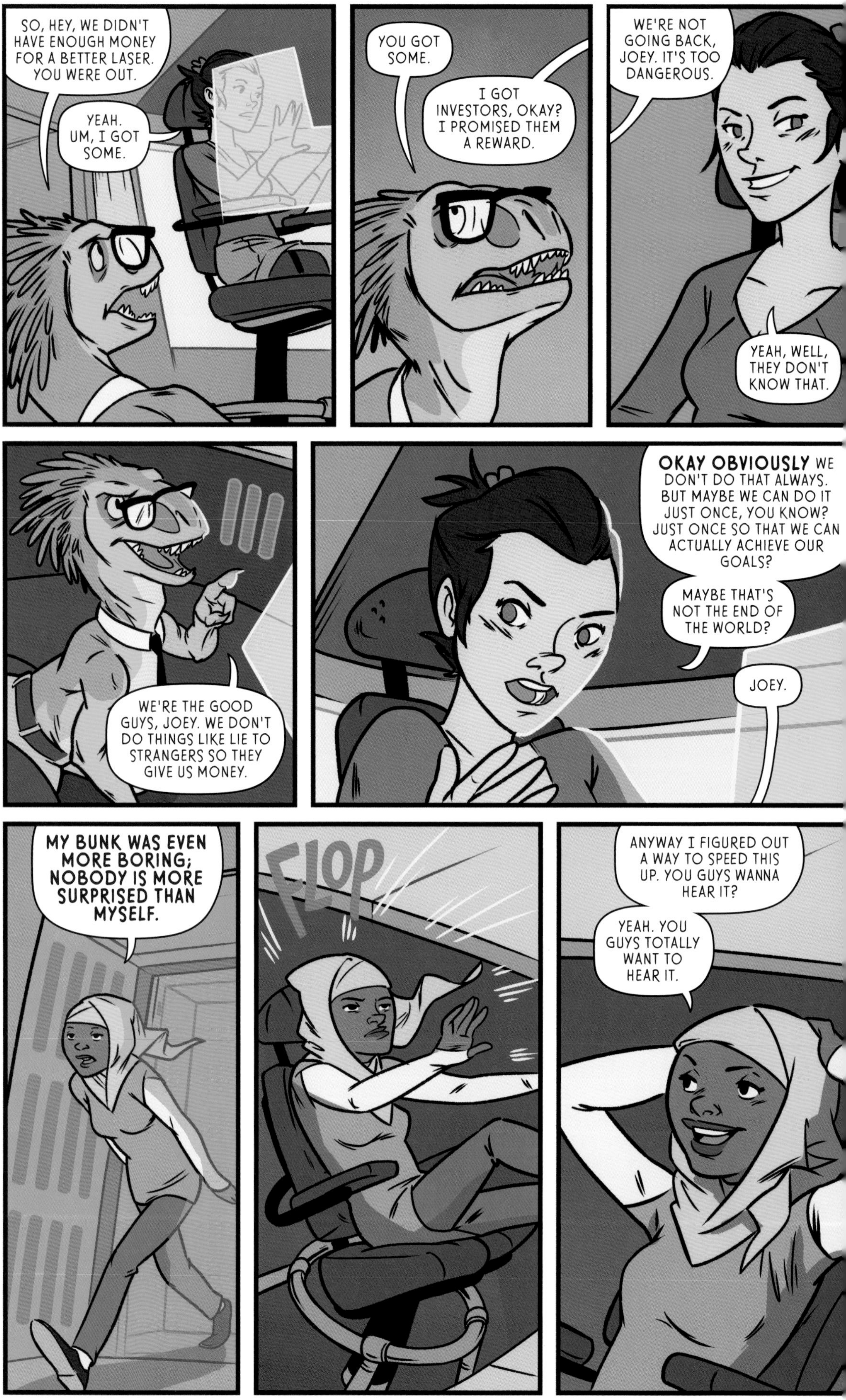
SO, HEY, WE DIDN'T HAVE ENOUGH MONEY FOR A BETTER LASER. YOU WERE OUT.
YEAH. UM, I GOT SOME.
YOU GOT SOME.
I GOT INVESTORS, OKAY? I PROMISED THEM A REWARD.
WE'RE NOT GOING BACK, JOEY. IT'S TOO DANGEROUS.
YEAH, WELL, THEY DON'T KNOW THAT.
WE'RE THE GOOD GUYS, JOEY. WE DON'T DO THINGS LIKE LIE TO STRANGERS SO THEY GIVE US MONEY.
OKAY OBVIOUSLY WE DON'T DO THAT ALWAYS. BUT MAYBE WE CAN DO IT JUST ONCE, YOU KNOW? JUST ONCE SO THAT WE CAN ACTUALLY ACHIEVE OUR GOALS?
MAYBE THAT'S NOT THE END OF THE WORLD?
JOEY.
MY BUNK WAS EVEN MORE BORING; NOBODY IS MORE SURPRISED THAN MYSELF.
FLOP
ANYWAY I FIGURED OUT A WAY TO SPEED THIS UP. YOU GUYS WANNA HEAR IT?
YEAH. YOU GUYS TOTALLY WANT TO HEAR IT.

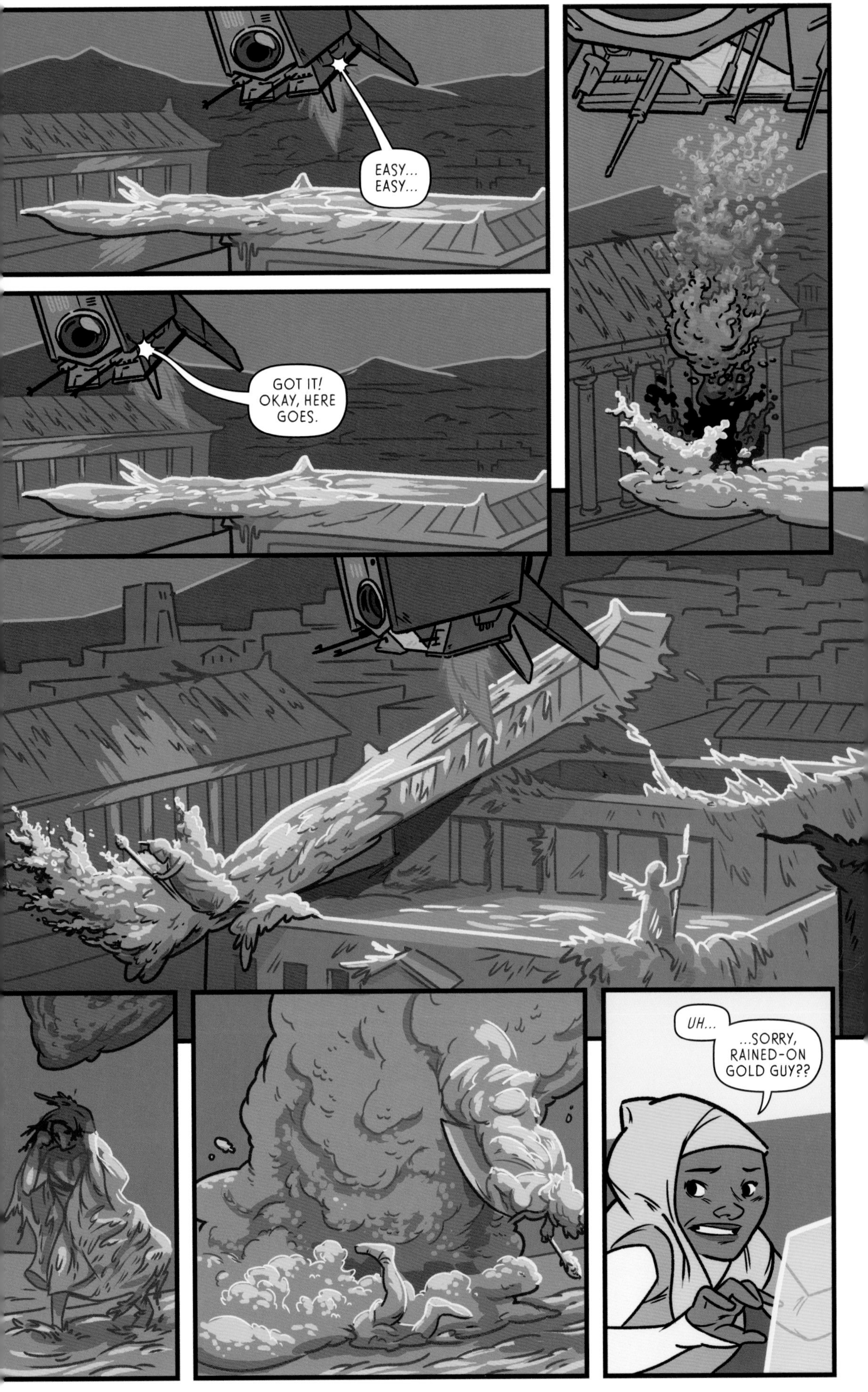
EASY...
EASY...
GOT IT! OKAY, HERE GOES.
UH...
...SORRY, RAINED-ON GOLD GUY??

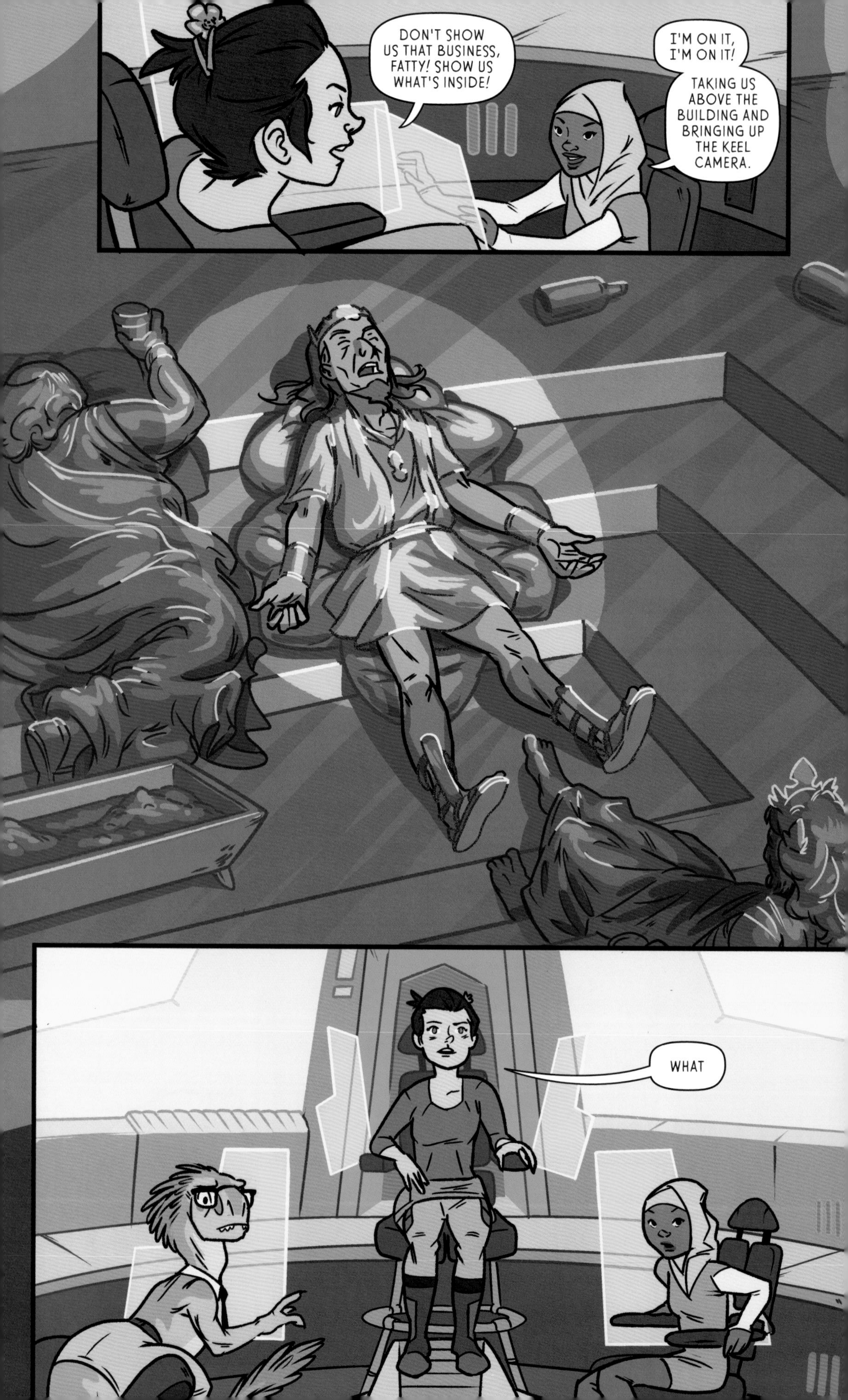
DON'T SHOW US THAT BUSINESS, FATTY! SHOW US WHAT'S INSIDE!
I'M ON IT, I'M ON IT!
TAKING US ABOVE THE BUILDING AND BRINGING UP THE KEEL CAMERA.
WHAT

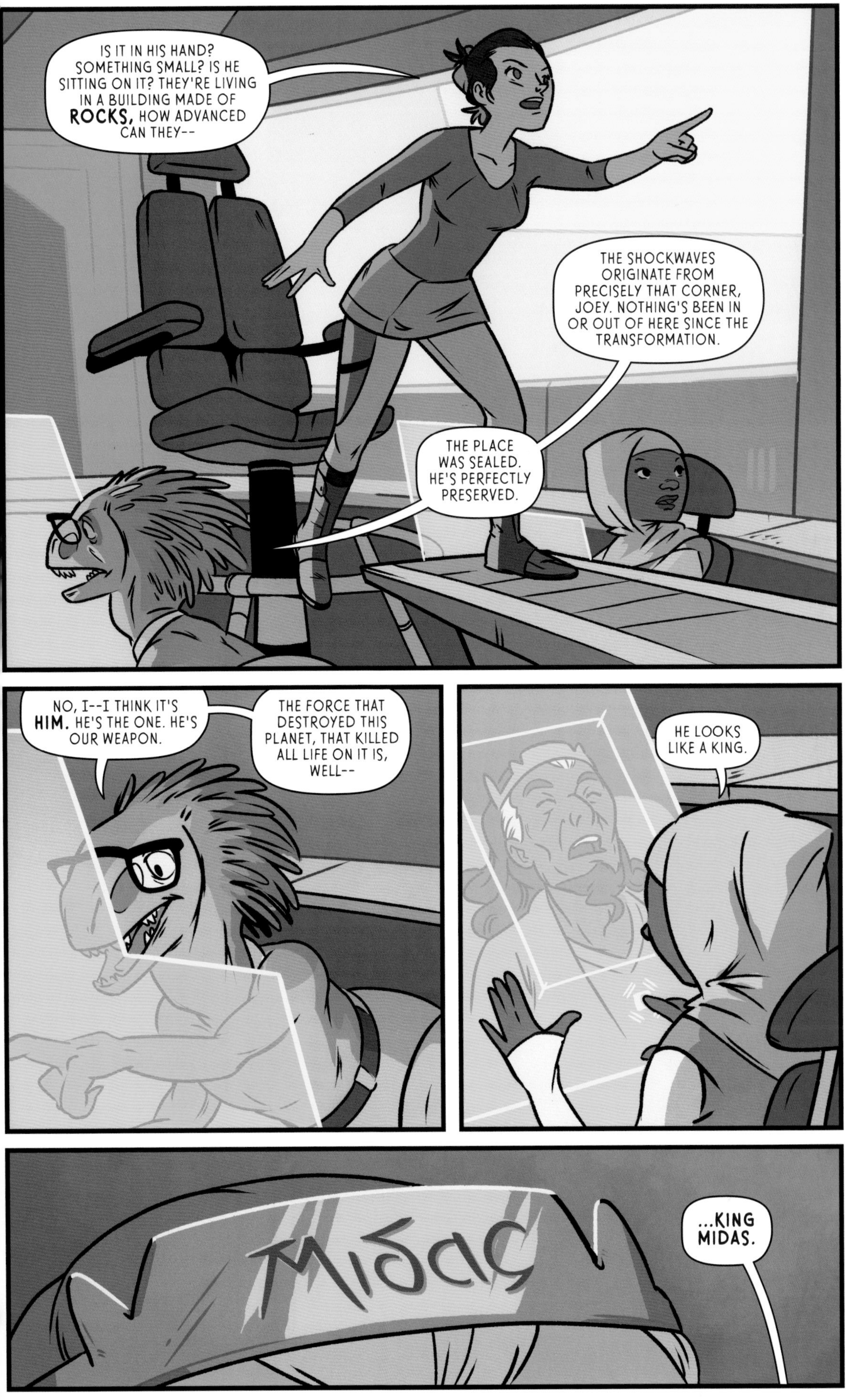
IS IT IN HIS HAND? SOMETHING SMALL? IS HE SITTING ON IT? THEY'RE LIVING IN A BUILDING MADE OF ROCKS, HOW ADVANCED CAN THEY--
THE SHOCKWAVES ORIGINATE FROM PRECISELY THAT CORNER, JOEY. NOTHING'S BEEN IN OR OUT OF HERE SINCE THE TRANSFORMATION.
THE PLACE WAS SEALED. HE'S PERFECTLY PRESERVED.
NO, I--I THINK IT'S HIM. HE'S THE ONE. HE'S OUR WEAPON.
THE FORCE THAT DESTROYED THIS PLANET, THAT KILLED ALL LIFE ON IT IS, WELL--
HE LOOKS LIKE A KING.
...KING MIDAS.

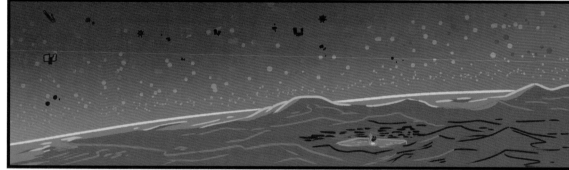

BRING 'EM UP, EVERYONE.

ACKNOWLEDGED. WEAPONS HOT.

TIME TO CONTACT: TEN MINUTES.

ALRIGHT. LET'S END THIS.

"A WHOLE PLANET FROZEN IN A SINGLE MOMENT…"

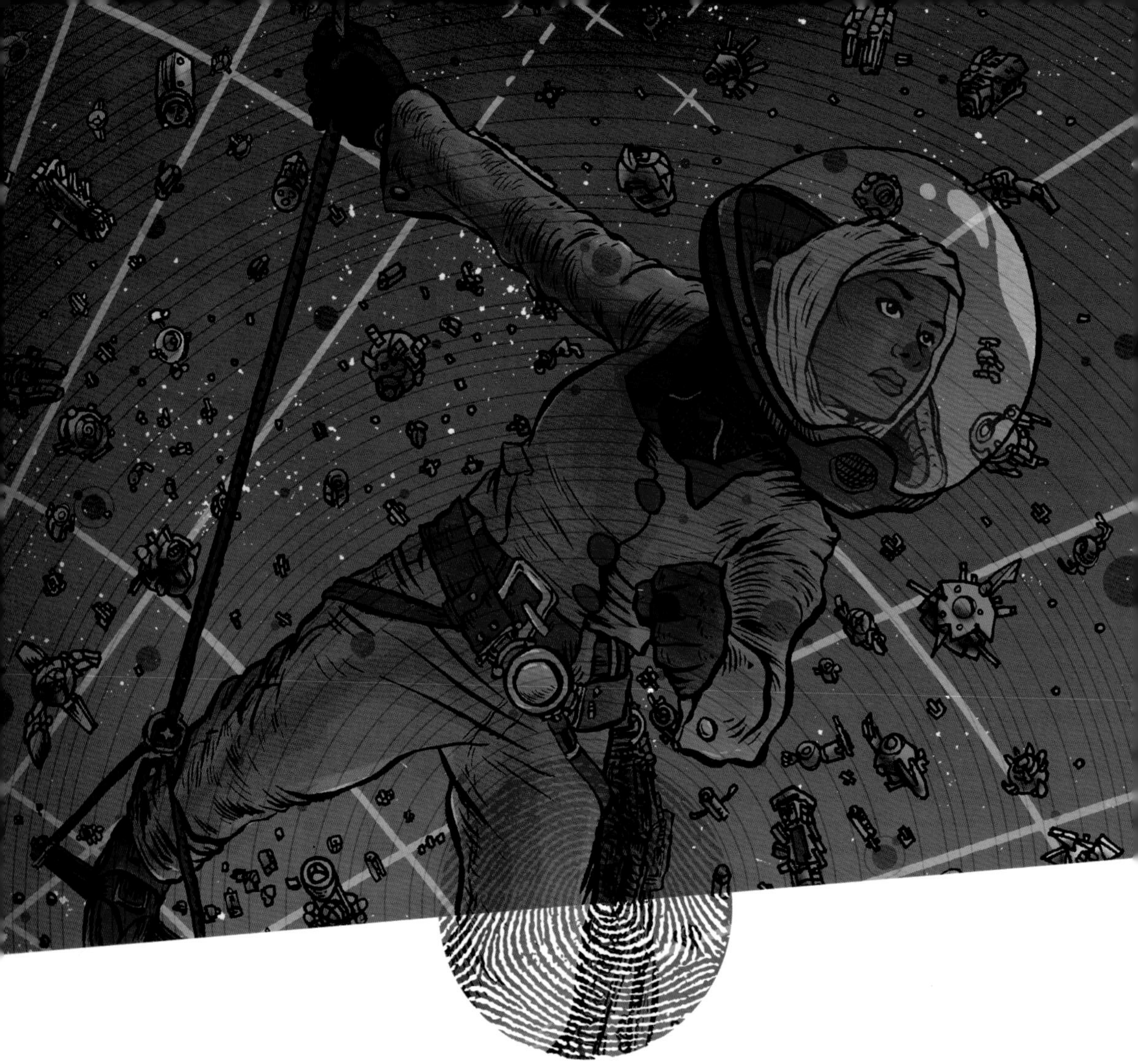

CHAPTER THREE

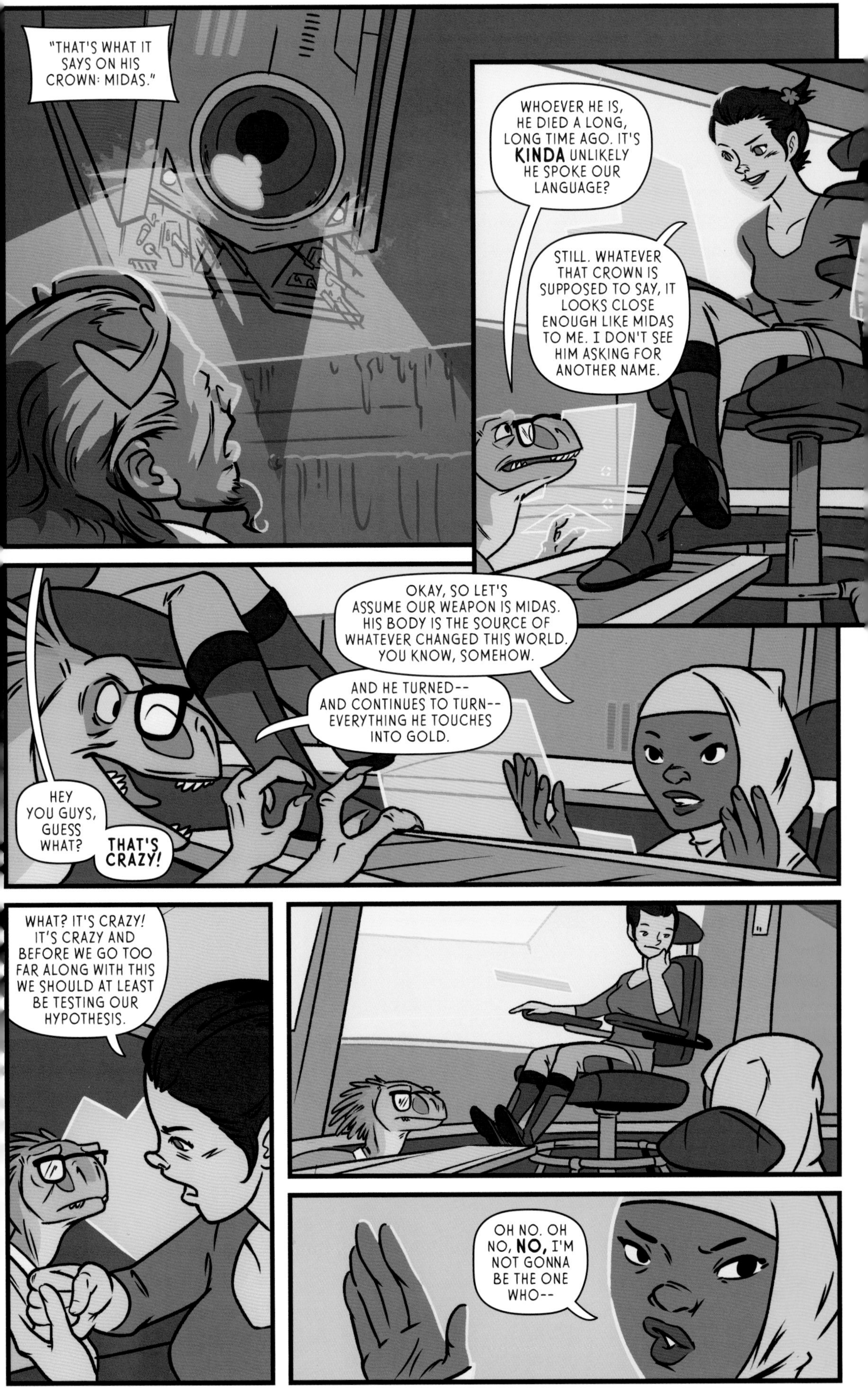
"THAT'S WHAT IT SAYS ON HIS CROWN: MIDAS."
WHOEVER HE IS, HE DIED A LONG, LONG TIME AGO. IT'S **KINDA** UNLIKELY HE SPOKE OUR LANGUAGE?
STILL. WHATEVER THAT CROWN IS SUPPOSED TO SAY, IT LOOKS CLOSE ENOUGH LIKE MIDAS TO ME. I DON'T SEE HIM ASKING FOR ANOTHER NAME.
OKAY, SO LET'S ASSUME OUR WEAPON IS MIDAS. HIS BODY IS THE SOURCE OF WHATEVER CHANGED THIS WORLD. YOU KNOW, SOMEHOW.
AND HE TURNED-- AND CONTINUES TO TURN-- EVERYTHING HE TOUCHES INTO GOLD.
HEY YOU GUYS, GUESS WHAT?
THAT'S CRAZY!
WHAT? IT'S CRAZY! IT'S CRAZY AND BEFORE WE GO TOO FAR ALONG WITH THIS WE SHOULD AT LEAST BE TESTING OUR HYPOTHESIS.
OH NO. OH NO, **NO,** I'M NOT GONNA BE THE ONE WHO--

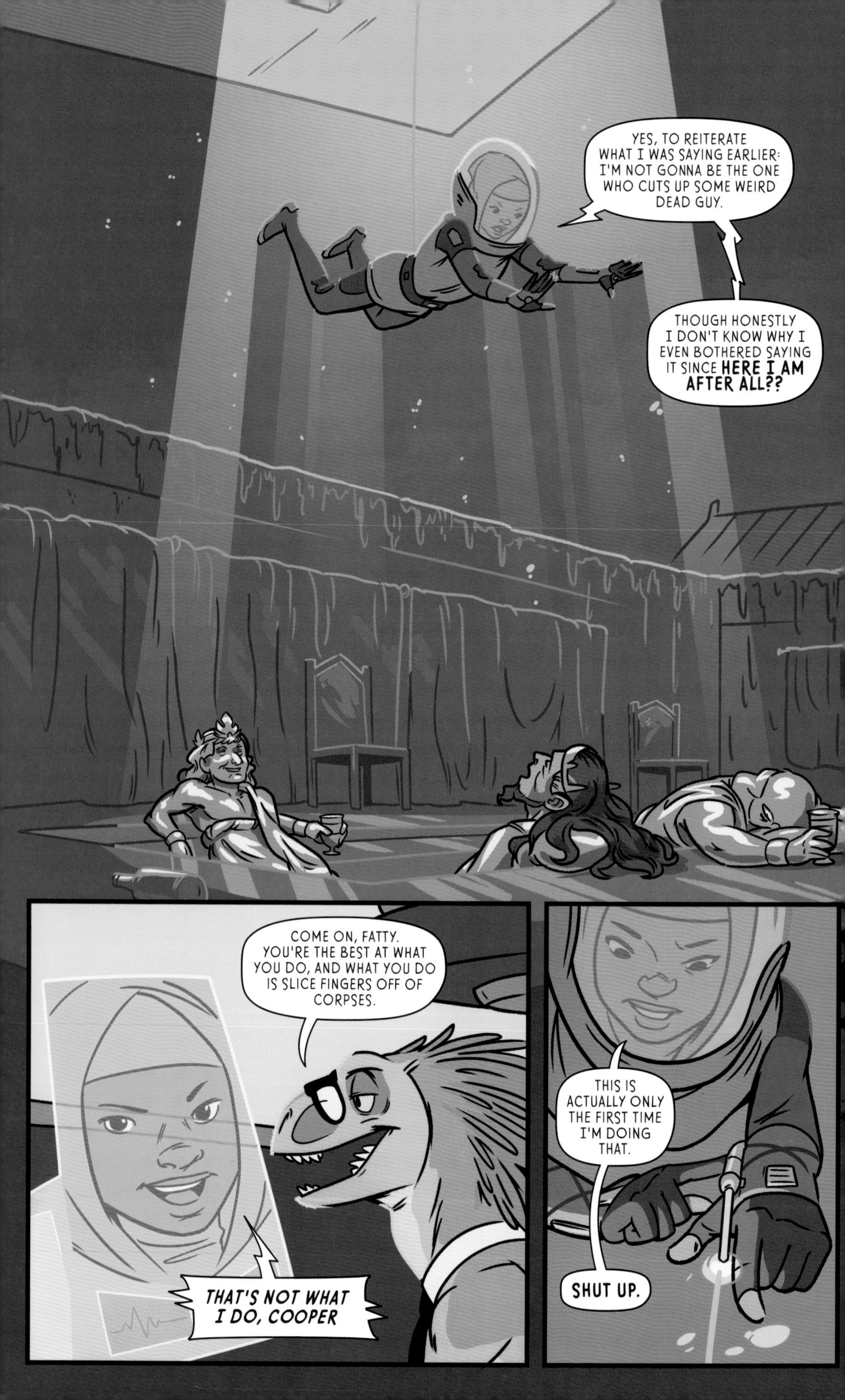
YES, TO REITERATE WHAT I WAS SAYING EARLIER: I'M NOT GONNA BE THE ONE WHO CUTS UP SOME WEIRD DEAD GUY.
THOUGH HONESTLY I DON'T KNOW WHY I EVEN BOTHERED SAYING IT SINCE **HERE I AM AFTER ALL??**
COME ON, FATTY. YOU'RE THE BEST AT WHAT YOU DO, AND WHAT YOU DO IS SLICE FINGERS OFF OF CORPSES.
THAT'S NOT WHAT I DO, COOPER
THIS IS ACTUALLY ONLY THE FIRST TIME I'M DOING THAT.
SHUT UP.

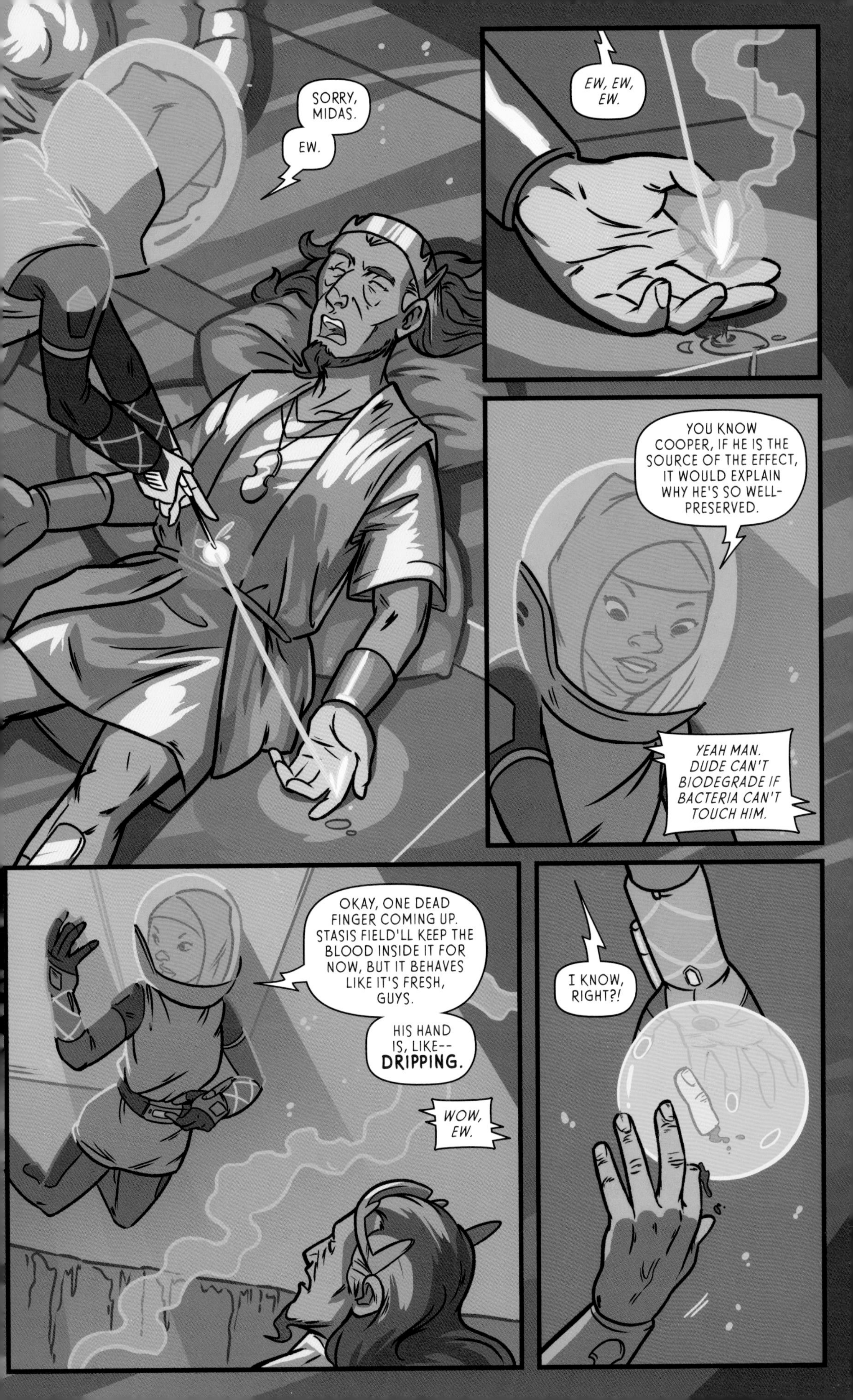
SORRY, MIDAS.
EW.
EW, EW, EW.
YOU KNOW COOPER, IF HE IS THE SOURCE OF THE EFFECT, IT WOULD EXPLAIN WHY HE'S SO WELL-PRESERVED.
YEAH MAN. DUDE CAN'T BIODEGRADE IF BACTERIA CAN'T TOUCH HIM.
OKAY, ONE DEAD FINGER COMING UP. STASIS FIELD'LL KEEP THE BLOOD INSIDE IT FOR NOW, BUT IT BEHAVES LIKE IT'S FRESH, GUYS.
HIS HAND IS, LIKE-- DRIPPING.
WOW, EW.
I KNOW, RIGHT?!

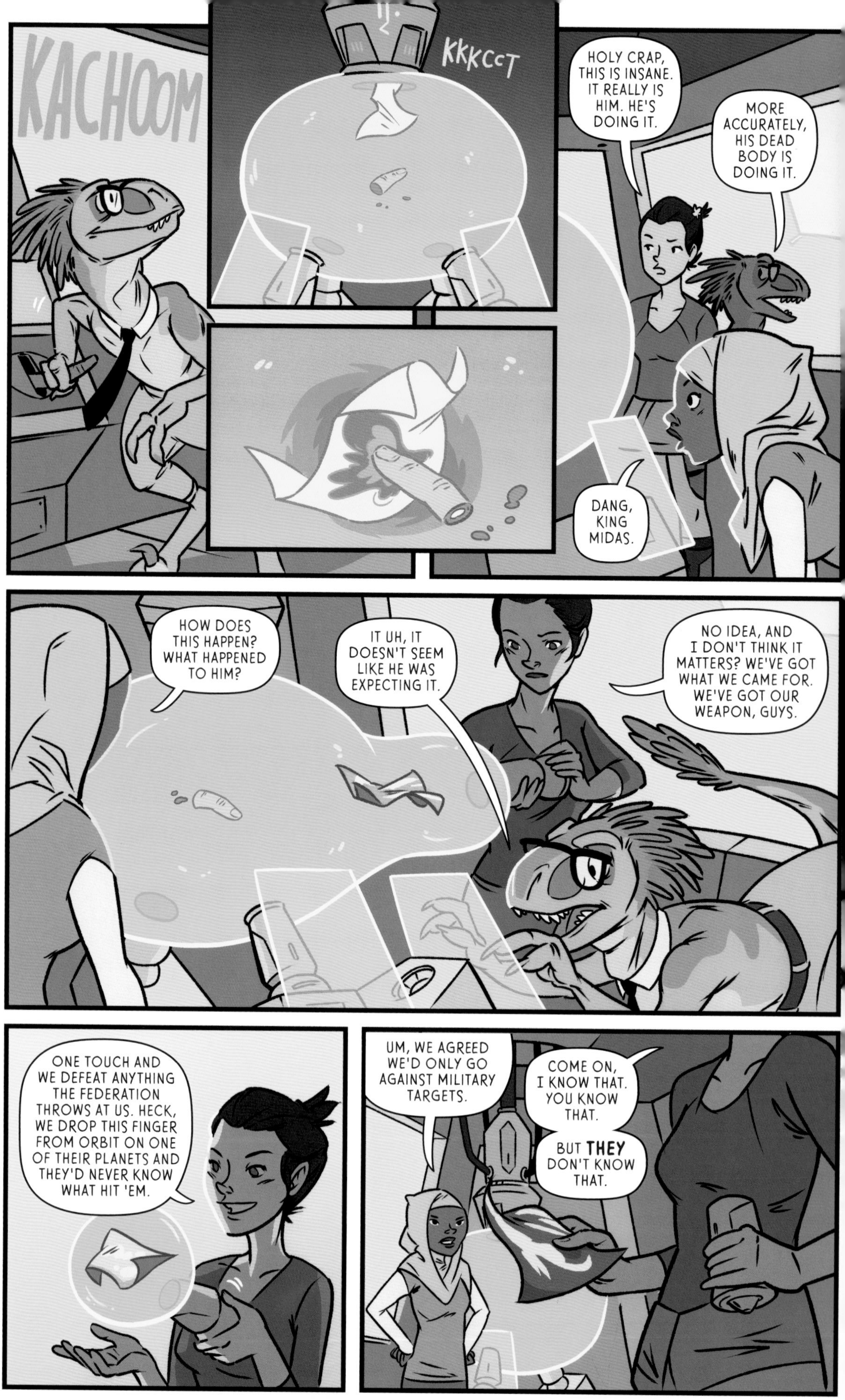
KACHOOM
KKKCCT
HOLY CRAP, THIS IS INSANE. IT REALLY IS HIM. HE'S DOING IT.
MORE ACCURATELY, HIS DEAD BODY IS DOING IT.
DANG, KING MIDAS.
HOW DOES THIS HAPPEN? WHAT HAPPENED TO HIM?
IT UH, IT DOESN'T SEEM LIKE HE WAS EXPECTING IT.
NO IDEA, AND I DON'T THINK IT MATTERS? WE'VE GOT WHAT WE CAME FOR. WE'VE GOT OUR WEAPON, GUYS.
ONE TOUCH AND WE DEFEAT ANYTHING THE FEDERATION THROWS AT US. HECK, WE DROP THIS FINGER FROM ORBIT ON ONE OF THEIR PLANETS AND THEY'D NEVER KNOW WHAT HIT 'EM.
UM, WE AGREED WE'D ONLY GO AGAINST MILITARY TARGETS.
COME ON, I KNOW THAT. YOU KNOW THAT.
BUT **THEY** DON'T KNOW THAT.

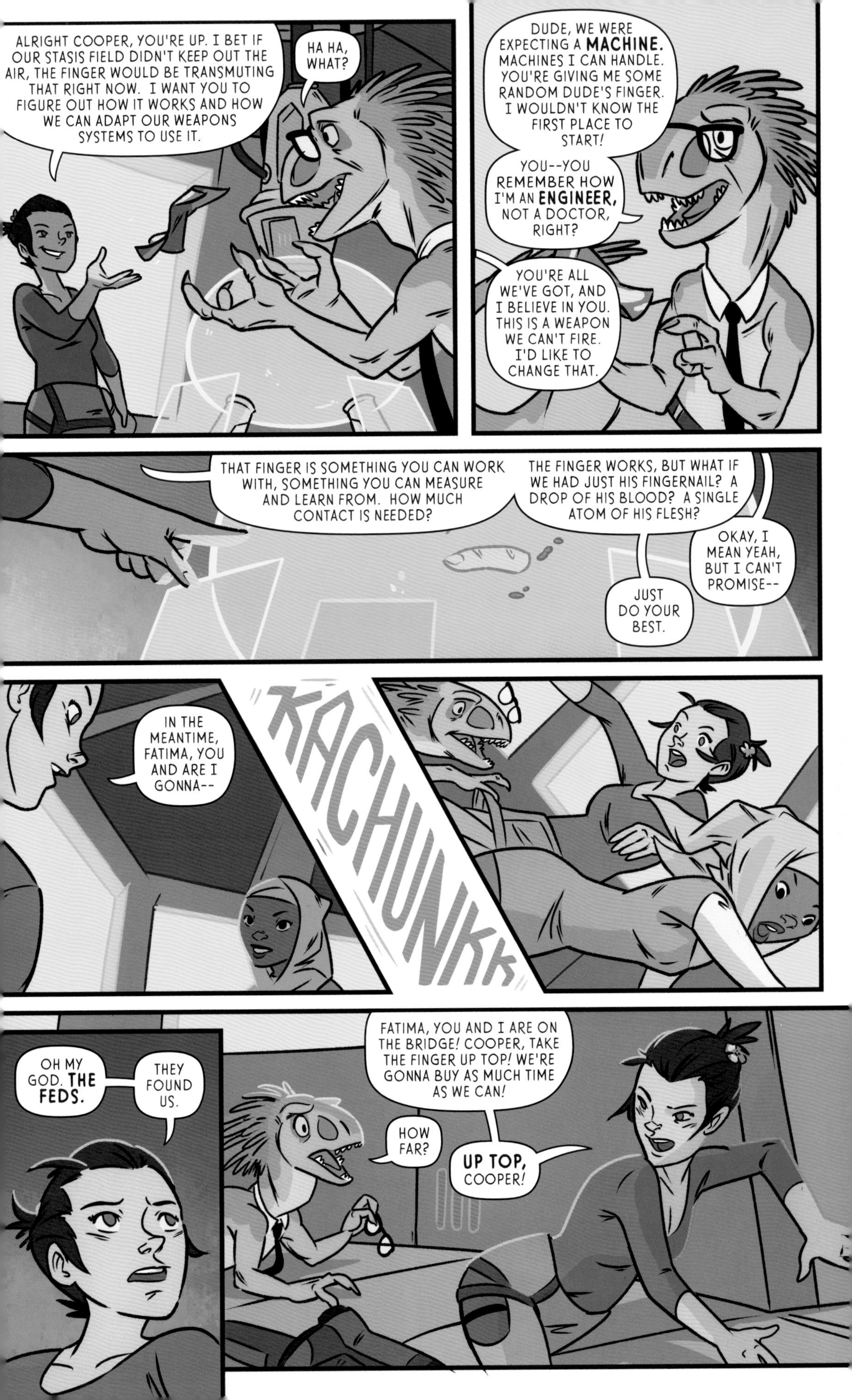
ALRIGHT COOPER, YOU'RE UP. I BET IF OUR STASIS FIELD DIDN'T KEEP OUT THE AIR, THE FINGER WOULD BE TRANSMUTING THAT RIGHT NOW. I WANT YOU TO FIGURE OUT HOW IT WORKS AND HOW WE CAN ADAPT OUR WEAPONS SYSTEMS TO USE IT.
HA HA, WHAT?
DUDE, WE WERE EXPECTING A **MACHINE.** MACHINES I CAN HANDLE. YOU'RE GIVING ME SOME RANDOM DUDE'S FINGER. I WOULDN'T KNOW THE FIRST PLACE TO START!
YOU--YOU REMEMBER HOW I'M AN **ENGINEER,** NOT A DOCTOR, RIGHT?
YOU'RE ALL WE'VE GOT, AND I BELIEVE IN YOU. THIS IS A WEAPON WE CAN'T FIRE. I'D LIKE TO CHANGE THAT.
THAT FINGER IS SOMETHING YOU CAN WORK WITH, SOMETHING YOU CAN MEASURE AND LEARN FROM. HOW MUCH CONTACT IS NEEDED?
THE FINGER WORKS, BUT WHAT IF WE HAD JUST HIS FINGERNAIL? A DROP OF HIS BLOOD? A SINGLE ATOM OF HIS FLESH?
OKAY, I MEAN YEAH, BUT I CAN'T PROMISE--
JUST DO YOUR BEST.
IN THE MEANTIME, FATIMA, YOU AND ARE I GONNA--
KACHUNKK
OH MY GOD. **THE FEDS.**
THEY FOUND US.
FATIMA, YOU AND I ARE ON THE BRIDGE! COOPER, TAKE THE FINGER UP TOP! WE'RE GONNA BUY AS MUCH TIME AS WE CAN!
HOW FAR?
UP TOP, COOPER!

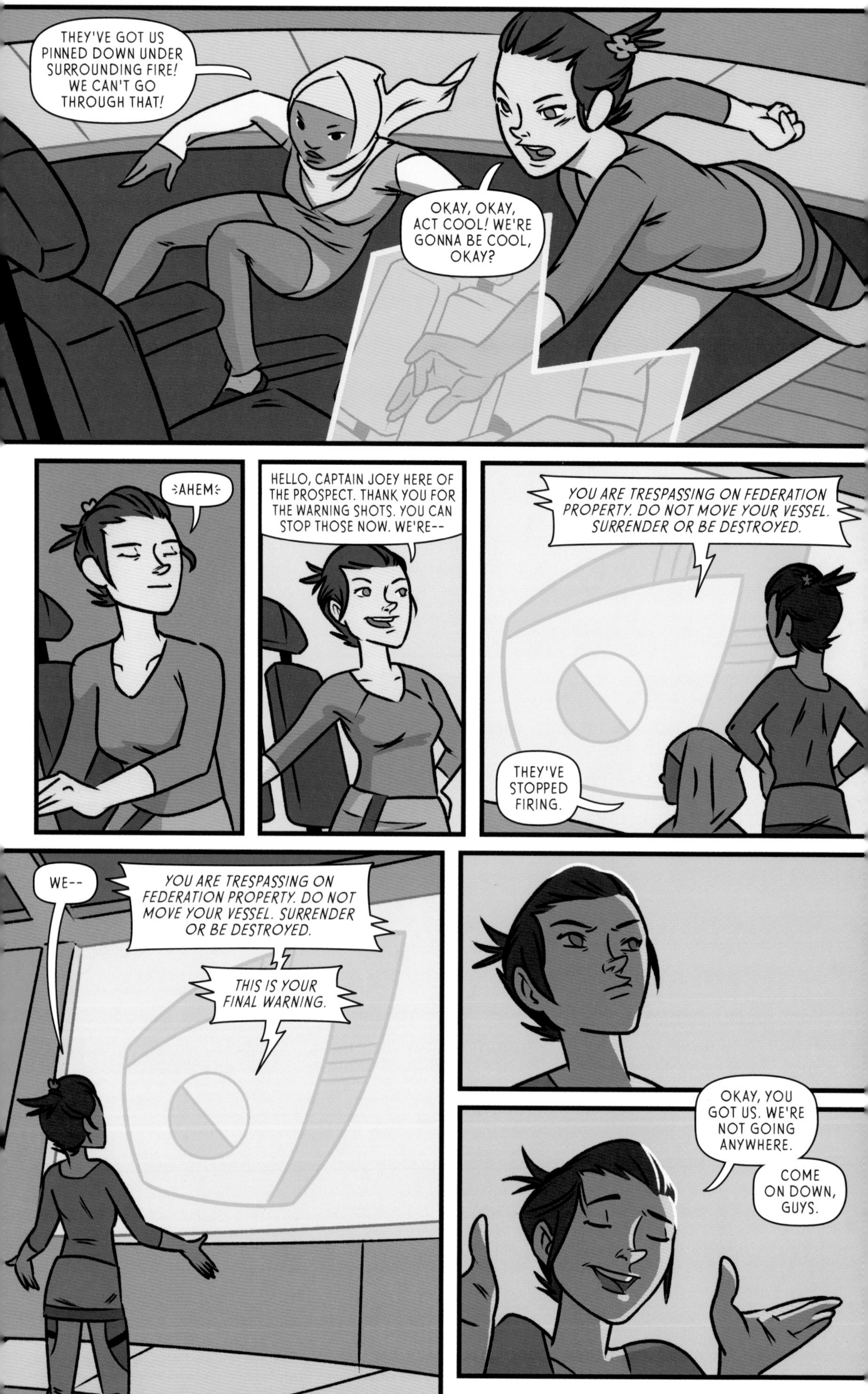
THEY'VE GOT US PINNED DOWN UNDER SURROUNDING FIRE! WE CAN'T GO THROUGH THAT!
OKAY, OKAY, ACT COOL! WE'RE GONNA BE COOL, OKAY?
AHEM
HELLO, CAPTAIN JOEY HERE OF THE PROSPECT. THANK YOU FOR THE WARNING SHOTS. YOU CAN STOP THOSE NOW. WE'RE--
YOU ARE TRESPASSING ON FEDERATION PROPERTY. DO NOT MOVE YOUR VESSEL. SURRENDER OR BE DESTROYED.
THEY'VE STOPPED FIRING.
WE--
YOU ARE TRESPASSING ON FEDERATION PROPERTY. DO NOT MOVE YOUR VESSEL. SURRENDER OR BE DESTROYED.
THIS IS YOUR FINAL WARNING.
OKAY, YOU GOT US. WE'RE NOT GOING ANYWHERE.
COME ON DOWN, GUYS.

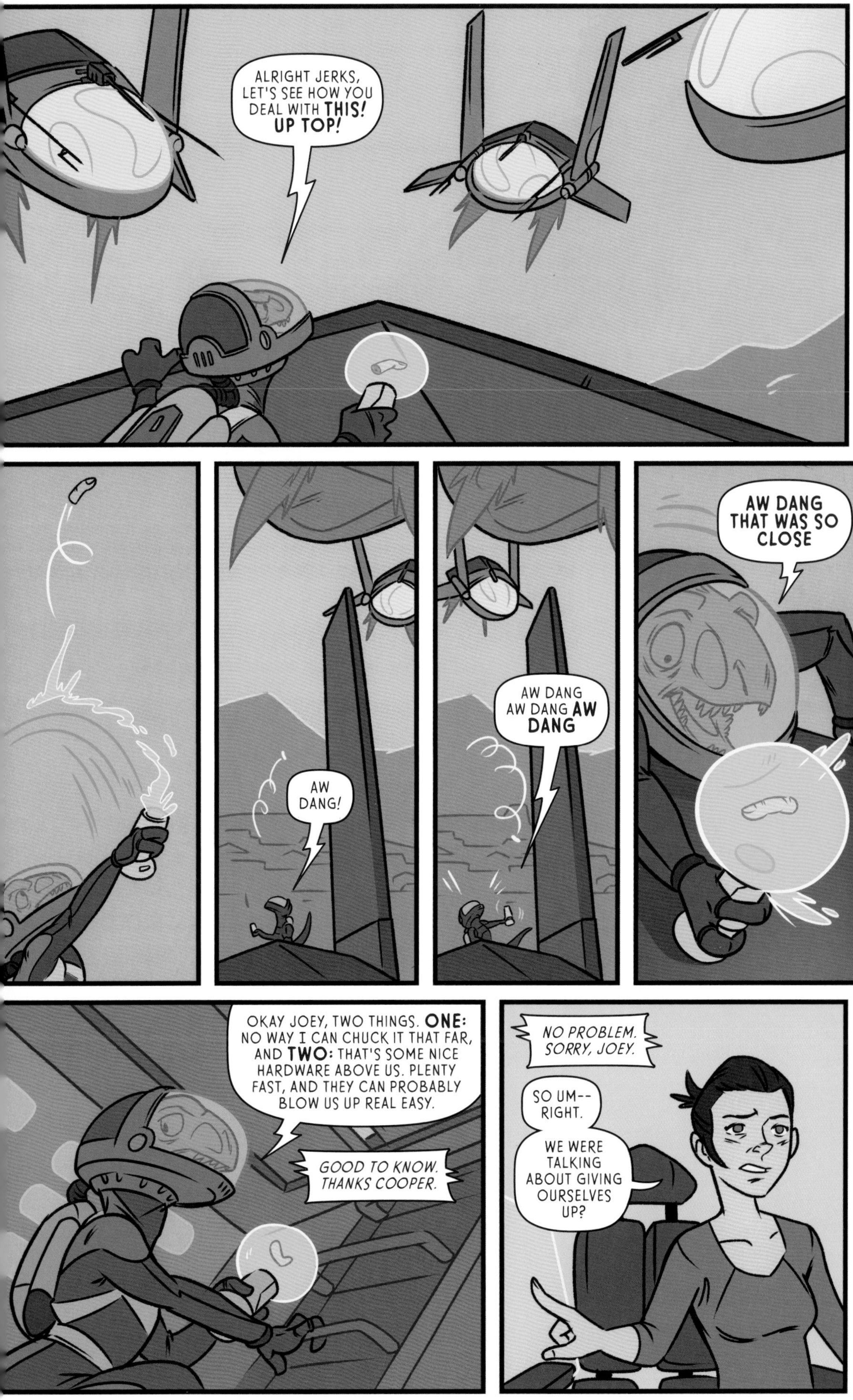
ALRIGHT JERKS, LET'S SEE HOW YOU DEAL WITH **THIS! UP TOP!**
AW DANG!
AW DANG AW DANG **AW DANG**
AW DANG THAT WAS SO CLOSE
OKAY JOEY, TWO THINGS. **ONE:** NO WAY I CAN CHUCK IT THAT FAR, AND **TWO:** THAT'S SOME NICE HARDWARE ABOVE US. PLENTY FAST, AND THEY CAN PROBABLY BLOW US UP REAL EASY.
GOOD TO KNOW. THANKS COOPER.
NO PROBLEM. SORRY, JOEY.
SO UM-- RIGHT.
WE WERE TALKING ABOUT GIVING OURSELVES UP?

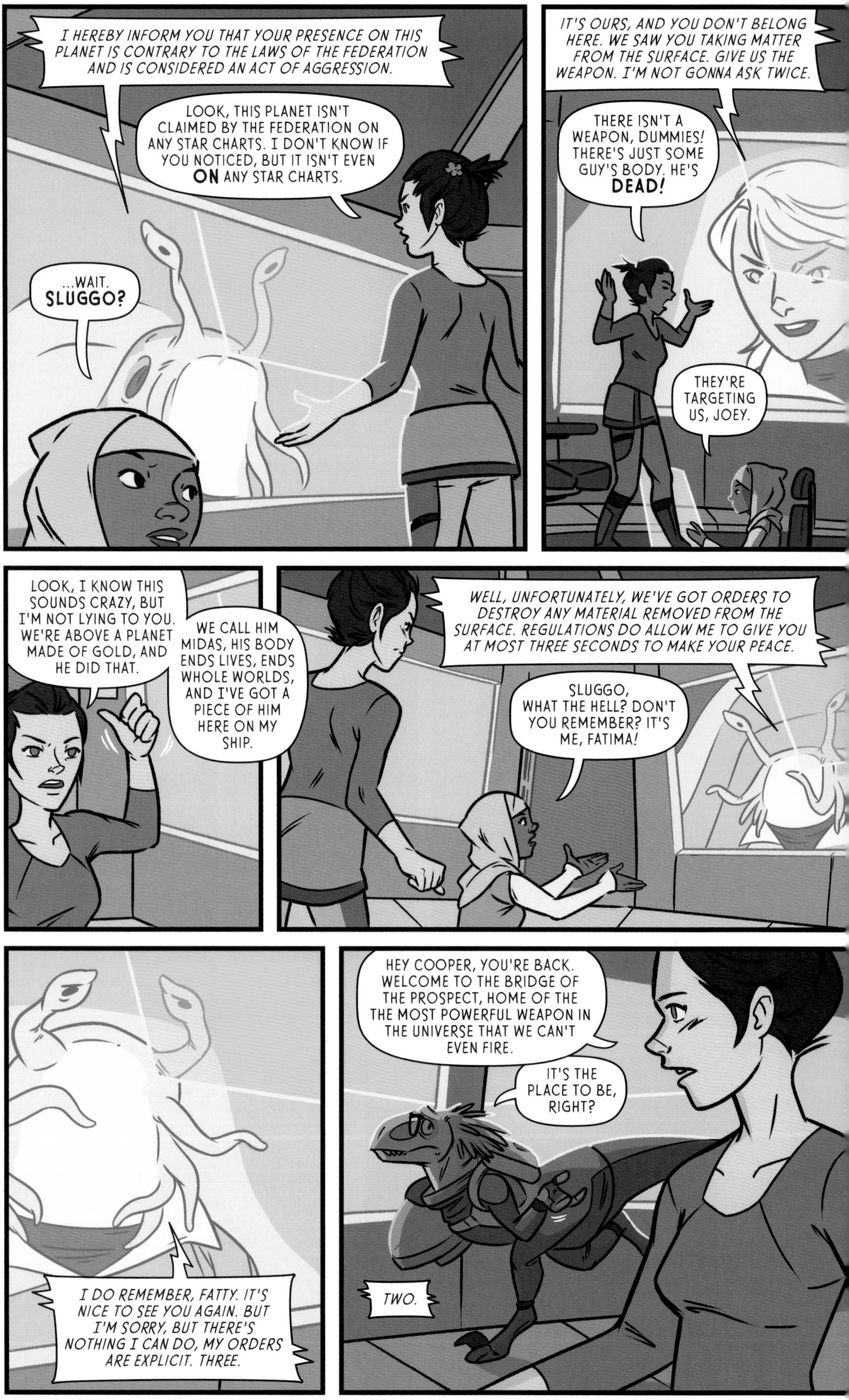
I HEREBY INFORM YOU THAT YOUR PRESENCE ON THIS PLANET IS CONTRARY TO THE LAWS OF THE FEDERATION AND IS CONSIDERED AN ACT OF AGGRESSION.
LOOK, THIS PLANET ISN'T CLAIMED BY THE FEDERATION ON ANY STAR CHARTS. I DON'T KNOW IF YOU NOTICED, BUT IT ISN'T EVEN **ON** ANY STAR CHARTS.
...WAIT. **SLUGGO?**
IT'S OURS, AND YOU DON'T BELONG HERE. WE SAW YOU TAKING MATTER FROM THE SURFACE. GIVE US THE WEAPON. I'M NOT GONNA ASK TWICE.
THERE ISN'T A WEAPON, DUMMIES! THERE'S JUST SOME GUY'S BODY. HE'S **DEAD!**
THEY'RE TARGETING US, JOEY.
LOOK, I KNOW THIS SOUNDS CRAZY, BUT I'M NOT LYING TO YOU. WE'RE ABOVE A PLANET MADE OF GOLD, AND HE DID THAT.
WE CALL HIM MIDAS, HIS BODY ENDS LIVES, ENDS WHOLE WORLDS, AND I'VE GOT A PIECE OF HIM HERE ON MY SHIP.
WELL, UNFORTUNATELY, WE'VE GOT ORDERS TO DESTROY ANY MATERIAL REMOVED FROM THE SURFACE. REGULATIONS DO ALLOW ME TO GIVE YOU AT MOST THREE SECONDS TO MAKE YOUR PEACE.
SLUGGO, WHAT THE HELL? DON'T YOU REMEMBER? IT'S ME, FATIMA!
I DO REMEMBER, FATTY. IT'S NICE TO SEE YOU AGAIN. BUT I'M SORRY, BUT THERE'S NOTHING I CAN DO, MY ORDERS ARE EXPLICIT. THREE.
HEY COOPER, YOU'RE BACK. WELCOME TO THE BRIDGE OF THE PROSPECT, HOME OF THE THE MOST POWERFUL WEAPON IN THE UNIVERSE THAT WE CAN'T EVEN FIRE.
IT'S THE PLACE TO BE, RIGHT?
TWO.

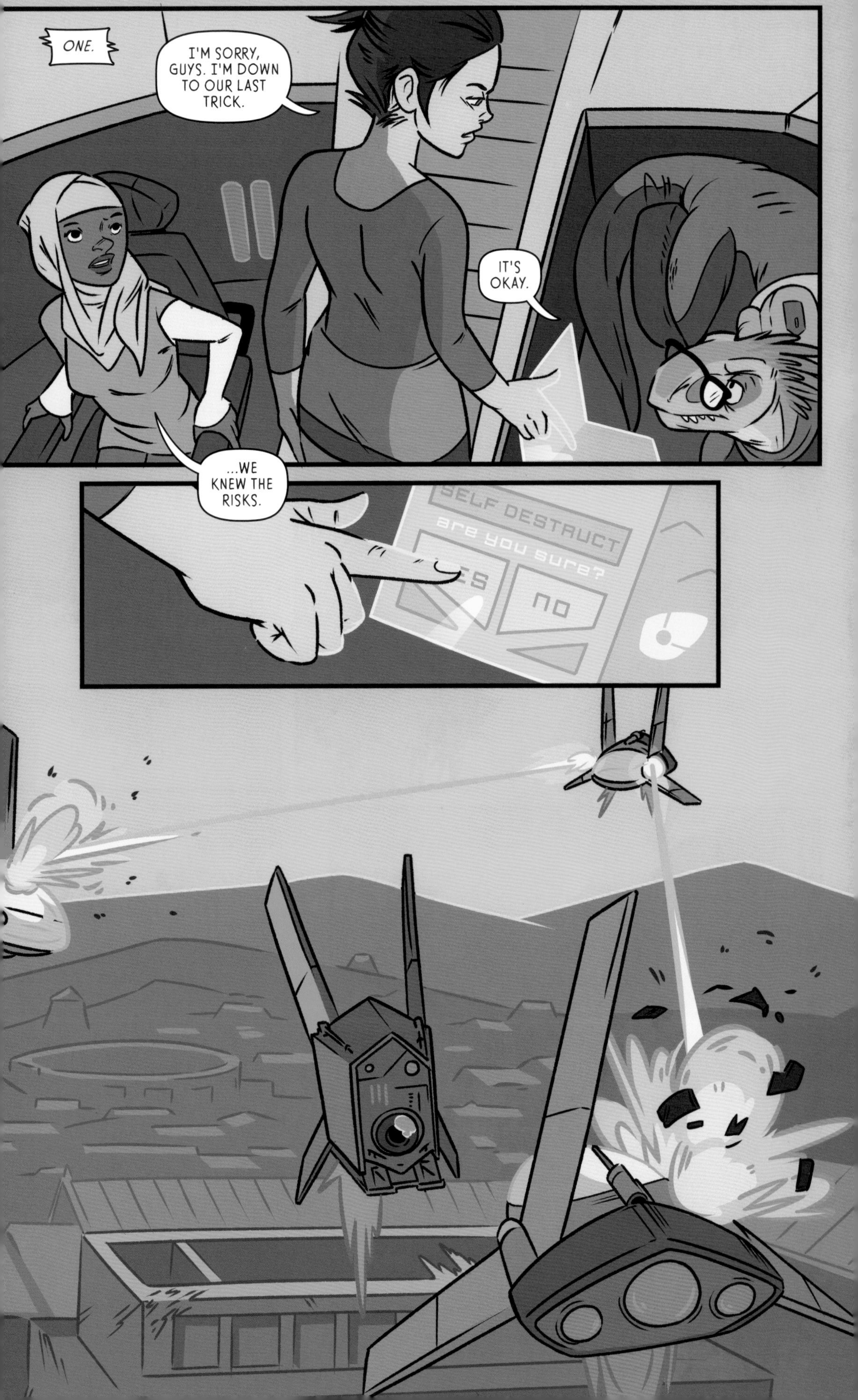
ONE.
I'M SORRY, GUYS. I'M DOWN TO OUR LAST TRICK.
IT'S OKAY.
...WE KNEW THE RISKS.
SELF DESTRUCT
are you sure?
NO

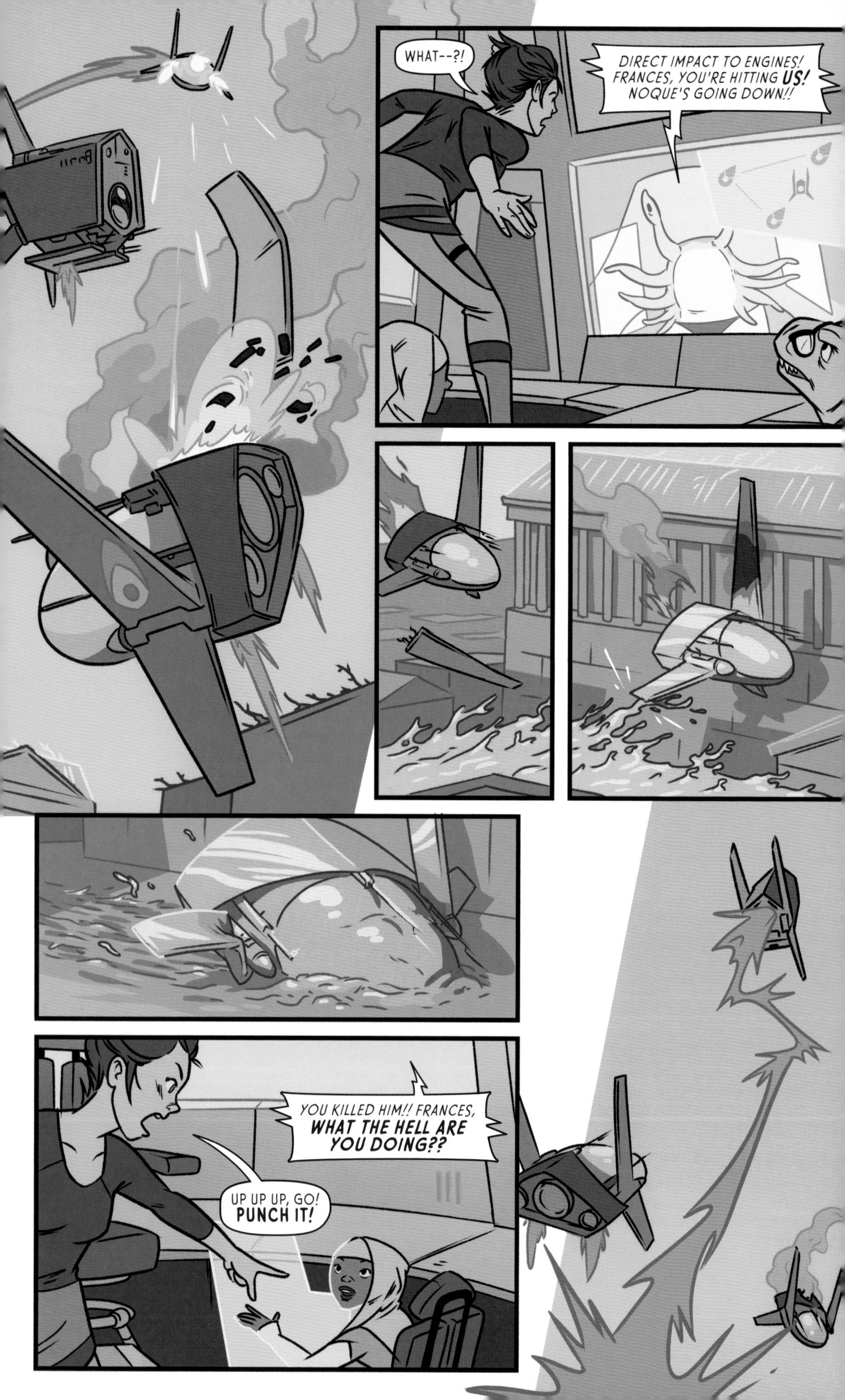
WHAT--?!
DIRECT IMPACT TO ENGINES! FRANCES, YOU'RE HITTING US! NOQUE'S GOING DOWN!!
YOU KILLED HIM!! FRANCES, WHAT THE HELL ARE YOU DOING??
UP UP UP, GO! PUNCH IT!

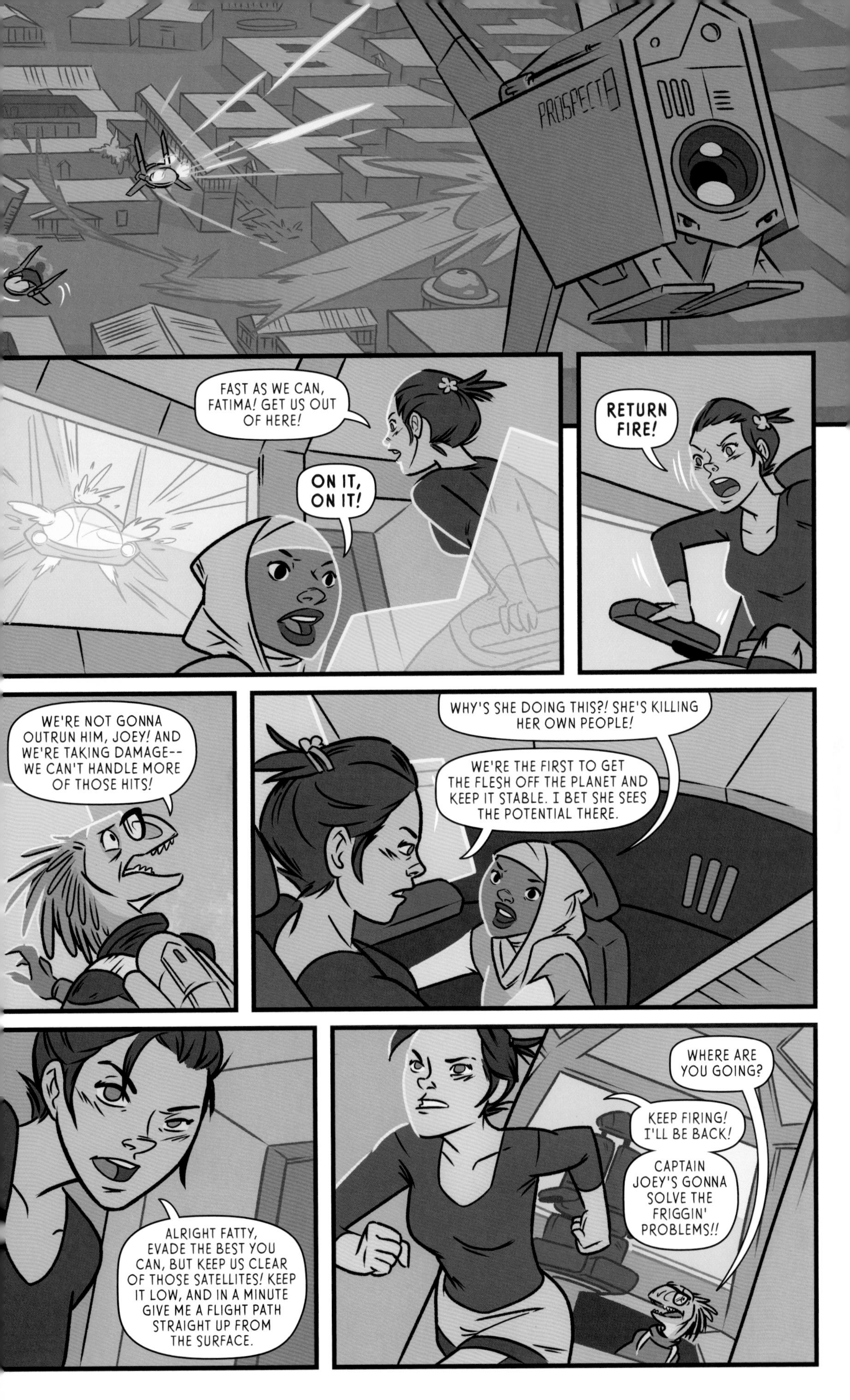
PROSPECTA
FAST AS WE CAN, FATIMA! GET US OUT OF HERE!
ON IT, ON IT!
RETURN FIRE!
WE'RE NOT GONNA OUTRUN HIM, JOEY! AND WE'RE TAKING DAMAGE-- WE CAN'T HANDLE MORE OF THOSE HITS!
WHY'S SHE DOING THIS?! SHE'S KILLING HER OWN PEOPLE!
WE'RE THE FIRST TO GET THE FLESH OFF THE PLANET AND KEEP IT STABLE. I BET SHE SEES THE POTENTIAL THERE.
ALRIGHT FATTY, EVADE THE BEST YOU CAN, BUT KEEP US CLEAR OF THOSE SATELLITES! KEEP IT LOW, AND IN A MINUTE GIVE ME A FLIGHT PATH STRAIGHT UP FROM THE SURFACE.
WHERE ARE YOU GOING?
KEEP FIRING! I'LL BE BACK!
CAPTAIN JOEY'S GONNA SOLVE THE FRIGGIN' PROBLEMS!!

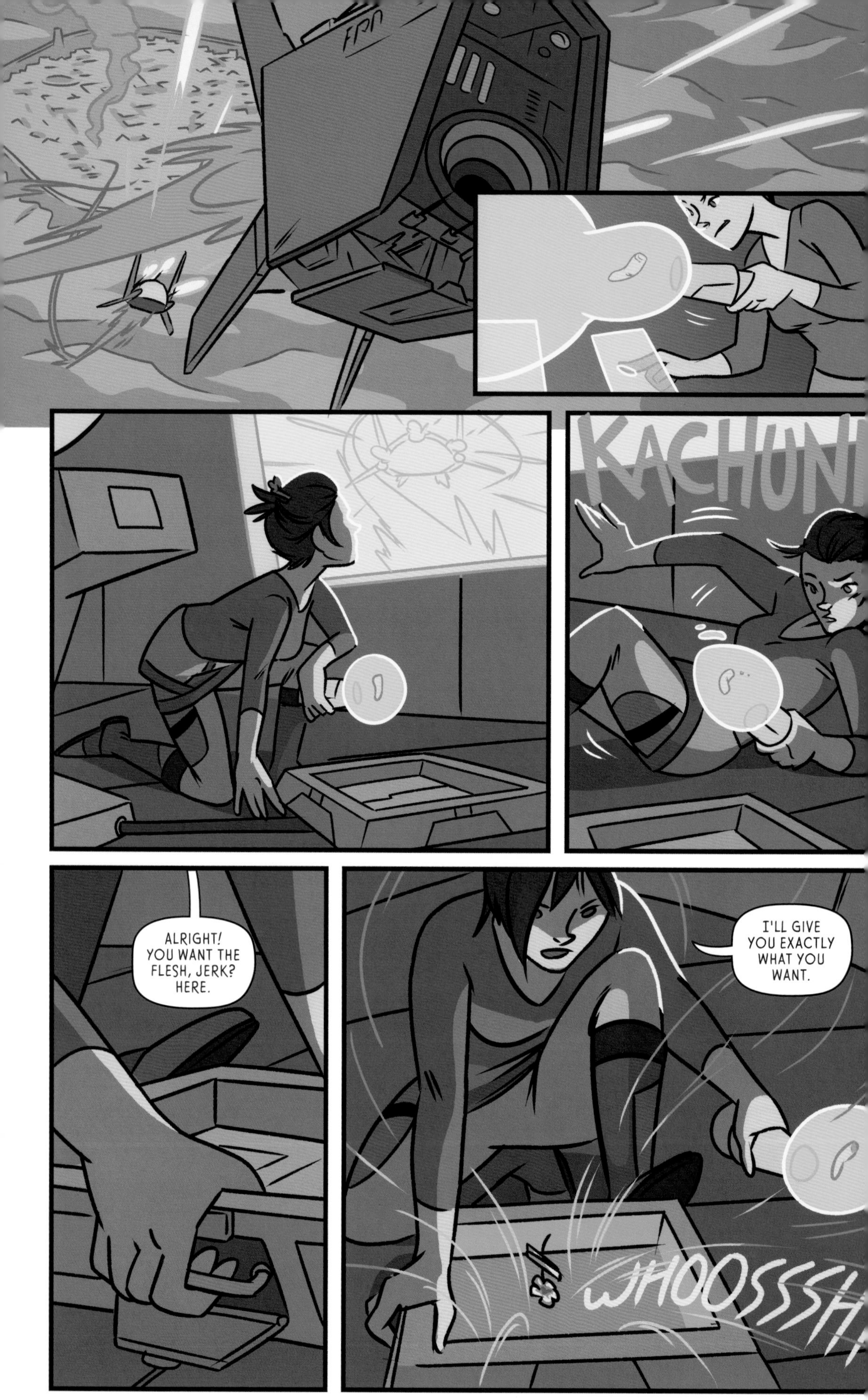
FRN
KACHUNK
ALRIGHT! YOU WANT THE FLESH, JERK? HERE.
I'LL GIVE YOU EXACTLY WHAT YOU WANT.
WHOOSSSH

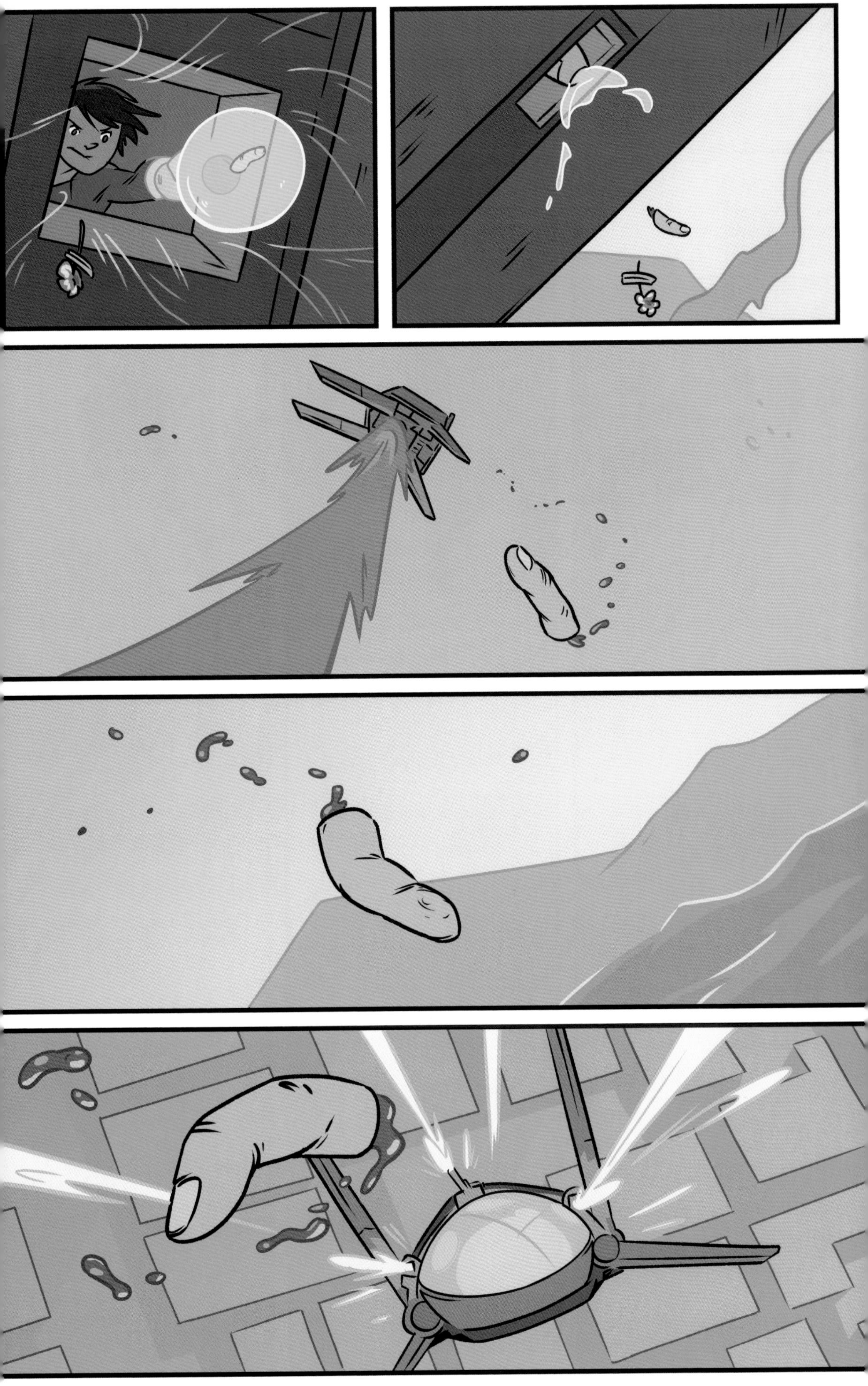

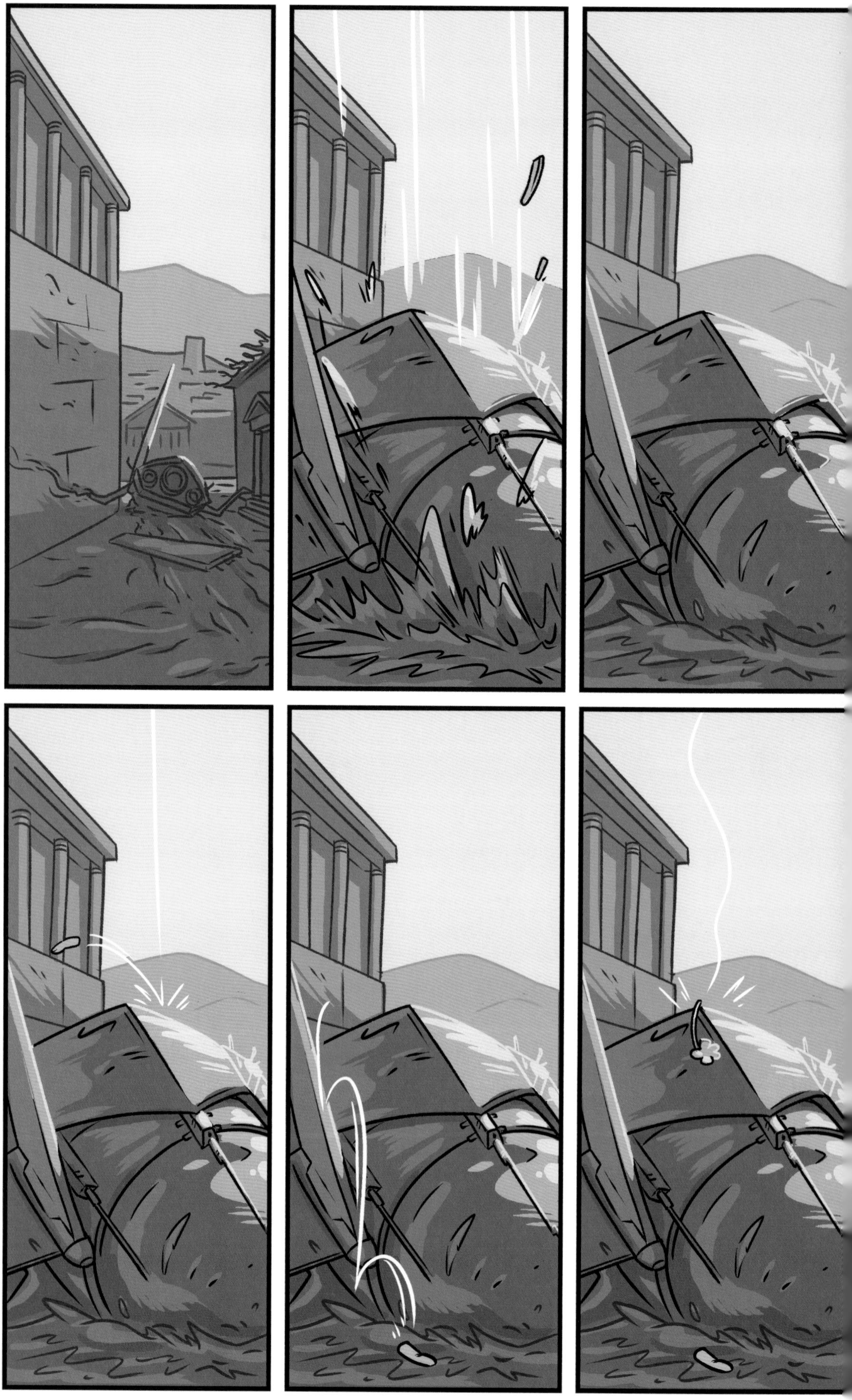

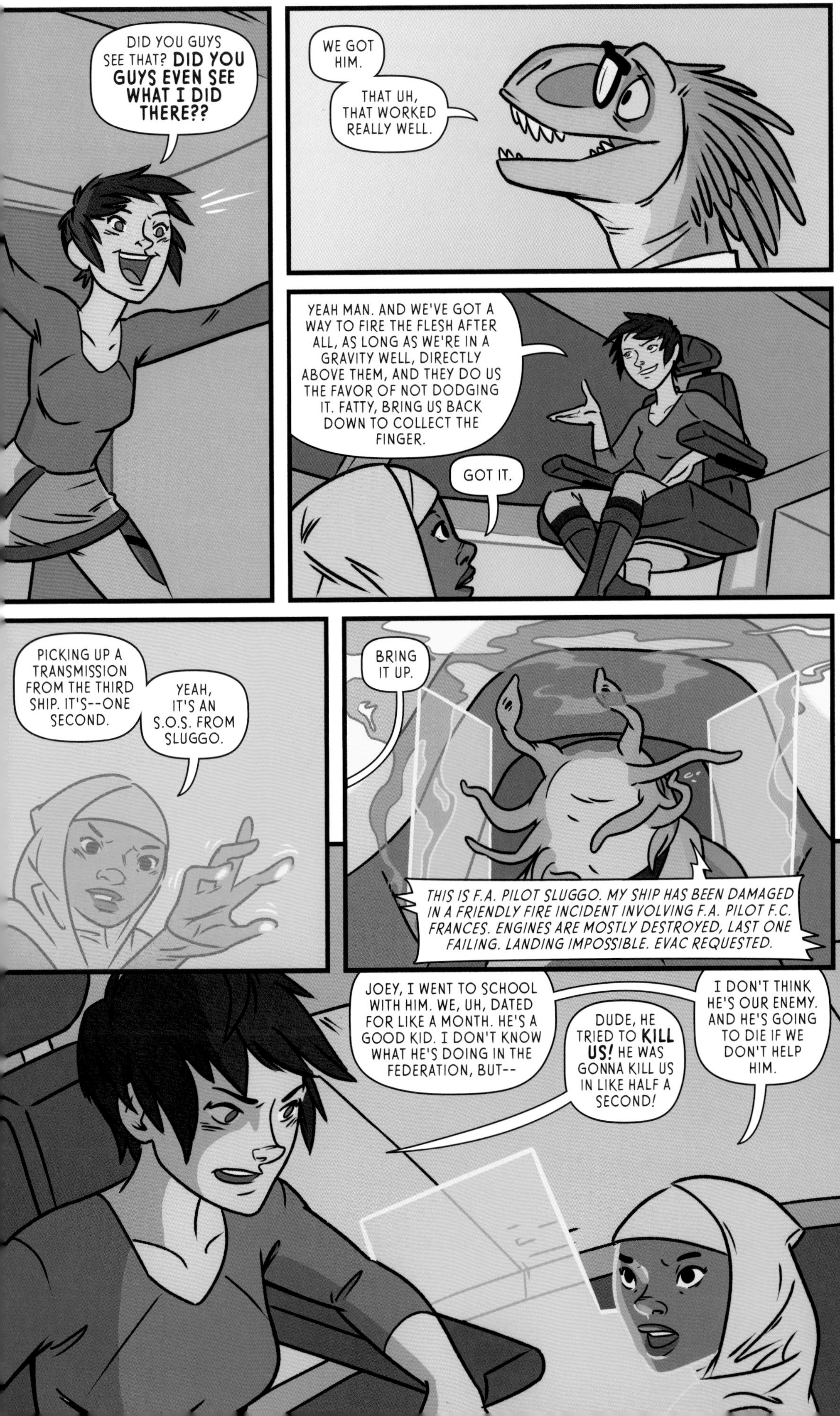
DID YOU GUYS SEE THAT? DID YOU GUYS EVEN SEE WHAT I DID THERE??
WE GOT HIM.
THAT UH, THAT WORKED REALLY WELL.
YEAH MAN. AND WE'VE GOT A WAY TO FIRE THE FLESH AFTER ALL, AS LONG AS WE'RE IN A GRAVITY WELL, DIRECTLY ABOVE THEM, AND THEY DO US THE FAVOR OF NOT DODGING IT. FATTY, BRING US BACK DOWN TO COLLECT THE FINGER.
GOT IT.
PICKING UP A TRANSMISSION FROM THE THIRD SHIP. IT'S--ONE SECOND.
YEAH, IT'S AN S.O.S. FROM SLUGGO.
BRING IT UP.
THIS IS F.A. PILOT SLUGGO. MY SHIP HAS BEEN DAMAGED IN A FRIENDLY FIRE INCIDENT INVOLVING F.A. PILOT F.C. FRANCES. ENGINES ARE MOSTLY DESTROYED, LAST ONE FAILING. LANDING IMPOSSIBLE. EVAC REQUESTED.
JOEY, I WENT TO SCHOOL WITH HIM. WE, UH, DATED FOR LIKE A MONTH. HE'S A GOOD KID. I DON'T KNOW WHAT HE'S DOING IN THE FEDERATION, BUT--
DUDE, HE TRIED TO KILL US! HE WAS GONNA KILL US IN LIKE HALF A SECOND!
I DON'T THINK HE'S OUR ENEMY. AND HE'S GOING TO DIE IF WE DON'T HELP HIM.

HMM...

HMMM...

JOEY!

OKAY FINE

PROSPECTE

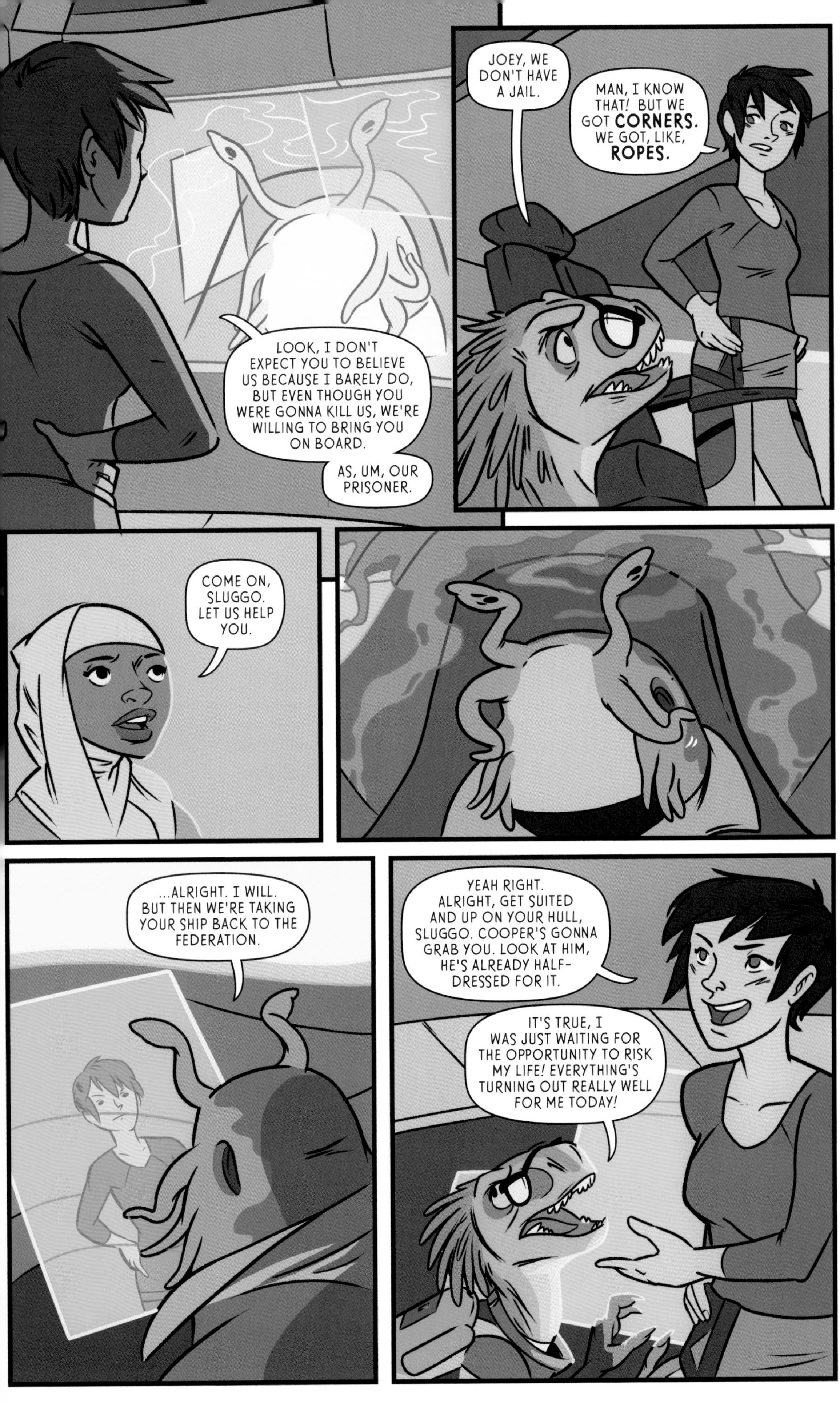
LOOK, I DON'T EXPECT YOU TO BELIEVE US BECAUSE I BARELY DO, BUT EVEN THOUGH YOU WERE GONNA KILL US, WE'RE WILLING TO BRING YOU ON BOARD.
AS, UM, OUR PRISONER.
JOEY, WE DON'T HAVE A JAIL.
MAN, I KNOW THAT! BUT WE GOT **CORNERS.** WE GOT, LIKE, **ROPES.**
COME ON, SLUGGO. LET US HELP YOU.
...ALRIGHT. I WILL. BUT THEN WE'RE TAKING YOUR SHIP BACK TO THE FEDERATION.
YEAH RIGHT. ALRIGHT, GET SUITED AND UP ON YOUR HULL, SLUGGO. COOPER'S GONNA GRAB YOU. LOOK AT HIM, HE'S ALREADY HALF-DRESSED FOR IT.
IT'S TRUE, I WAS JUST WAITING FOR THE OPPORTUNITY TO RISK MY LIFE! EVERYTHING'S TURNING OUT REALLY WELL FOR ME TODAY!

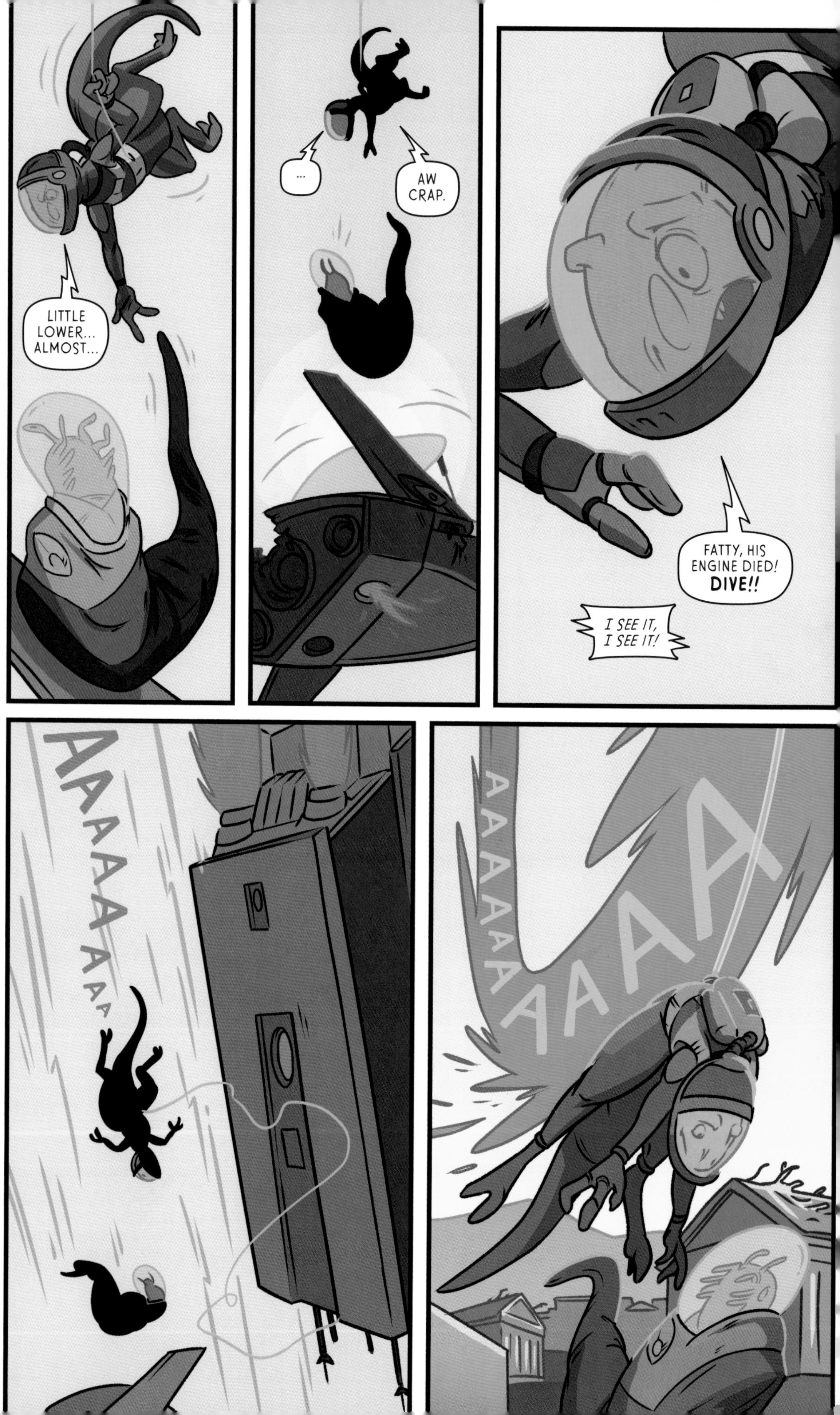
LITTLE LOWER... ALMOST...
...
AW CRAP.
FATTY, HIS ENGINE DIED! DIVE!!
I SEE IT, I SEE IT!
AAAAAAAAA
AAAAAAAAAAA

AHHHHHHH YES THAT'S WHAT I'M TALKING ABOUT!

HI SLUGGO, I'M COOPER. I'M THE DUDE WHO JUST SAVED YOUR LIFE.

COME ON. I WANNA INTRODUCE YOU TO MY FRIENDS.

SHORTLY.

WELCOME ABOARD. THIS IS THE **PROSPECT.**

GOOD TO BE BACK, FATTY. SLUGGO, THIS IS OUR CAPTAIN JOEY AND I BELIEVE YOU'VE MET FATIMA?

HELLO CAPTAIN. HELLO FATTY.

COOPER.

RIGHT.

I, UM, HAVE TO TIE YOU UP.

I'M SORRY ABOUT THIS, BUT THIS ISN'T EXACTLY GOING AS WE PLANNED. WE'RE NOT SET UP FOR PRISONERS, AND I'M NOT CONVINCED THAT YOU DON'T KNOW MORE ABOUT THE ATTACK ON US THAN YOU'VE SAID. SO I DON'T TRUST YOU.

SO YOU'RE GONNA STAY TIED UP FOR NOW.

I DON'T KNOW WHAT YOU KNOW ABOUT MY PEOPLE, BUT WE'RE NOT THE FASTEST IN THE WORLD. CHECK ME FOR WEAPONS; I'M NOT GOING TO ATTACK YOU. AND EVEN IF I TRIED, YOU'VE GOT A **DINOSAUR** IN A TIE OVER THERE. I THINK HE CAN TAKE ME.

I LIKE HIM!

LOOK, SLUGGO, CARDS ON THE TABLE: THE PROSPECT'S A TOUGH SHIP. WE SURVIVED THE ATTACK THAT TOOK OUT TWO OF YOURS. BUT THAT UNEXPECTED FIGHT WITH YOUR FRIEND DAMAGED MOST OF OUR DEFENSES AND MANY OF OUR OFFENSES. WE'RE HURT. AND HONESTLY?

I DON'T THINK WE CAN MAKE IT OUT.

TK
TK
TK

WE'LL BE DESTROYED BY THOSE SATELLITES IF WE TRY TO LEAVE, WE CAN'T STAY HERE ON A PLANET THAT'LL KILL US IF WE TOUCH IT, AND WE CAN'T USE OUR WEAPON UNLESS SOMEONE GETS DIRECTLY BENEATH US. CAN YOU HELP US ESCAPE?

...MAYBE.

I WON'T HELP WITH THE WEAPON, BUT I CAN GET YOU OUT. AND WHEN WE'RE OUT, IF YOU PROMISE TO HAVE A CONVERSATION WITH ME ABOUT TURNING YOURSELVES INTO THE FEDERATION, I'LL BE HAPPY.

YEAH, WE'RE NOT GONNA DO THAT.

HERE'S MY CARDS ON THE TABLE: YOU'RE DEAD IF YOU DON'T. IT'S NOT LIKE THE FEDERATION IS JUST GOING TO FORGET YOU WERE HERE, STEALING FROM THEM.

LOOK, I DON'T THINK I HAVE MUCH OF A CHOICE. I'LL HELP YOU LEAVE. THERE'S AN OVERRIDE SIGNAL WE USED TO GET IN THAT I CAN SEND TO THE SATELLITES. GET ME AT YOUR COMPUTERS AND I'LL SEND IT, ON ONE CONDITION:

YOU HAVE TO UNTIE ME.

...

COME ON! IT'S LIKE--I DON'T KNOW ABOUT YOU GUYS, BUT I CAN'T TYPE WITH BOTH ARMS TIED BEHIND MY BACK?

LATER...
FINGER'S PICKED UP AND BACK IN STASIS, JOEY. AND HERE'S YOUR FLOWER.
IF YOU WERE THE GOOD GUYS, SLUGGO, THEN I DOUBT YOUR FRIEND WOULD'VE HAD ORDERS TO KILL EVERYONE, **INCLUDING YOU.** CLASSIC FEDERATION: FEWER WITNESSES, EASIER CLEANUP.
THEY WOULDN'T GIVE ORDERS LIKE THAT! FRANCES WENT **ROGUE.** BESIDES, YOU'RE THE ONE WHO CAME HERE SEEKING A WEAPON TO DESTROY THE FEDERATION! **YOU'RE** THE TERRORISTS IN THIS SCENARIO!!
THAT'S RICH.
FATTY, BRING US ABOUT...
...AND LET'S DO WHAT WE CAME HERE FOR.
ALRIGHT, WE'RE THROUGH. **NOW** CAN WE TALK ABOUT OUR NEXT DESTINATION? IF I SIGNAL FOR AN ESCORT TO TAKE US TO FEDERATION SPACE, I THINK I CAN GUARANTEE--
WAIT.
WAIT, SOMETHING'S WRONG. THERE'S SOMETHING OUT HERE.
SOMETHING BIG. GUYS--

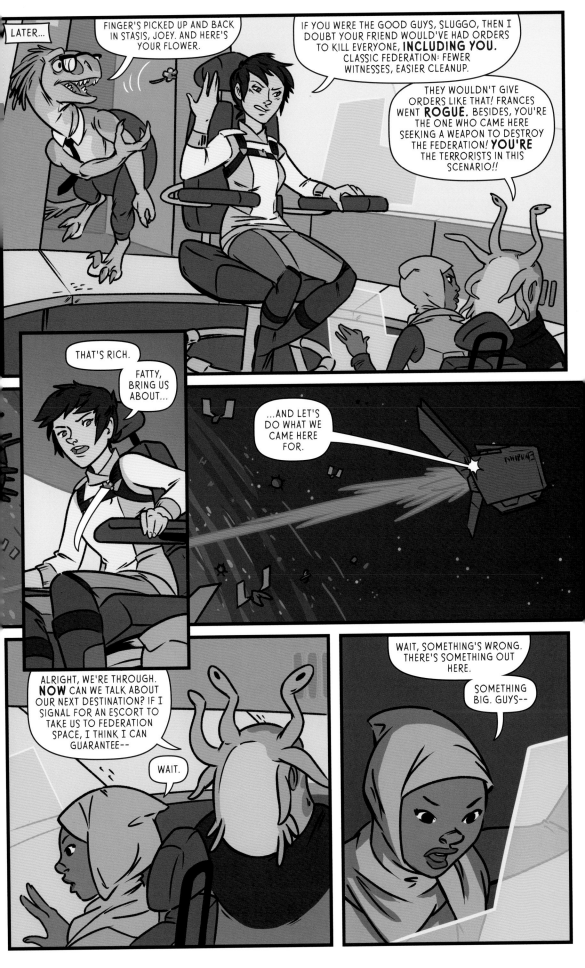

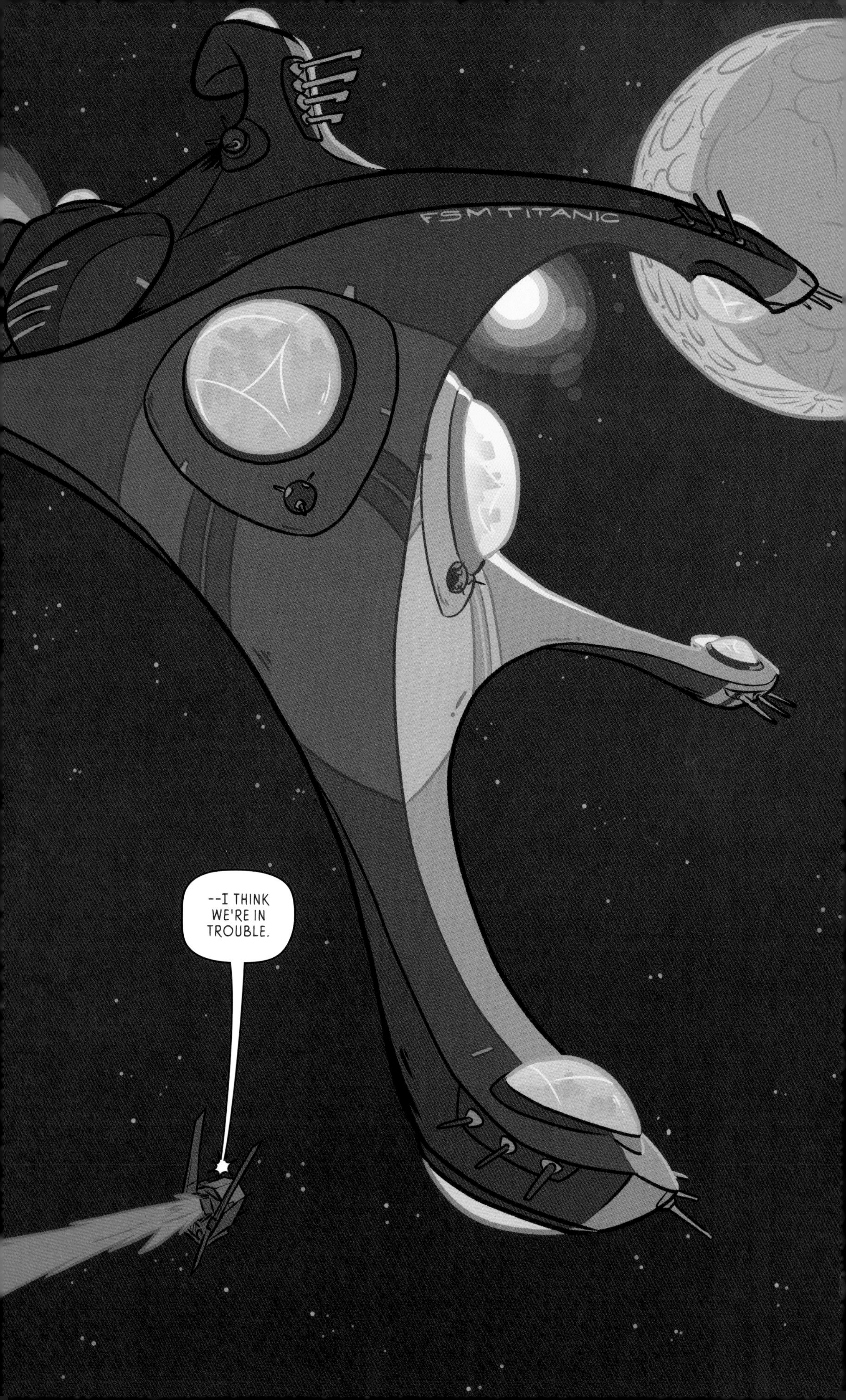
FSM TITANIC
--I THINK WE'RE IN TROUBLE.

"DANG, KING MIDAS."

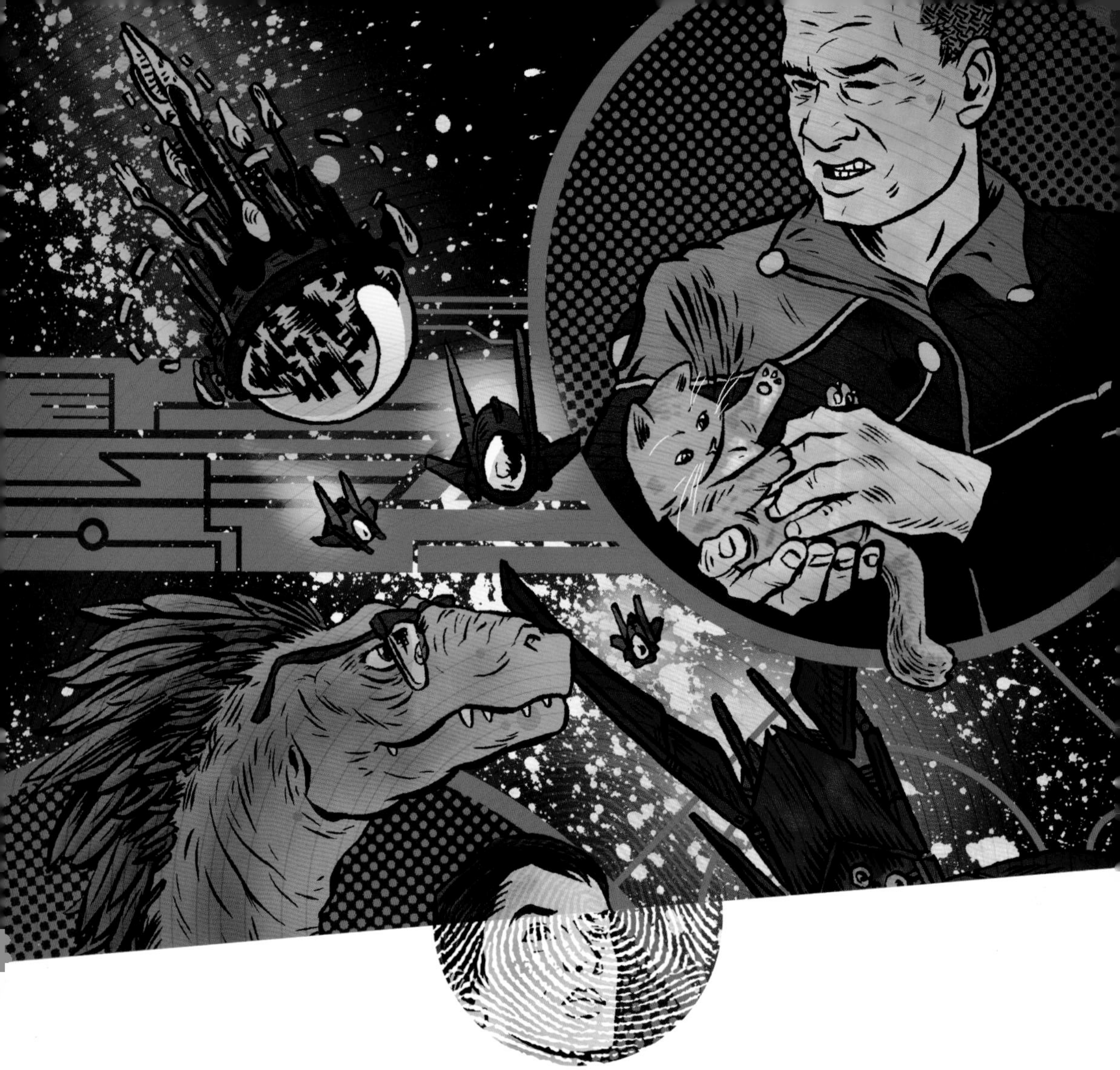

CHAPTER FOUR

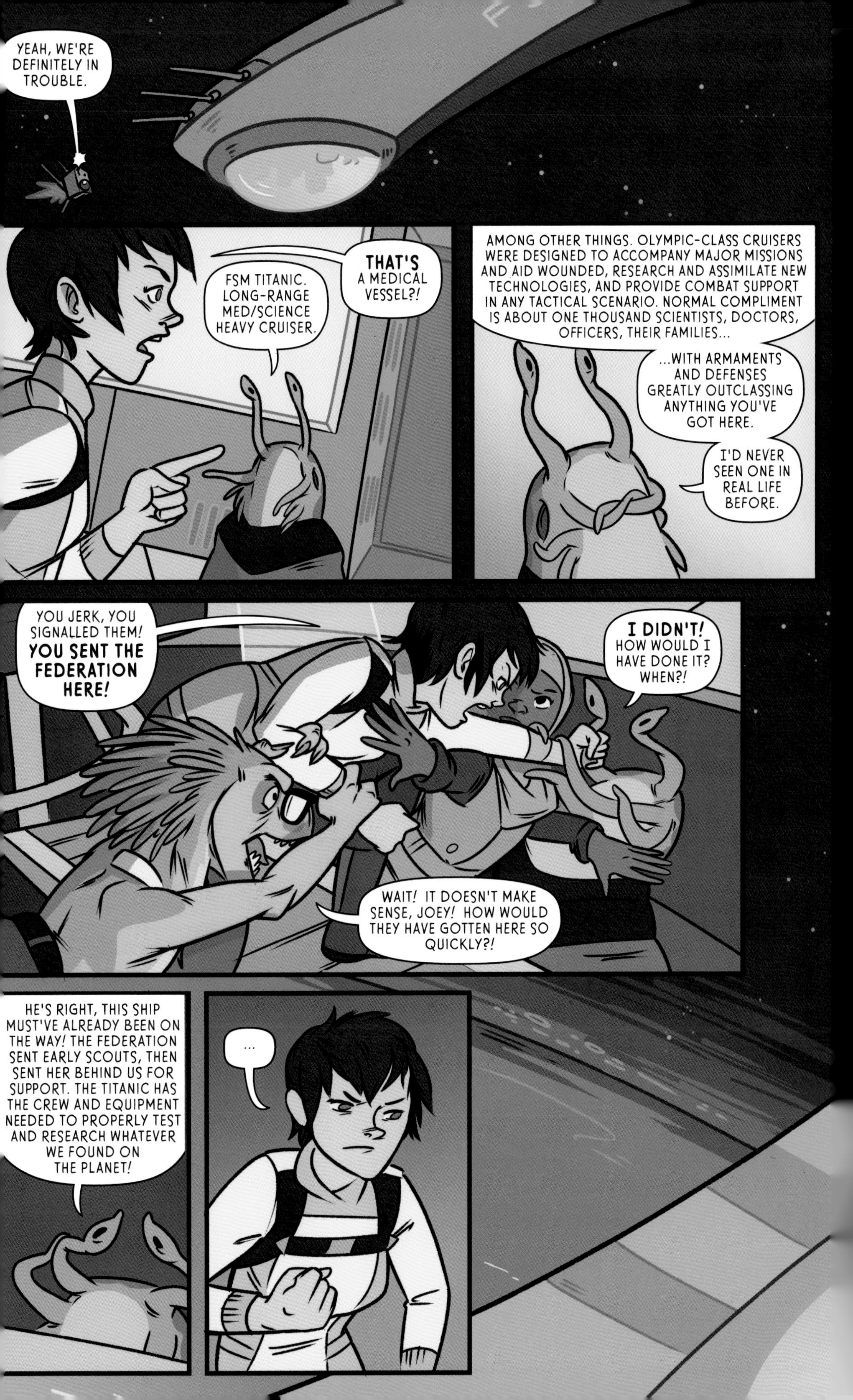
YEAH, WE'RE DEFINITELY IN TROUBLE.
FSM TITANIC. LONG-RANGE MED/SCIENCE HEAVY CRUISER.
THAT'S A MEDICAL VESSEL?!
AMONG OTHER THINGS. OLYMPIC-CLASS CRUISERS WERE DESIGNED TO ACCOMPANY MAJOR MISSIONS AND AID WOUNDED, RESEARCH AND ASSIMILATE NEW TECHNOLOGIES, AND PROVIDE COMBAT SUPPORT IN ANY TACTICAL SCENARIO. NORMAL COMPLIMENT IS ABOUT ONE THOUSAND SCIENTISTS, DOCTORS, OFFICERS, THEIR FAMILIES...
...WITH ARMAMENTS AND DEFENSES GREATLY OUTCLASSING ANYTHING YOU'VE GOT HERE.
I'D NEVER SEEN ONE IN REAL LIFE BEFORE.
YOU JERK, YOU SIGNALLED THEM! YOU SENT THE FEDERATION HERE!
I DIDN'T! HOW WOULD I HAVE DONE IT? WHEN?!
WAIT! IT DOESN'T MAKE SENSE, JOEY! HOW WOULD THEY HAVE GOTTEN HERE SO QUICKLY?!
HE'S RIGHT, THIS SHIP MUST'VE ALREADY BEEN ON THE WAY! THE FEDERATION SENT EARLY SCOUTS, THEN SENT HER BEHIND US FOR SUPPORT. THE TITANIC HAS THE CREW AND EQUIPMENT NEEDED TO PROPERLY TEST AND RESEARCH WHATEVER WE FOUND ON THE PLANET!
...

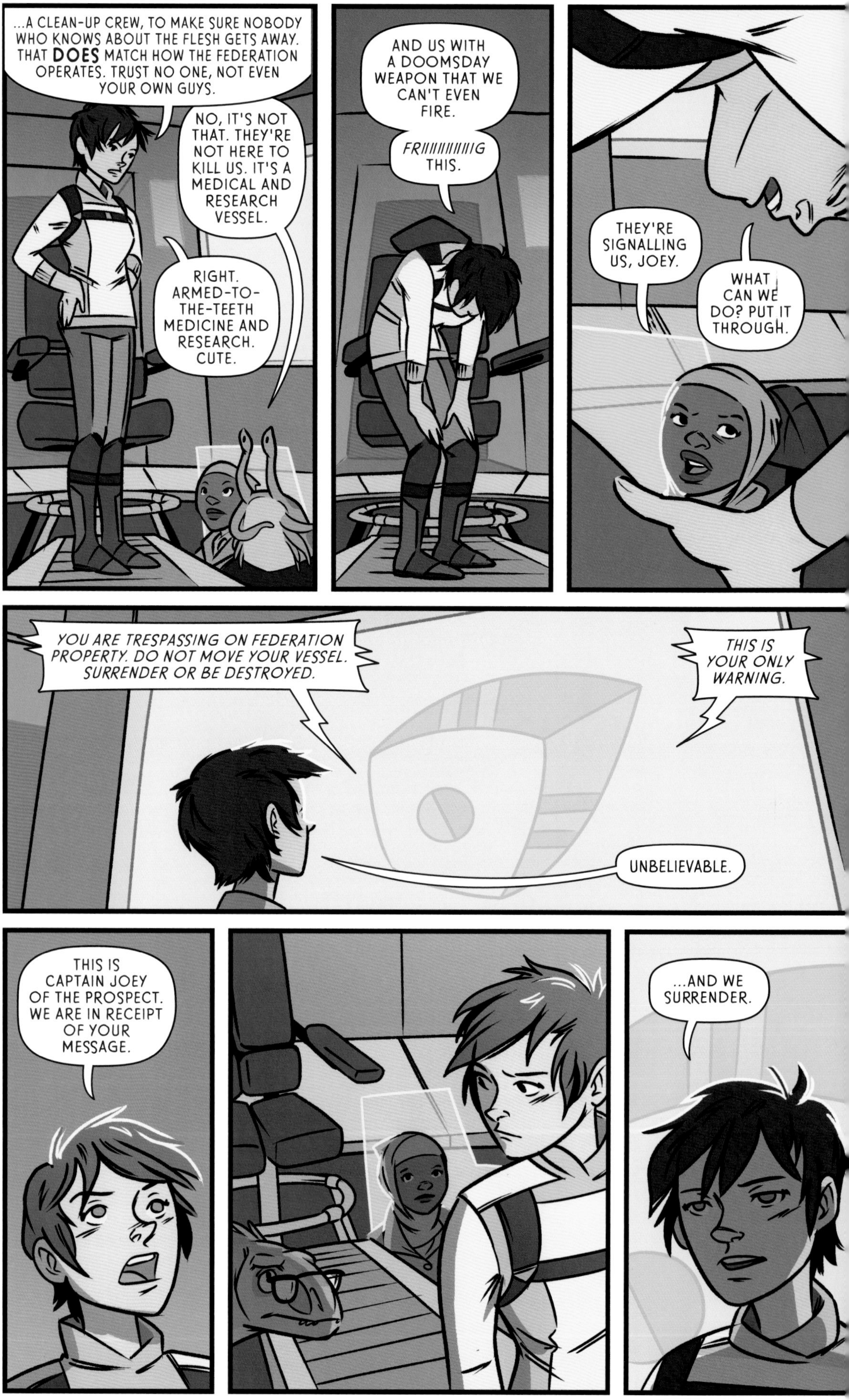
...A CLEAN-UP CREW, TO MAKE SURE NOBODY WHO KNOWS ABOUT THE FLESH GETS AWAY. THAT DOES MATCH HOW THE FEDERATION OPERATES. TRUST NO ONE, NOT EVEN YOUR OWN GUYS.
NO, IT'S NOT THAT. THEY'RE NOT HERE TO KILL US. IT'S A MEDICAL AND RESEARCH VESSEL.
RIGHT. ARMED-TO-THE-TEETH MEDICINE AND RESEARCH. CUTE.
AND US WITH A DOOMSDAY WEAPON THAT WE CAN'T EVEN FIRE.
FRIIIIIIIIIIIG THIS.
THEY'RE SIGNALLING US, JOEY.
WHAT CAN WE DO? PUT IT THROUGH.
YOU ARE TRESPASSING ON FEDERATION PROPERTY. DO NOT MOVE YOUR VESSEL. SURRENDER OR BE DESTROYED.
THIS IS YOUR ONLY WARNING.
UNBELIEVABLE.
THIS IS CAPTAIN JOEY OF THE PROSPECT. WE ARE IN RECEIPT OF YOUR MESSAGE.
...AND WE SURRENDER.

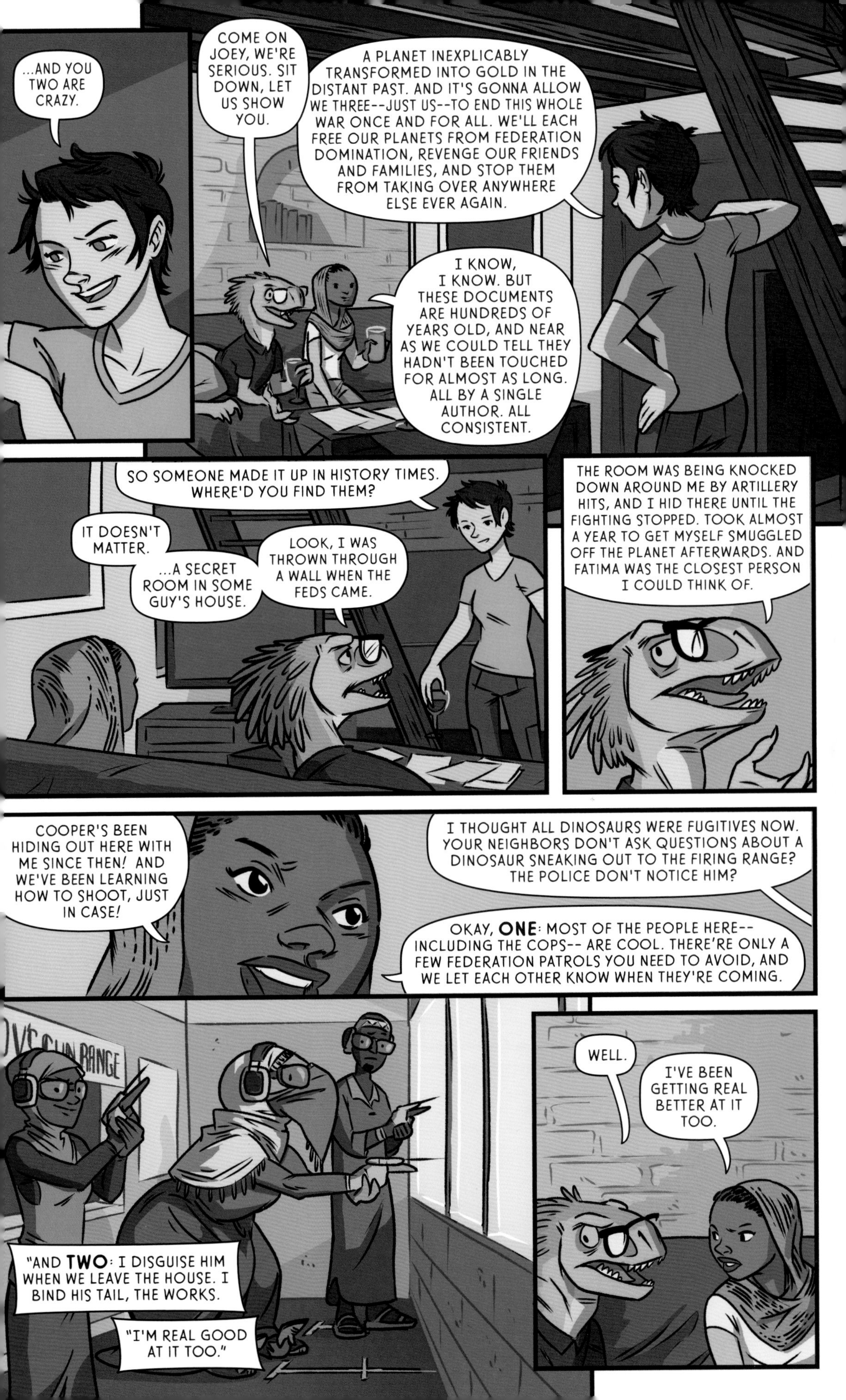
...AND YOU TWO ARE CRAZY.
COME ON JOEY, WE'RE SERIOUS. SIT DOWN, LET US SHOW YOU.
A PLANET INEXPLICABLY TRANSFORMED INTO GOLD IN THE DISTANT PAST. AND IT'S GONNA ALLOW WE THREE--JUST US--TO END THIS WHOLE WAR ONCE AND FOR ALL. WE'LL EACH FREE OUR PLANETS FROM FEDERATION DOMINATION, REVENGE OUR FRIENDS AND FAMILIES, AND STOP THEM FROM TAKING OVER ANYWHERE ELSE EVER AGAIN.
I KNOW, I KNOW. BUT THESE DOCUMENTS ARE HUNDREDS OF YEARS OLD, AND NEAR AS WE COULD TELL THEY HADN'T BEEN TOUCHED FOR ALMOST AS LONG. ALL BY A SINGLE AUTHOR. ALL CONSISTENT.
SO SOMEONE MADE IT UP IN HISTORY TIMES. WHERE'D YOU FIND THEM?
IT DOESN'T MATTER.
...A SECRET ROOM IN SOME GUY'S HOUSE.
LOOK, I WAS THROWN THROUGH A WALL WHEN THE FEDS CAME.
THE ROOM WAS BEING KNOCKED DOWN AROUND ME BY ARTILLERY HITS, AND I HID THERE UNTIL THE FIGHTING STOPPED. TOOK ALMOST A YEAR TO GET MYSELF SMUGGLED OFF THE PLANET AFTERWARDS. AND FATIMA WAS THE CLOSEST PERSON I COULD THINK OF.
COOPER'S BEEN HIDING OUT HERE WITH ME SINCE THEN! AND WE'VE BEEN LEARNING HOW TO SHOOT, JUST IN CASE!
I THOUGHT ALL DINOSAURS WERE FUGITIVES NOW. YOUR NEIGHBORS DON'T ASK QUESTIONS ABOUT A DINOSAUR SNEAKING OUT TO THE FIRING RANGE? THE POLICE DON'T NOTICE HIM?
OKAY, ONE: MOST OF THE PEOPLE HERE--INCLUDING THE COPS-- ARE COOL. THERE'RE ONLY A FEW FEDERATION PATROLS YOU NEED TO AVOID, AND WE LET EACH OTHER KNOW WHEN THEY'RE COMING.
GUN RANGE
"AND TWO: I DISGUISE HIM WHEN WE LEAVE THE HOUSE. I BIND HIS TAIL, THE WORKS.
"I'M REAL GOOD AT IT TOO."
WELL.
I'VE BEEN GETTING REAL BETTER AT IT TOO.

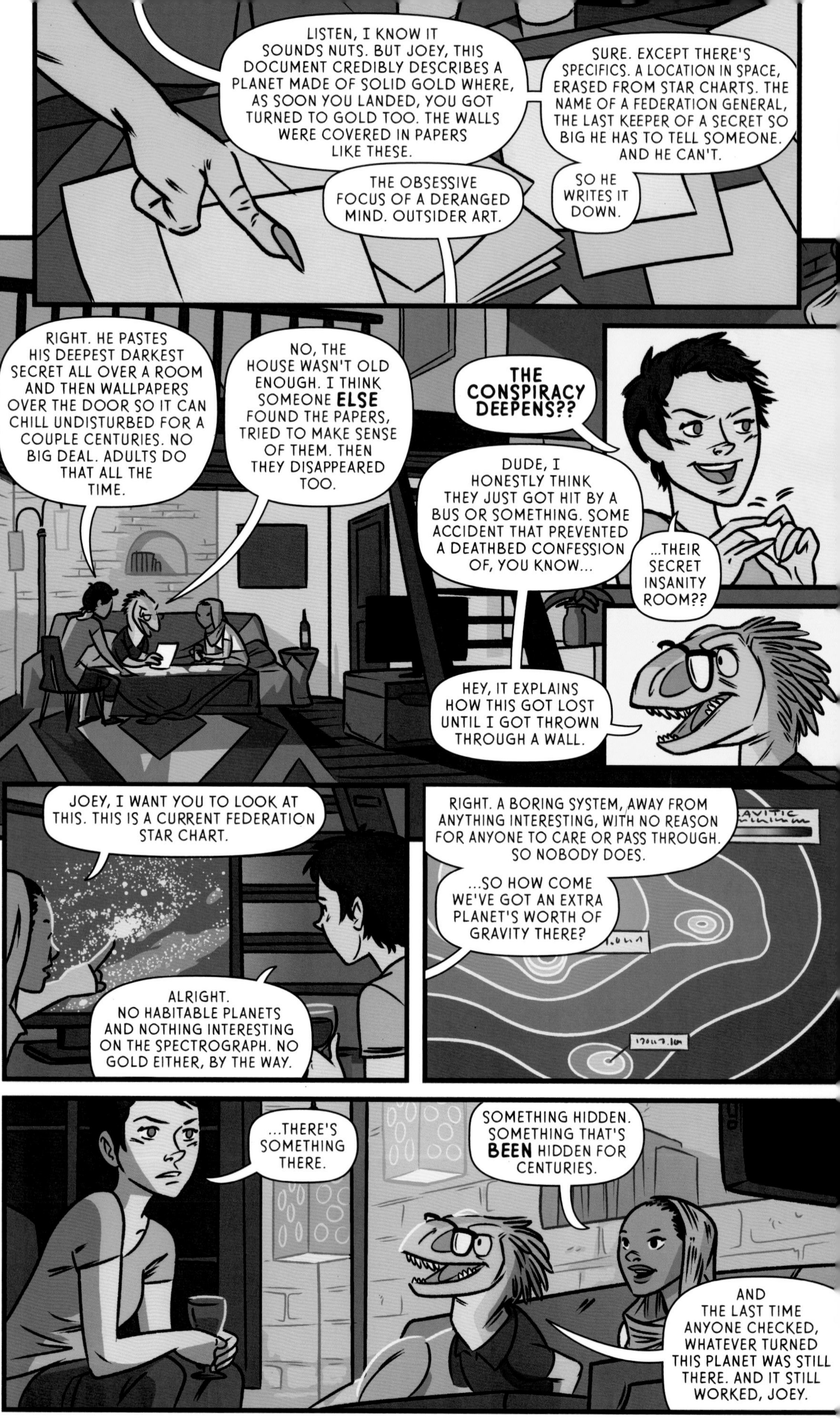
LISTEN, I KNOW IT SOUNDS NUTS. BUT JOEY, THIS DOCUMENT CREDIBLY DESCRIBES A PLANET MADE OF SOLID GOLD WHERE, AS SOON YOU LANDED, YOU GOT TURNED TO GOLD TOO. THE WALLS WERE COVERED IN PAPERS LIKE THESE.
THE OBSESSIVE FOCUS OF A DERANGED MIND. OUTSIDER ART.
SURE. EXCEPT THERE'S SPECIFICS. A LOCATION IN SPACE, ERASED FROM STAR CHARTS. THE NAME OF A FEDERATION GENERAL, THE LAST KEEPER OF A SECRET SO BIG HE HAS TO TELL SOMEONE. AND HE CAN'T.
SO HE WRITES IT DOWN.
RIGHT. HE PASTES HIS DEEPEST DARKEST SECRET ALL OVER A ROOM AND THEN WALLPAPERS OVER THE DOOR SO IT CAN CHILL UNDISTURBED FOR A COUPLE CENTURIES. NO BIG DEAL. ADULTS DO THAT ALL THE TIME.
NO, THE HOUSE WASN'T OLD ENOUGH. I THINK SOMEONE **ELSE** FOUND THE PAPERS, TRIED TO MAKE SENSE OF THEM. THEN THEY DISAPPEARED TOO.
THE CONSPIRACY DEEPENS??
DUDE, I HONESTLY THINK THEY JUST GOT HIT BY A BUS OR SOMETHING. SOME ACCIDENT THAT PREVENTED A DEATHBED CONFESSION OF, YOU KNOW...
...THEIR SECRET INSANITY ROOM??
HEY, IT EXPLAINS HOW THIS GOT LOST UNTIL I GOT THROWN THROUGH A WALL.
JOEY, I WANT YOU TO LOOK AT THIS. THIS IS A CURRENT FEDERATION STAR CHART.
ALRIGHT. NO HABITABLE PLANETS AND NOTHING INTERESTING ON THE SPECTROGRAPH. NO GOLD EITHER, BY THE WAY.
RIGHT. A BORING SYSTEM, AWAY FROM ANYTHING INTERESTING, WITH NO REASON FOR ANYONE TO CARE OR PASS THROUGH. SO NOBODY DOES.
...SO HOW COME WE'VE GOT AN EXTRA PLANET'S WORTH OF GRAVITY THERE?
...THERE'S SOMETHING THERE.
SOMETHING HIDDEN. SOMETHING THAT'S **BEEN** HIDDEN FOR CENTURIES.
AND THE LAST TIME ANYONE CHECKED, WHATEVER TURNED THIS PLANET WAS STILL THERE. AND IT STILL WORKED, JOEY.

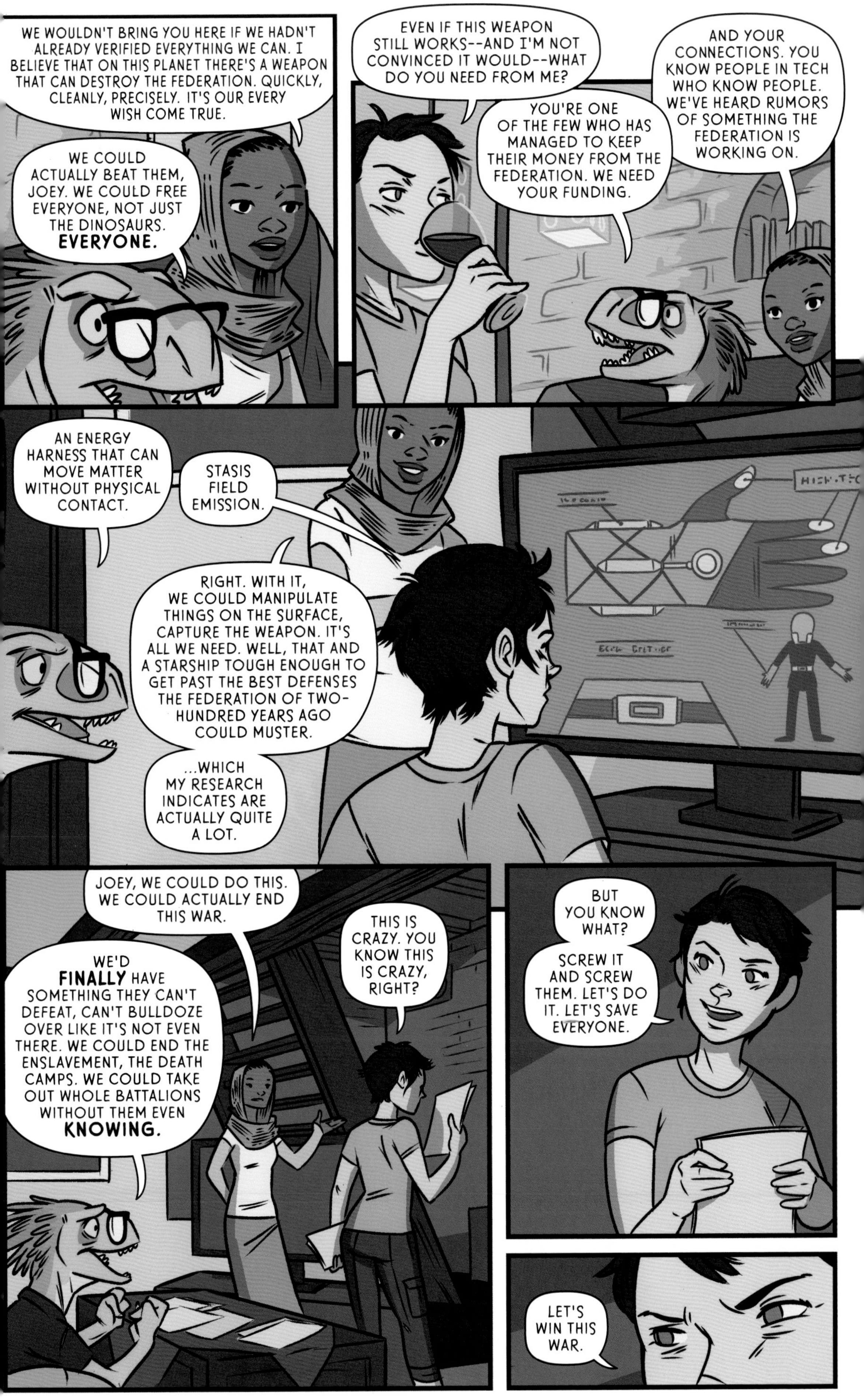
WE WOULDN'T BRING YOU HERE IF WE HADN'T ALREADY VERIFIED EVERYTHING WE CAN. I BELIEVE THAT ON THIS PLANET THERE'S A WEAPON THAT CAN DESTROY THE FEDERATION. QUICKLY, CLEANLY, PRECISELY. IT'S OUR EVERY WISH COME TRUE.
WE COULD ACTUALLY BEAT THEM, JOEY. WE COULD FREE EVERYONE, NOT JUST THE DINOSAURS. **EVERYONE.**
EVEN IF THIS WEAPON STILL WORKS--AND I'M NOT CONVINCED IT WOULD--WHAT DO YOU NEED FROM ME?
YOU'RE ONE OF THE FEW WHO HAS MANAGED TO KEEP THEIR MONEY FROM THE FEDERATION. WE NEED YOUR FUNDING.
AND YOUR CONNECTIONS. YOU KNOW PEOPLE IN TECH WHO KNOW PEOPLE. WE'VE HEARD RUMORS OF SOMETHING THE FEDERATION IS WORKING ON.
AN ENERGY HARNESS THAT CAN MOVE MATTER WITHOUT PHYSICAL CONTACT.
STASIS FIELD EMISSION.
RIGHT. WITH IT, WE COULD MANIPULATE THINGS ON THE SURFACE, CAPTURE THE WEAPON. IT'S ALL WE NEED. WELL, THAT AND A STARSHIP TOUGH ENOUGH TO GET PAST THE BEST DEFENSES THE FEDERATION OF TWO-HUNDRED YEARS AGO COULD MUSTER.
...WHICH MY RESEARCH INDICATES ARE ACTUALLY QUITE A LOT.
JOEY, WE COULD DO THIS. WE COULD ACTUALLY END THIS WAR.
WE'D **FINALLY** HAVE SOMETHING THEY CAN'T DEFEAT, CAN'T BULLDOZE OVER LIKE IT'S NOT EVEN THERE. WE COULD END THE ENSLAVEMENT, THE DEATH CAMPS. WE COULD TAKE OUT WHOLE BATTALIONS WITHOUT THEM EVEN **KNOWING.**
THIS IS CRAZY. YOU KNOW THIS IS CRAZY, RIGHT?
BUT YOU KNOW WHAT?
SCREW IT AND SCREW THEM. LET'S DO IT. LET'S SAVE EVERYONE.
LET'S WIN THIS WAR.

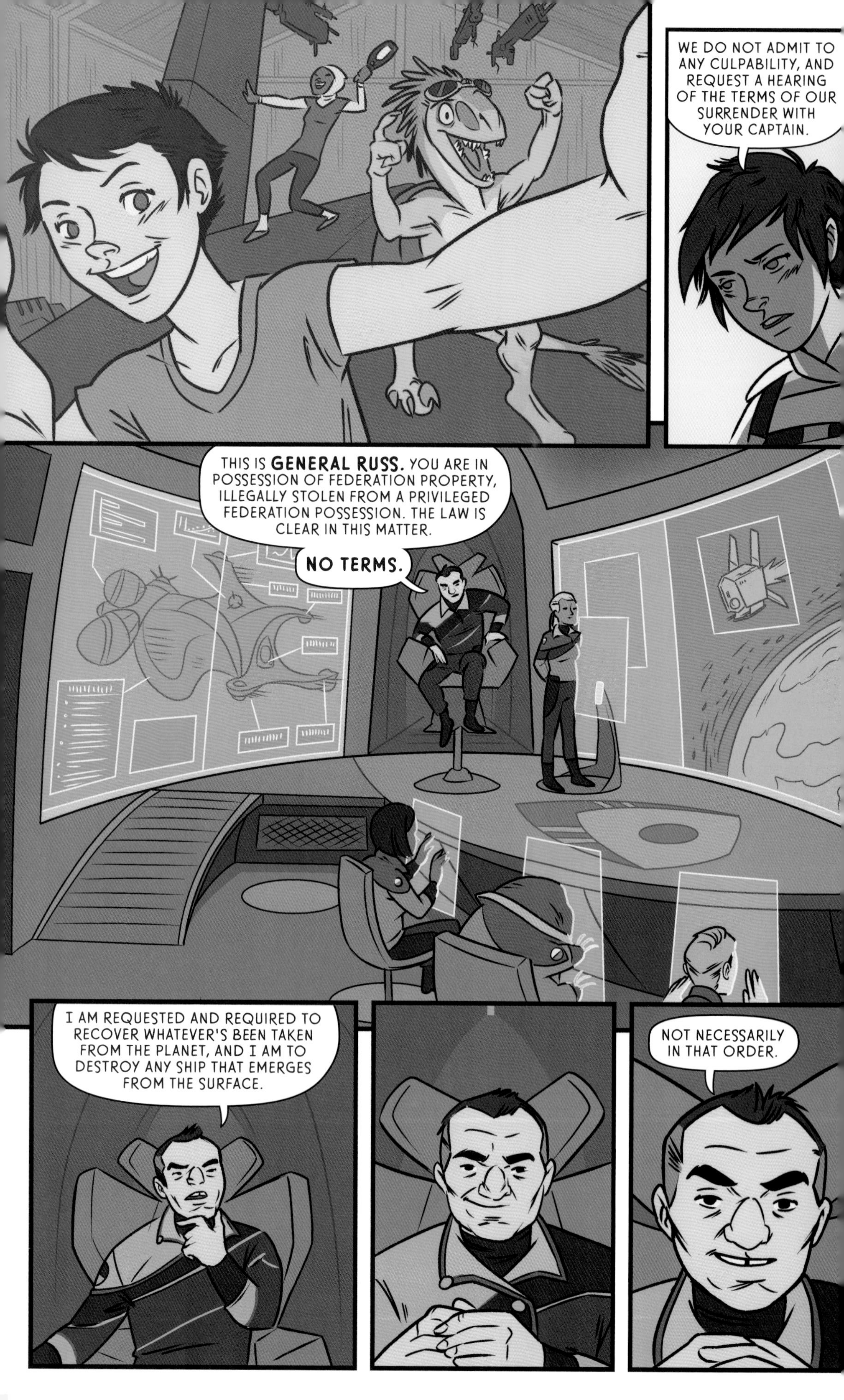
WE DO NOT ADMIT TO ANY CULPABILITY, AND REQUEST A HEARING OF THE TERMS OF OUR SURRENDER WITH YOUR CAPTAIN.
THIS IS GENERAL RUSS. YOU ARE IN POSSESSION OF FEDERATION PROPERTY, ILLEGALLY STOLEN FROM A PRIVILEGED FEDERATION POSSESSION. THE LAW IS CLEAR IN THIS MATTER.
NO TERMS.
I AM REQUESTED AND REQUIRED TO RECOVER WHATEVER'S BEEN TAKEN FROM THE PLANET, AND I AM TO DESTROY ANY SHIP THAT EMERGES FROM THE SURFACE.
NOT NECESSARILY IN THAT ORDER.

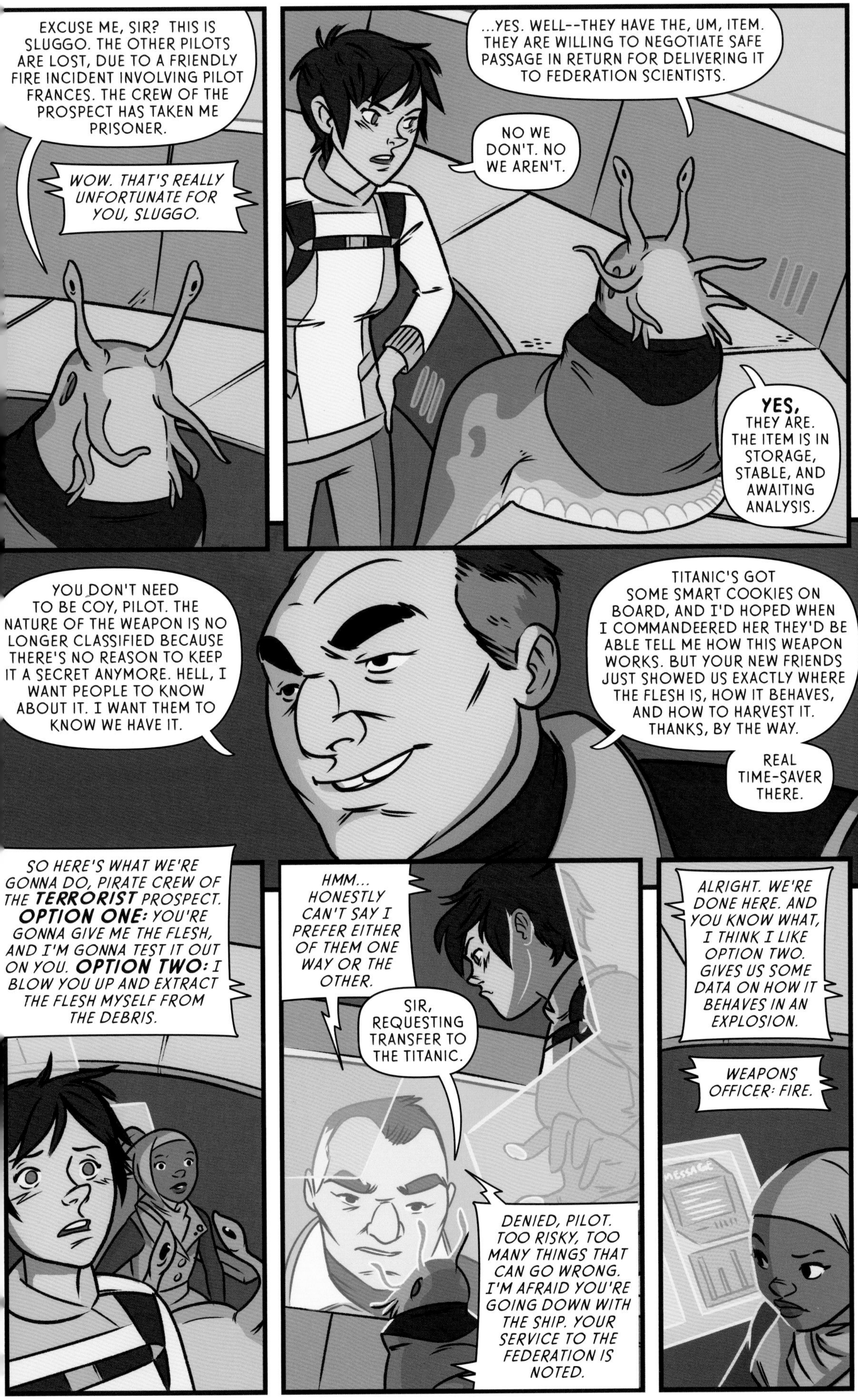
EXCUSE ME, SIR? THIS IS SLUGGO. THE OTHER PILOTS ARE LOST, DUE TO A FRIENDLY FIRE INCIDENT INVOLVING PILOT FRANCES. THE CREW OF THE PROSPECT HAS TAKEN ME PRISONER.
WOW. THAT'S REALLY UNFORTUNATE FOR YOU, SLUGGO.
...YES. WELL--THEY HAVE THE, UM, ITEM. THEY ARE WILLING TO NEGOTIATE SAFE PASSAGE IN RETURN FOR DELIVERING IT TO FEDERATION SCIENTISTS.
NO WE DON'T. NO WE AREN'T.
YES, THEY ARE. THE ITEM IS IN STORAGE, STABLE, AND AWAITING ANALYSIS.
YOU DON'T NEED TO BE COY, PILOT. THE NATURE OF THE WEAPON IS NO LONGER CLASSIFIED BECAUSE THERE'S NO REASON TO KEEP IT A SECRET ANYMORE. HELL, I WANT PEOPLE TO KNOW ABOUT IT. I WANT THEM TO KNOW WE HAVE IT.
TITANIC'S GOT SOME SMART COOKIES ON BOARD, AND I'D HOPED WHEN I COMMANDEERED HER THEY'D BE ABLE TELL ME HOW THIS WEAPON WORKS. BUT YOUR NEW FRIENDS JUST SHOWED US EXACTLY WHERE THE FLESH IS, HOW IT BEHAVES, AND HOW TO HARVEST IT. THANKS, BY THE WAY.
REAL TIME-SAVER THERE.
SO HERE'S WHAT WE'RE GONNA DO, PIRATE CREW OF THE TERRORIST PROSPECT. OPTION ONE: YOU'RE GONNA GIVE ME THE FLESH, AND I'M GONNA TEST IT OUT ON YOU. OPTION TWO: I BLOW YOU UP AND EXTRACT THE FLESH MYSELF FROM THE DEBRIS.
HMM... HONESTLY CAN'T SAY I PREFER EITHER OF THEM ONE WAY OR THE OTHER.
SIR, REQUESTING TRANSFER TO THE TITANIC.
DENIED, PILOT. TOO RISKY, TOO MANY THINGS THAT CAN GO WRONG. I'M AFRAID YOU'RE GOING DOWN WITH THE SHIP. YOUR SERVICE TO THE FEDERATION IS NOTED.
ALRIGHT. WE'RE DONE HERE. AND YOU KNOW WHAT, I THINK I LIKE OPTION TWO. GIVES US SOME DATA ON HOW IT BEHAVES IN AN EXPLOSION.
WEAPONS OFFICER: FIRE.
MESSAGE

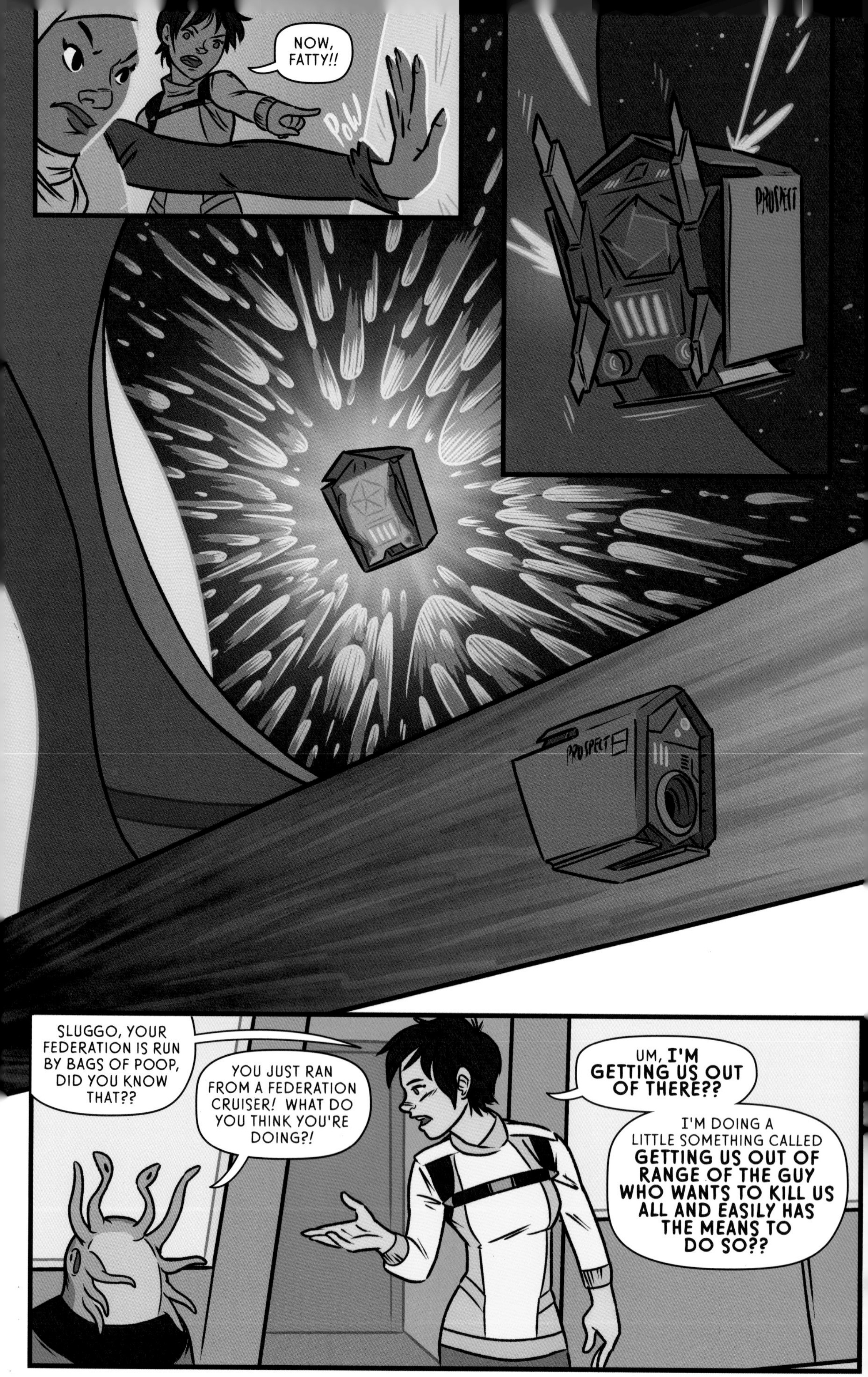
NOW, FATTY!!
POW
PROSPECT
PROSPECT
SLUGGO, YOUR FEDERATION IS RUN BY BAGS OF POOP, DID YOU KNOW THAT??
YOU JUST RAN FROM A FEDERATION CRUISER! WHAT DO YOU THINK YOU'RE DOING?!
UM, I'M GETTING US OUT OF THERE??
I'M DOING A LITTLE SOMETHING CALLED GETTING US OUT OF RANGE OF THE GUY WHO WANTS TO KILL US ALL AND EASILY HAS THE MEANS TO DO SO??

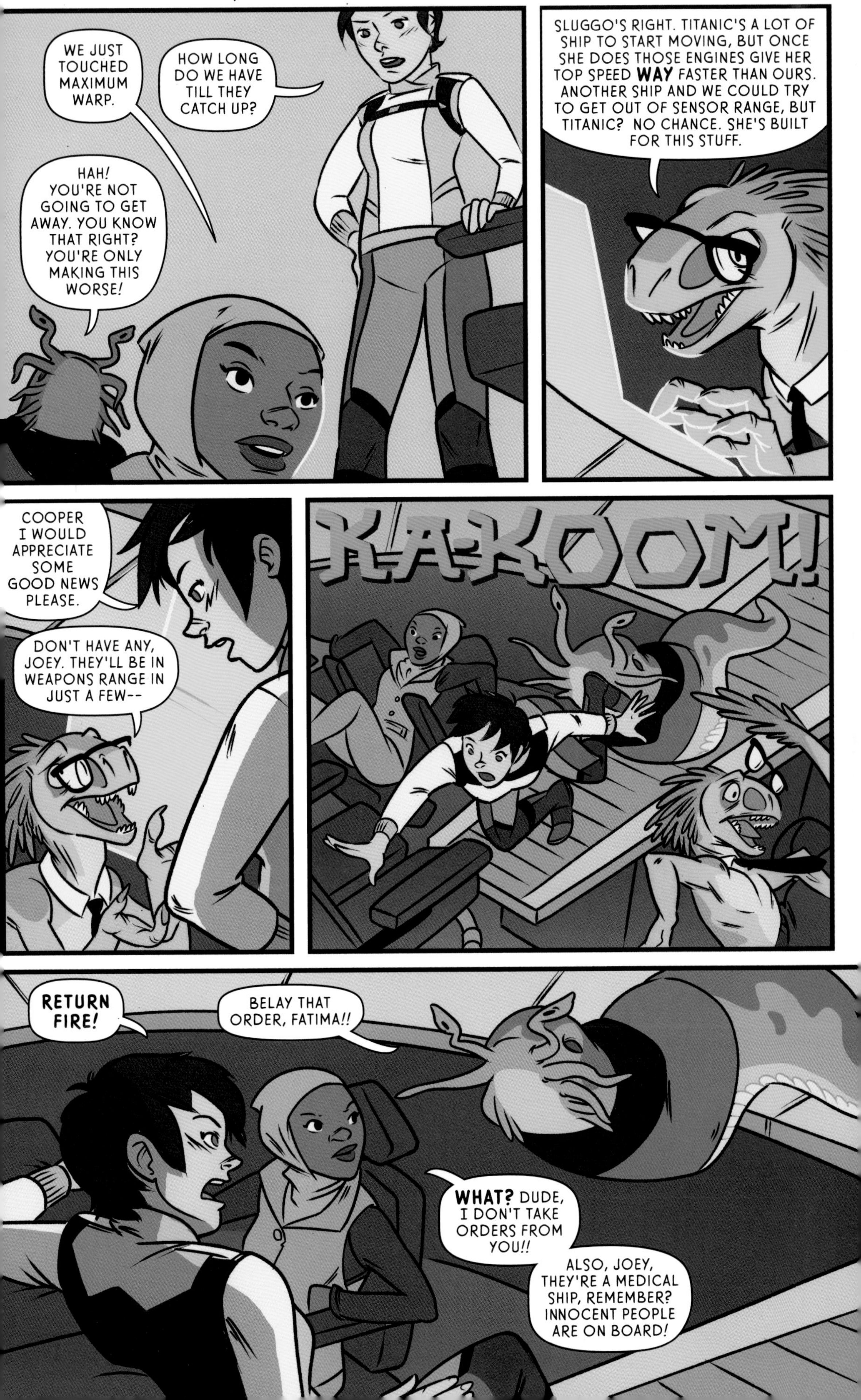
WE JUST TOUCHED MAXIMUM WARP.
HOW LONG DO WE HAVE TILL THEY CATCH UP?
HAH! YOU'RE NOT GOING TO GET AWAY. YOU KNOW THAT RIGHT? YOU'RE ONLY MAKING THIS WORSE!
SLUGGO'S RIGHT. TITANIC'S A LOT OF SHIP TO START MOVING, BUT ONCE SHE DOES THOSE ENGINES GIVE HER TOP SPEED **WAY** FASTER THAN OURS. ANOTHER SHIP AND WE COULD TRY TO GET OUT OF SENSOR RANGE, BUT TITANIC? NO CHANCE. SHE'S BUILT FOR THIS STUFF.
COOPER I WOULD APPRECIATE SOME GOOD NEWS PLEASE.
DON'T HAVE ANY, JOEY. THEY'LL BE IN WEAPONS RANGE IN JUST A FEW--
KA-KOOM!
RETURN FIRE!
BELAY THAT ORDER, FATIMA!!
WHAT? DUDE, I DON'T TAKE ORDERS FROM YOU!!
ALSO, JOEY, THEY'RE A MEDICAL SHIP, REMEMBER? INNOCENT PEOPLE ARE ON BOARD!

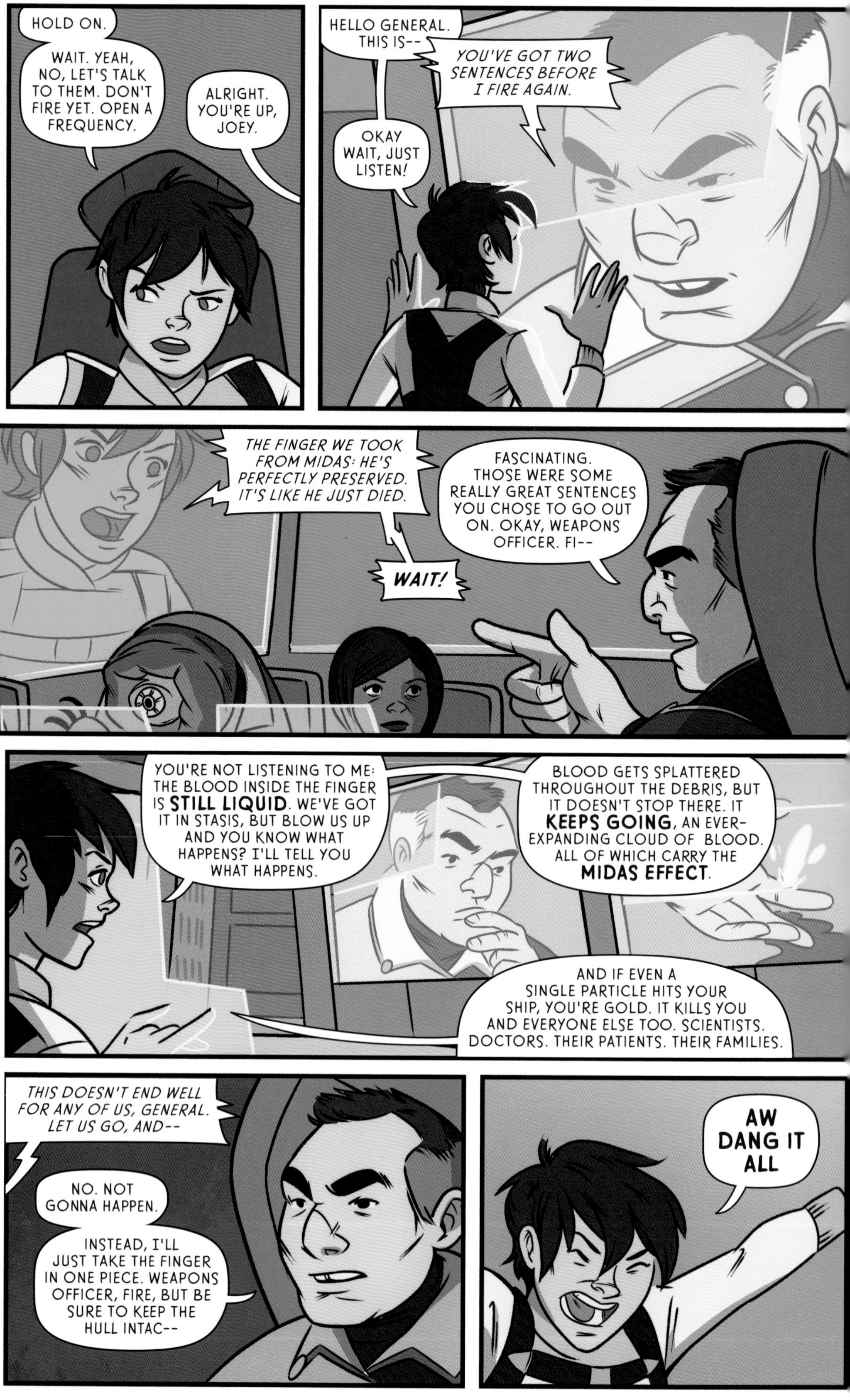
HOLD ON.
WAIT. YEAH, NO, LET'S TALK TO THEM. DON'T FIRE YET. OPEN A FREQUENCY.
ALRIGHT. YOU'RE UP, JOEY.
HELLO GENERAL. THIS IS--
YOU'VE GOT TWO SENTENCES BEFORE I FIRE AGAIN.
OKAY WAIT, JUST LISTEN!
THE FINGER WE TOOK FROM MIDAS: HE'S PERFECTLY PRESERVED. IT'S LIKE HE JUST DIED.
FASCINATING. THOSE WERE SOME REALLY GREAT SENTENCES YOU CHOSE TO GO OUT ON. OKAY, WEAPONS OFFICER. FI--
WAIT!
YOU'RE NOT LISTENING TO ME: THE BLOOD INSIDE THE FINGER IS STILL LIQUID. WE'VE GOT IT IN STASIS, BUT BLOW US UP AND YOU KNOW WHAT HAPPENS? I'LL TELL YOU WHAT HAPPENS.
BLOOD GETS SPLATTERED THROUGHOUT THE DEBRIS, BUT IT DOESN'T STOP THERE. IT KEEPS GOING, AN EVER-EXPANDING CLOUD OF BLOOD. ALL OF WHICH CARRY THE MIDAS EFFECT.
AND IF EVEN A SINGLE PARTICLE HITS YOUR SHIP, YOU'RE GOLD. IT KILLS YOU AND EVERYONE ELSE TOO. SCIENTISTS. DOCTORS. THEIR PATIENTS. THEIR FAMILIES.
THIS DOESN'T END WELL FOR ANY OF US, GENERAL. LET US GO, AND--
NO. NOT GONNA HAPPEN.
INSTEAD, I'LL JUST TAKE THE FINGER IN ONE PIECE. WEAPONS OFFICER, FIRE, BUT BE SURE TO KEEP THE HULL INTAC--
AW DANG IT ALL

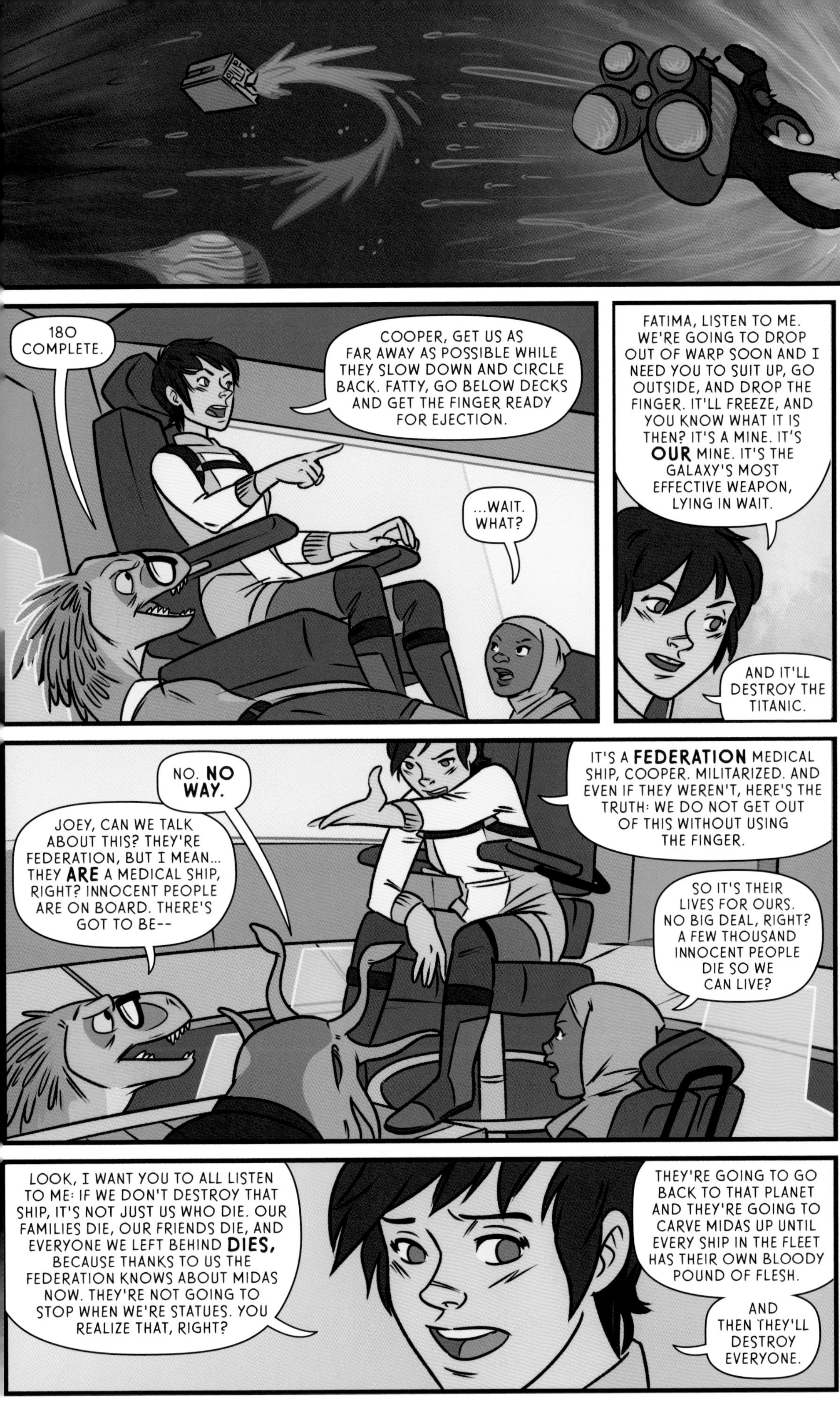
180 COMPLETE.
COOPER, GET US AS FAR AWAY AS POSSIBLE WHILE THEY SLOW DOWN AND CIRCLE BACK. FATTY, GO BELOW DECKS AND GET THE FINGER READY FOR EJECTION.
...WAIT. WHAT?
FATIMA, LISTEN TO ME. WE'RE GOING TO DROP OUT OF WARP SOON AND I NEED YOU TO SUIT UP, GO OUTSIDE, AND DROP THE FINGER. IT'LL FREEZE, AND YOU KNOW WHAT IT IS THEN? IT'S A MINE. IT'S OUR MINE. IT'S THE GALAXY'S MOST EFFECTIVE WEAPON, LYING IN WAIT.
AND IT'LL DESTROY THE TITANIC.
NO. NO WAY.
JOEY, CAN WE TALK ABOUT THIS? THEY'RE FEDERATION, BUT I MEAN... THEY ARE A MEDICAL SHIP, RIGHT? INNOCENT PEOPLE ARE ON BOARD. THERE'S GOT TO BE--
IT'S A FEDERATION MEDICAL SHIP, COOPER. MILITARIZED. AND EVEN IF THEY WEREN'T, HERE'S THE TRUTH: WE DO NOT GET OUT OF THIS WITHOUT USING THE FINGER.
SO IT'S THEIR LIVES FOR OURS. NO BIG DEAL, RIGHT? A FEW THOUSAND INNOCENT PEOPLE DIE SO WE CAN LIVE?
LOOK, I WANT YOU TO ALL LISTEN TO ME: IF WE DON'T DESTROY THAT SHIP, IT'S NOT JUST US WHO DIE. OUR FAMILIES DIE, OUR FRIENDS DIE, AND EVERYONE WE LEFT BEHIND DIES, BECAUSE THANKS TO US THE FEDERATION KNOWS ABOUT MIDAS NOW. THEY'RE NOT GOING TO STOP WHEN WE'RE STATUES. YOU REALIZE THAT, RIGHT?
THEY'RE GOING TO GO BACK TO THAT PLANET AND THEY'RE GOING TO CARVE MIDAS UP UNTIL EVERY SHIP IN THE FLEET HAS THEIR OWN BLOODY POUND OF FLESH.
AND THEN THEY'LL DESTROY EVERYONE.

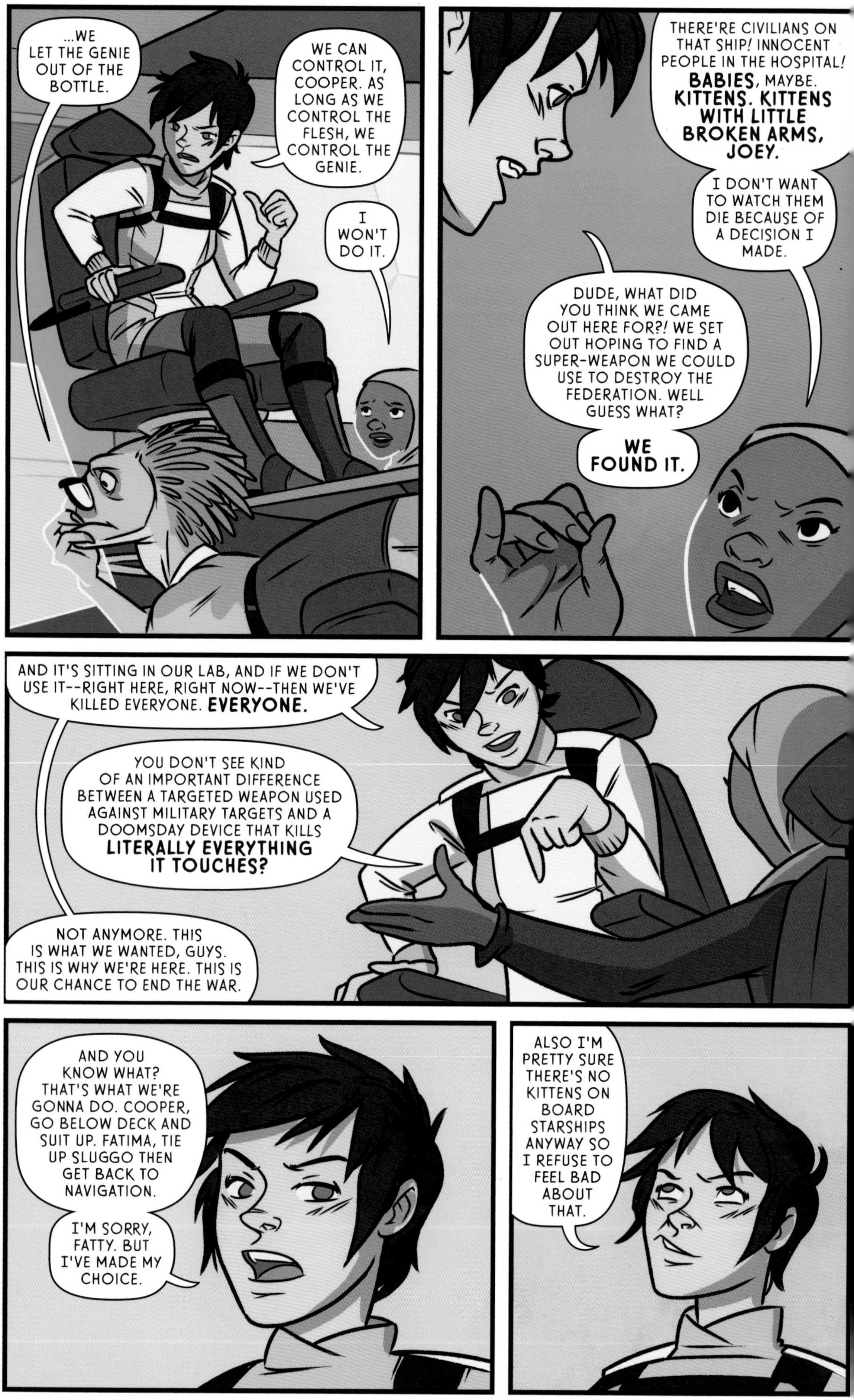
...WE LET THE GENIE OUT OF THE BOTTLE.
WE CAN CONTROL IT, COOPER. AS LONG AS WE CONTROL THE FLESH, WE CONTROL THE GENIE.
I WON'T DO IT.
THERE'RE CIVILIANS ON THAT SHIP! INNOCENT PEOPLE IN THE HOSPITAL! **BABIES**, MAYBE. **KITTENS. KITTENS WITH LITTLE BROKEN ARMS, JOEY.**
I DON'T WANT TO WATCH THEM DIE BECAUSE OF A DECISION I MADE.
DUDE, WHAT DID YOU THINK WE CAME OUT HERE FOR?! WE SET OUT HOPING TO FIND A SUPER-WEAPON WE COULD USE TO DESTROY THE FEDERATION. WELL GUESS WHAT?
WE FOUND IT.
AND IT'S SITTING IN OUR LAB, AND IF WE DON'T USE IT--RIGHT HERE, RIGHT NOW--THEN WE'VE KILLED EVERYONE. **EVERYONE.**
YOU DON'T SEE KIND OF AN IMPORTANT DIFFERENCE BETWEEN A TARGETED WEAPON USED AGAINST MILITARY TARGETS AND A DOOMSDAY DEVICE THAT KILLS **LITERALLY EVERYTHING IT TOUCHES?**
NOT ANYMORE. THIS IS WHAT WE WANTED, GUYS. THIS IS WHY WE'RE HERE. THIS IS OUR CHANCE TO END THE WAR.
AND YOU KNOW WHAT? THAT'S WHAT WE'RE GONNA DO. COOPER, GO BELOW DECK AND SUIT UP. FATIMA, TIE UP SLUGGO THEN GET BACK TO NAVIGATION.
I'M SORRY, FATTY. BUT I'VE MADE MY CHOICE.
ALSO I'M PRETTY SURE THERE'S NO KITTENS ON BOARD STARSHIPS ANYWAY SO I REFUSE TO FEEL BAD ABOUT THAT.

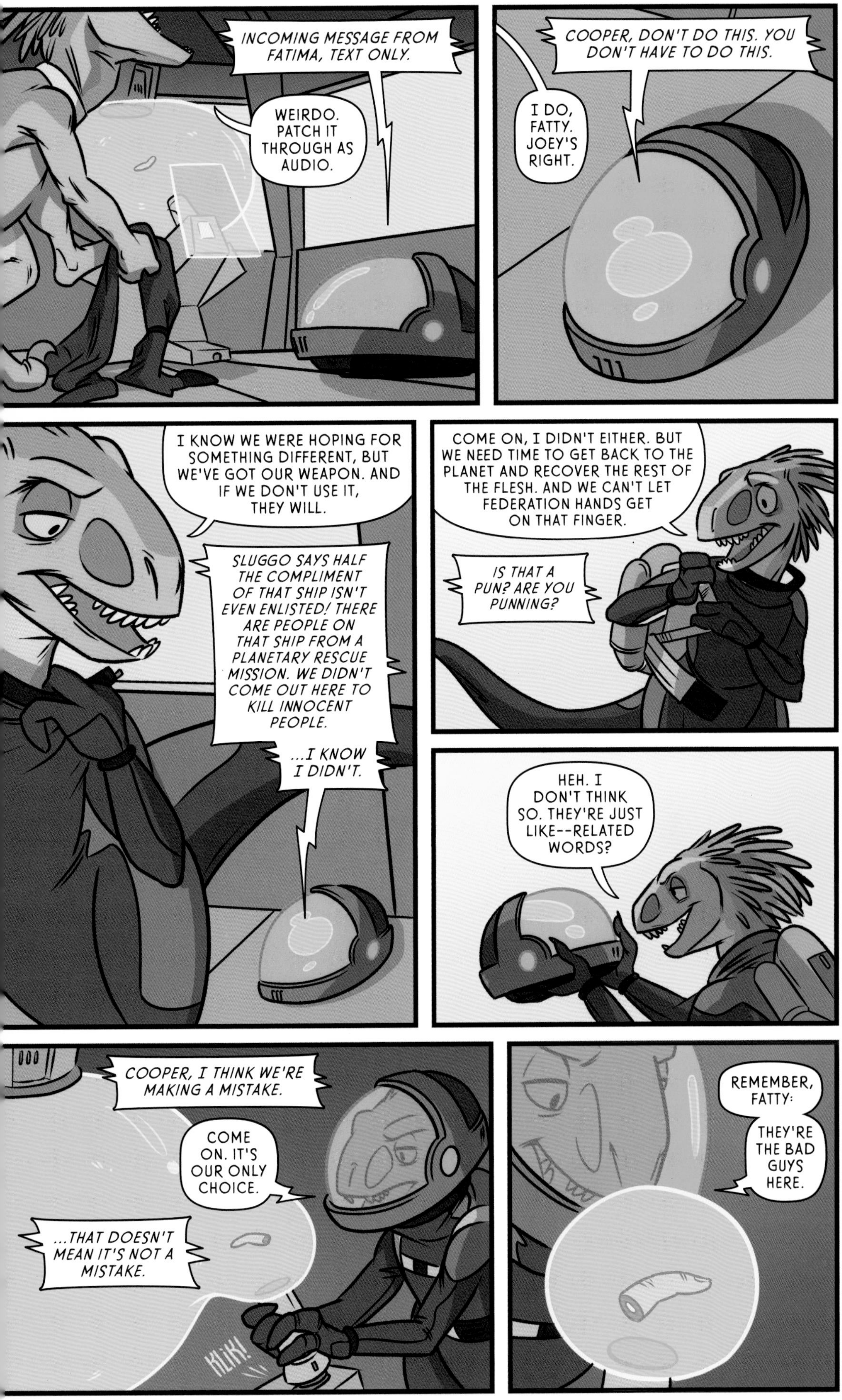
INCOMING MESSAGE FROM FATIMA, TEXT ONLY.
WEIRDO. PATCH IT THROUGH AS AUDIO.
COOPER, DON'T DO THIS. YOU DON'T HAVE TO DO THIS.
I DO, FATTY. JOEY'S RIGHT.
I KNOW WE WERE HOPING FOR SOMETHING DIFFERENT, BUT WE'VE GOT OUR WEAPON. AND IF WE DON'T USE IT, THEY WILL.
SLUGGO SAYS HALF THE COMPLIMENT OF THAT SHIP ISN'T EVEN ENLISTED! THERE ARE PEOPLE ON THAT SHIP FROM A PLANETARY RESCUE MISSION. WE DIDN'T COME OUT HERE TO KILL INNOCENT PEOPLE.
...I KNOW I DIDN'T.
COME ON, I DIDN'T EITHER. BUT WE NEED TIME TO GET BACK TO THE PLANET AND RECOVER THE REST OF THE FLESH. AND WE CAN'T LET FEDERATION HANDS GET ON THAT FINGER.
IS THAT A PUN? ARE YOU PUNNING?
HEH. I DON'T THINK SO. THEY'RE JUST LIKE--RELATED WORDS?
COOPER, I THINK WE'RE MAKING A MISTAKE.
COME ON. IT'S OUR ONLY CHOICE.
...THAT DOESN'T MEAN IT'S NOT A MISTAKE.
KLIK!
REMEMBER, FATTY:
THEY'RE THE BAD GUYS HERE.

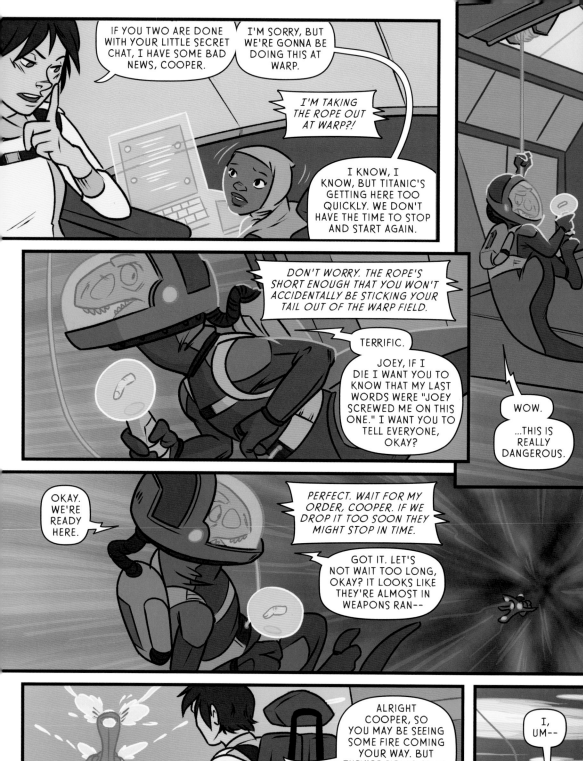

IF YOU TWO ARE DONE WITH YOUR LITTLE SECRET CHAT, I HAVE SOME BAD NEWS, COOPER.

I'M SORRY, BUT WE'RE GONNA BE DOING THIS AT WARP.

I'M TAKING THE ROPE OUT AT WARP?!

I KNOW, I KNOW, BUT TITANIC'S GETTING HERE TOO QUICKLY. WE DON'T HAVE THE TIME TO STOP AND START AGAIN.

DON'T WORRY. THE ROPE'S SHORT ENOUGH THAT YOU WON'T ACCIDENTALLY BE STICKING YOUR TAIL OUT OF THE WARP FIELD.

TERRIFIC.

JOEY, IF I DIE I WANT YOU TO KNOW THAT MY LAST WORDS WERE "JOEY SCREWED ME ON THIS ONE." I WANT YOU TO TELL EVERYONE, OKAY?

WOW.

...THIS IS REALLY DANGEROUS.

OKAY. WE'RE READY HERE.

PERFECT. WAIT FOR MY ORDER, COOPER. IF WE DROP IT TOO SOON THEY MIGHT STOP IN TIME.

GOT IT. LET'S NOT WAIT TOO LONG, OKAY? IT LOOKS LIKE THEY'RE ALMOST IN WEAPONS RAN--

THEY'VE OPENED FIRE!!

ALRIGHT COOPER, SO YOU MAY BE SEEING SOME FIRE COMING YOUR WAY. BUT THEY'RE FIRING AT US, NOT AT YOU. YOU SHOULD BE FINE, OKAY?

I, UM--

...OKAY?

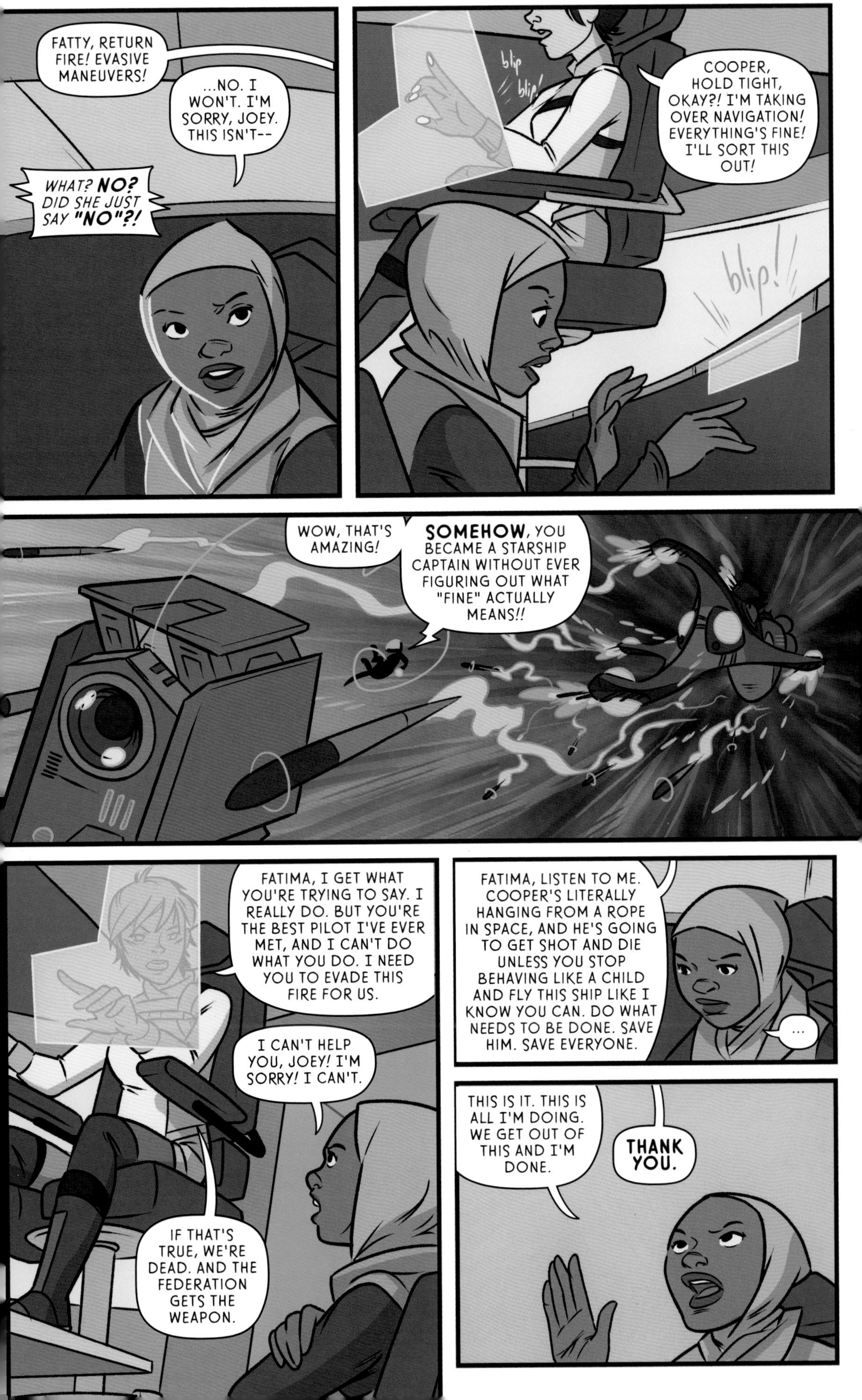
FATTY, RETURN FIRE! EVASIVE MANEUVERS!
...NO. I WON'T. I'M SORRY, JOEY. THIS ISN'T--
WHAT? NO? DID SHE JUST SAY "NO"?!
blip
blip!
COOPER, HOLD TIGHT, OKAY?! I'M TAKING OVER NAVIGATION! EVERYTHING'S FINE! I'LL SORT THIS OUT!
blip!
WOW, THAT'S AMAZING!
SOMEHOW, YOU BECAME A STARSHIP CAPTAIN WITHOUT EVER FIGURING OUT WHAT "FINE" ACTUALLY MEANS!!
FATIMA, I GET WHAT YOU'RE TRYING TO SAY. I REALLY DO. BUT YOU'RE THE BEST PILOT I'VE EVER MET, AND I CAN'T DO WHAT YOU DO. I NEED YOU TO EVADE THIS FIRE FOR US.
I CAN'T HELP YOU, JOEY! I'M SORRY! I CAN'T.
IF THAT'S TRUE, WE'RE DEAD. AND THE FEDERATION GETS THE WEAPON.
FATIMA, LISTEN TO ME. COOPER'S LITERALLY HANGING FROM A ROPE IN SPACE, AND HE'S GOING TO GET SHOT AND DIE UNLESS YOU STOP BEHAVING LIKE A CHILD AND FLY THIS SHIP LIKE I KNOW YOU CAN. DO WHAT NEEDS TO BE DONE. SAVE HIM. SAVE EVERYONE.
...
THIS IS IT. THIS IS ALL I'M DOING. WE GET OUT OF THIS AND I'M DONE.
THANK YOU.

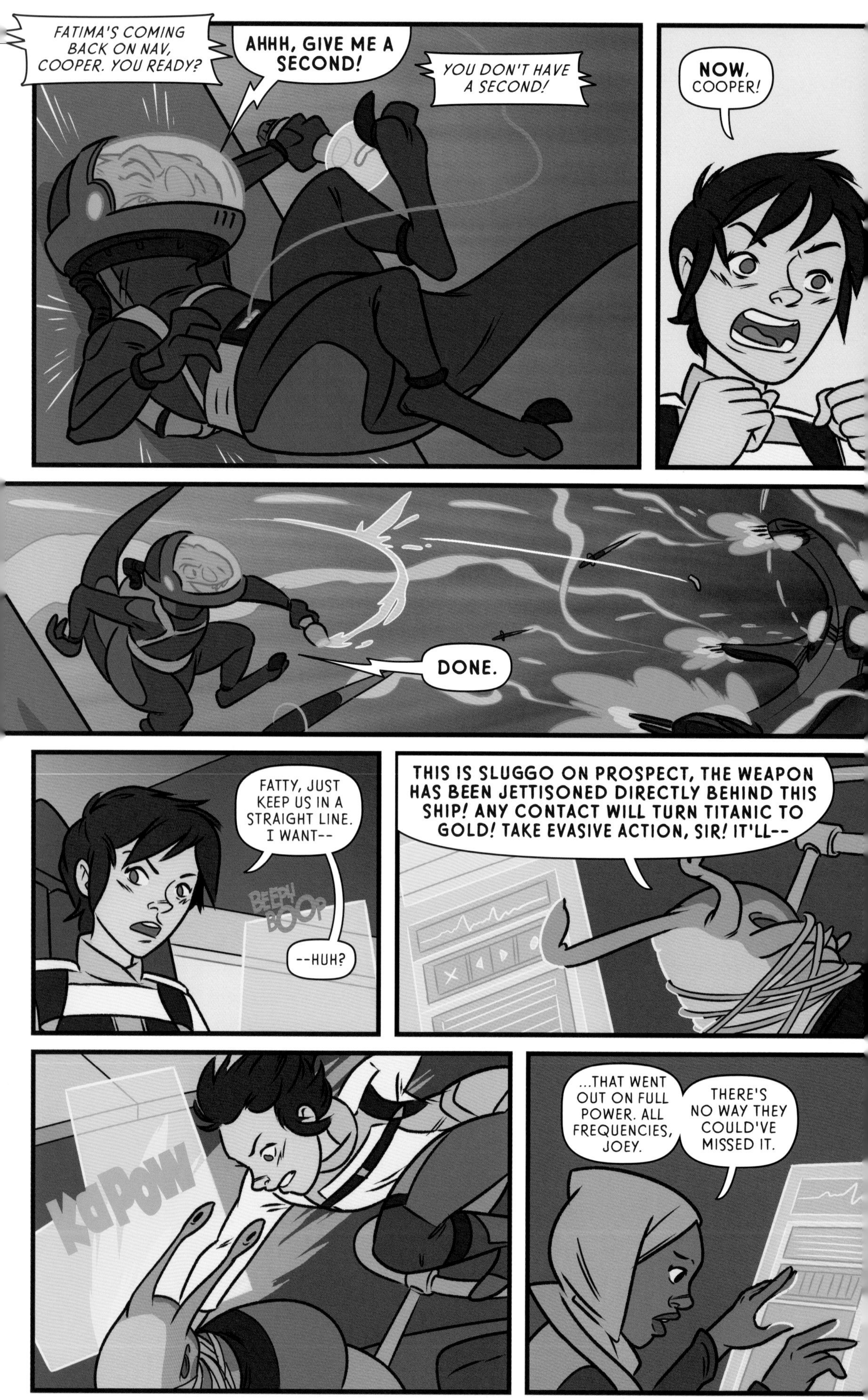
FATIMA'S COMING BACK ON NAV, COOPER. YOU READY?
AHHH, GIVE ME A SECOND!
YOU DON'T HAVE A SECOND!
NOW, COOPER!
DONE.
FATTY, JUST KEEP US IN A STRAIGHT LINE. I WANT--
BEEPH BOOP
--HUH?
THIS IS SLUGGO ON PROSPECT, THE WEAPON HAS BEEN JETTISONED DIRECTLY BEHIND THIS SHIP! ANY CONTACT WILL TURN TITANIC TO GOLD! TAKE EVASIVE ACTION, SIR! IT'LL--
KAPOW
...THAT WENT OUT ON FULL POWER. ALL FREQUENCIES, JOEY.
THERE'S NO WAY THEY COULD'VE MISSED IT.

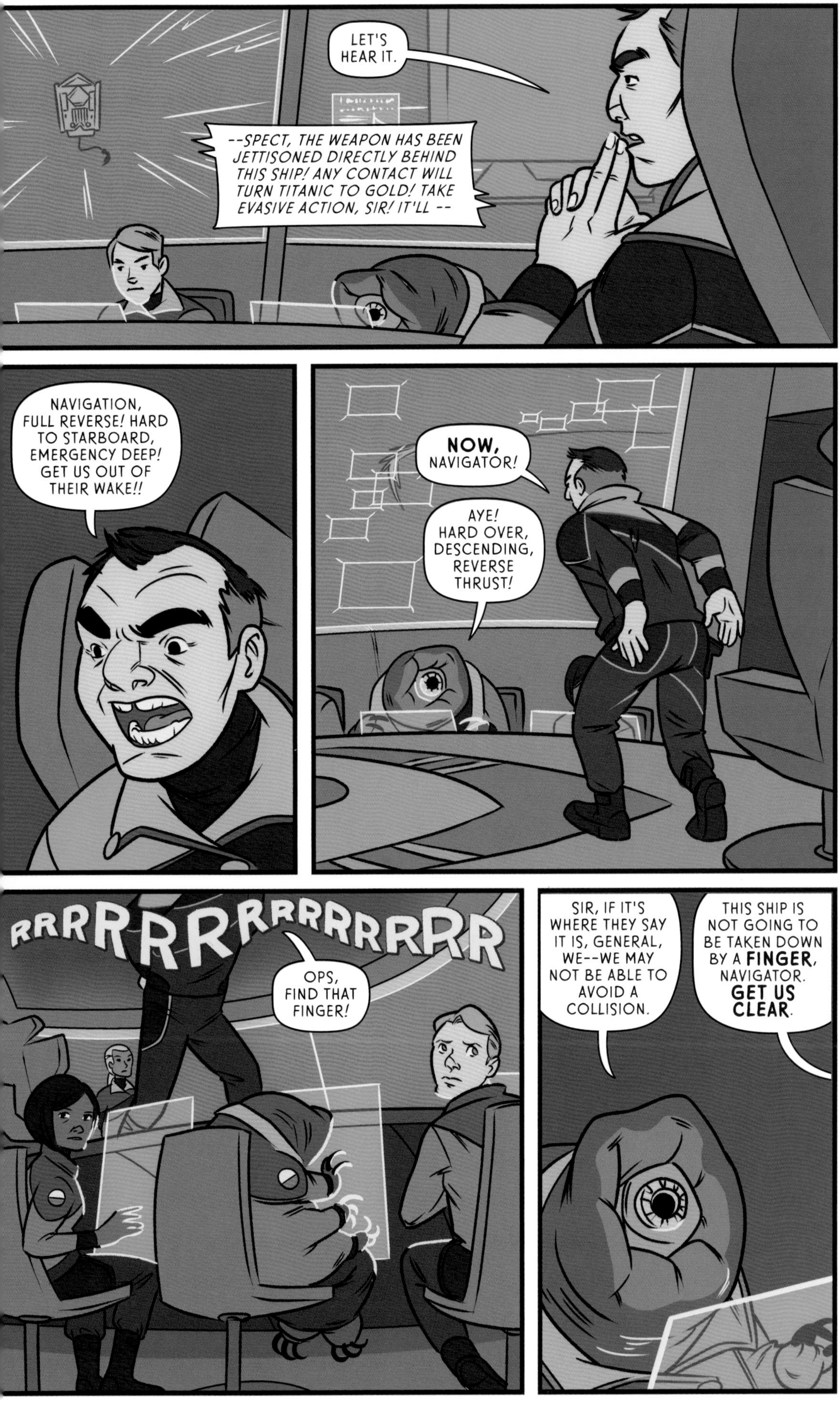
LET'S HEAR IT.
--SPECT, THE WEAPON HAS BEEN JETTISONED DIRECTLY BEHIND THIS SHIP! ANY CONTACT WILL TURN TITANIC TO GOLD! TAKE EVASIVE ACTION, SIR! IT'LL --
NAVIGATION, FULL REVERSE! HARD TO STARBOARD, EMERGENCY DEEP! GET US OUT OF THEIR WAKE!!
NOW, NAVIGATOR!
AYE! HARD OVER, DESCENDING, REVERSE THRUST!
RRRRRRRRRRRRRRR
OPS, FIND THAT FINGER!
SIR, IF IT'S WHERE THEY SAY IT IS, GENERAL, WE--WE MAY NOT BE ABLE TO AVOID A COLLISION.
THIS SHIP IS NOT GOING TO BE TAKEN DOWN BY A FINGER, NAVIGATOR. GET US CLEAR.

OPS... FOUND IT, FOUND IT!

WELL?! FIRE!!

USE CANNONFIRE, BULLETS WILL JUST BREAK IT UP!

COORDINATES PASSED TO WEAPONS.

AYE, FIRING CANNONS!

SIR, I'M HAVING TROUBLE TARGETING. OUR SYSTEMS WEREN'T DESIGNED FOR SOMETHING THIS SMALL, THIS CLOSE.

AIM MANUALLY, DAMN IT! KNOCK THAT FINGER OUT OF THE WAY!!

AYE!

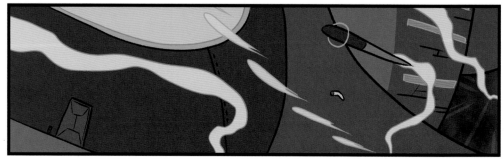

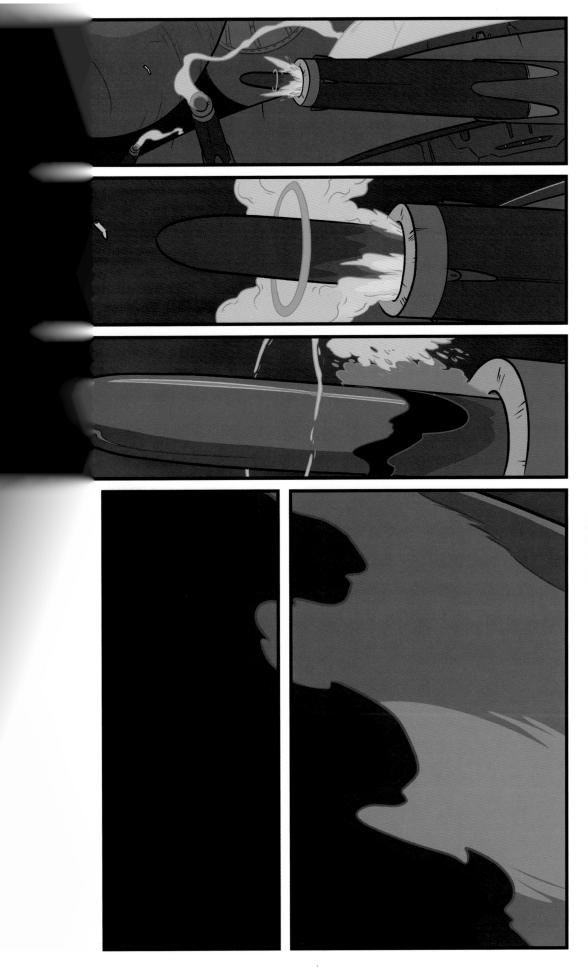

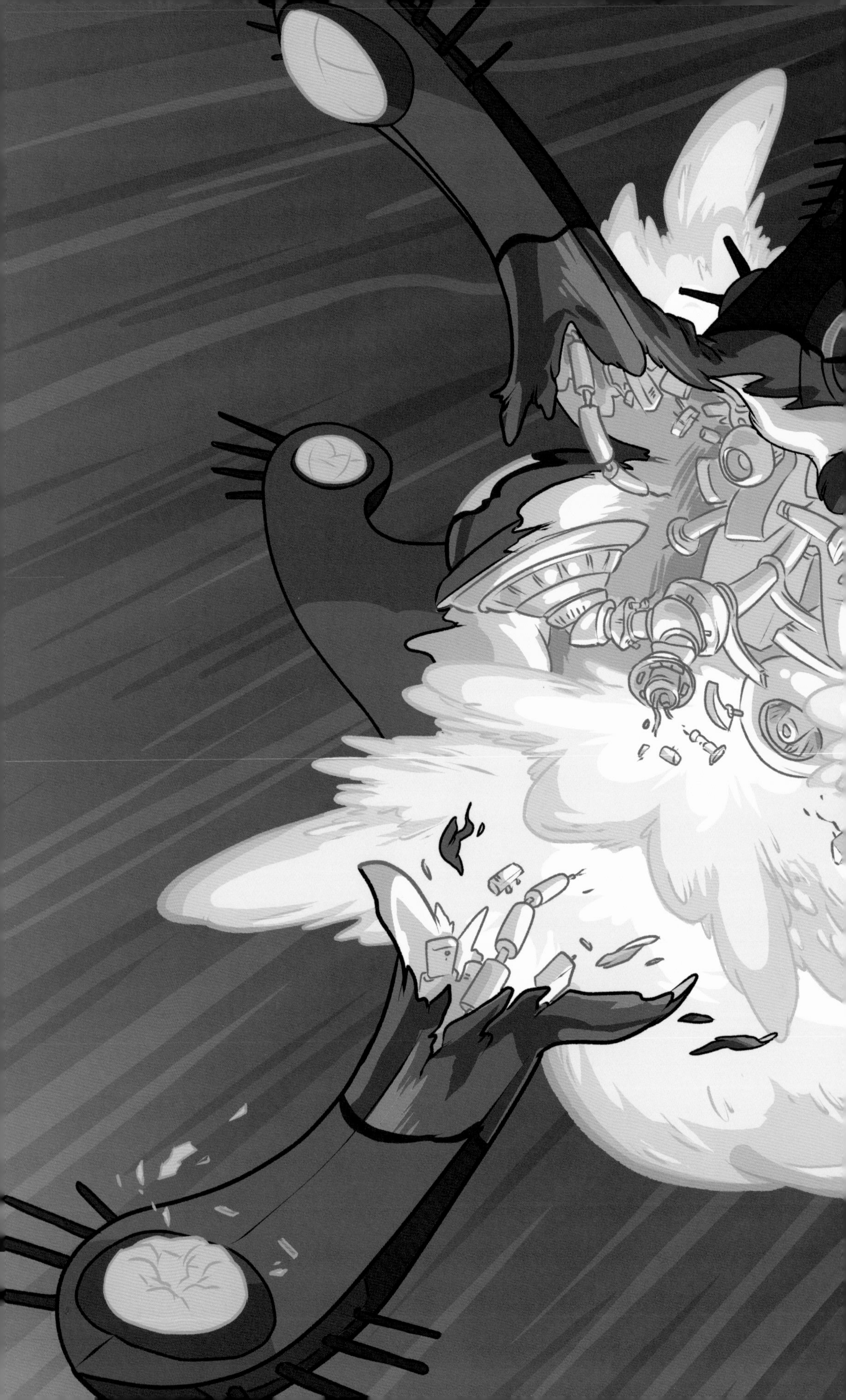

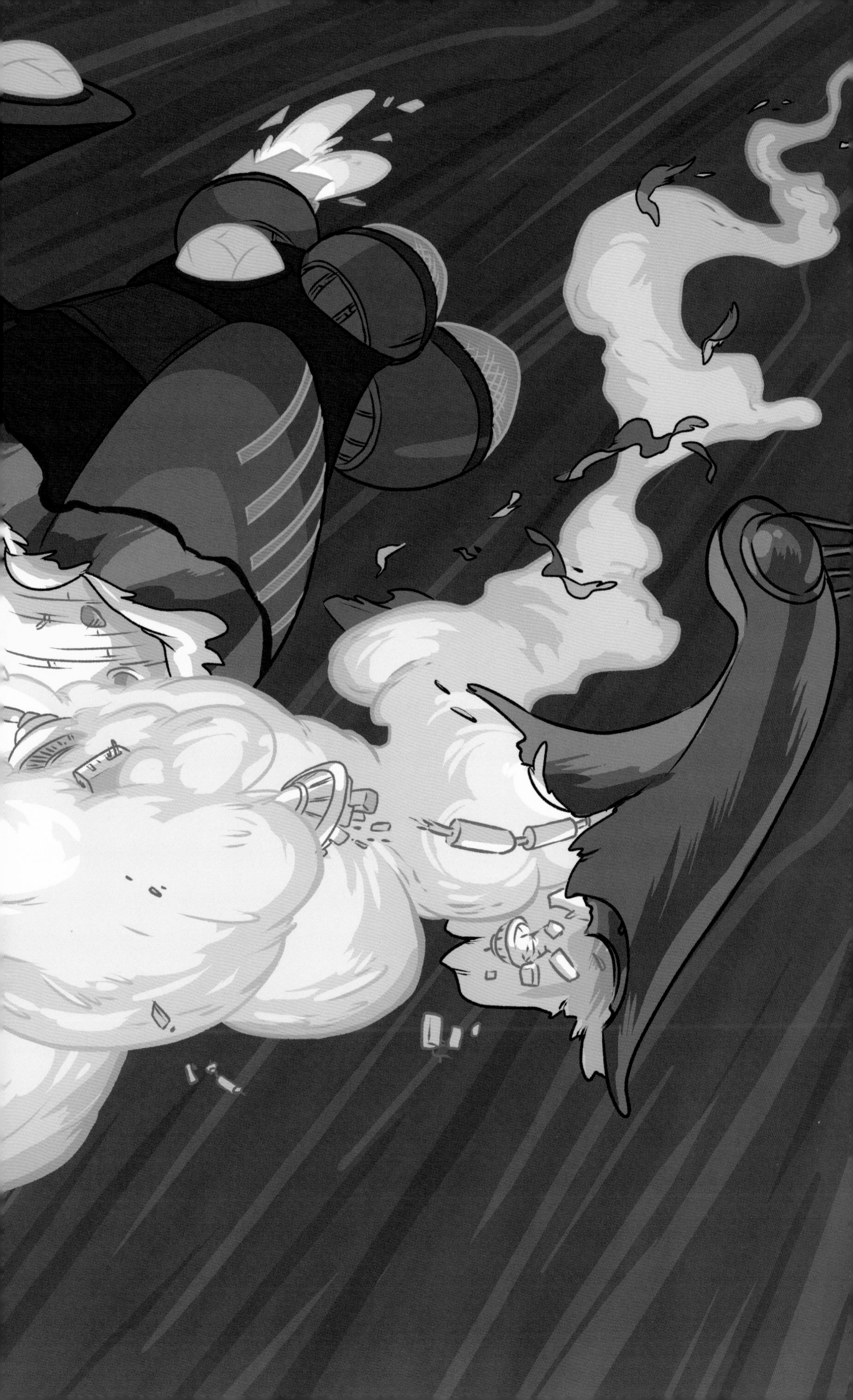

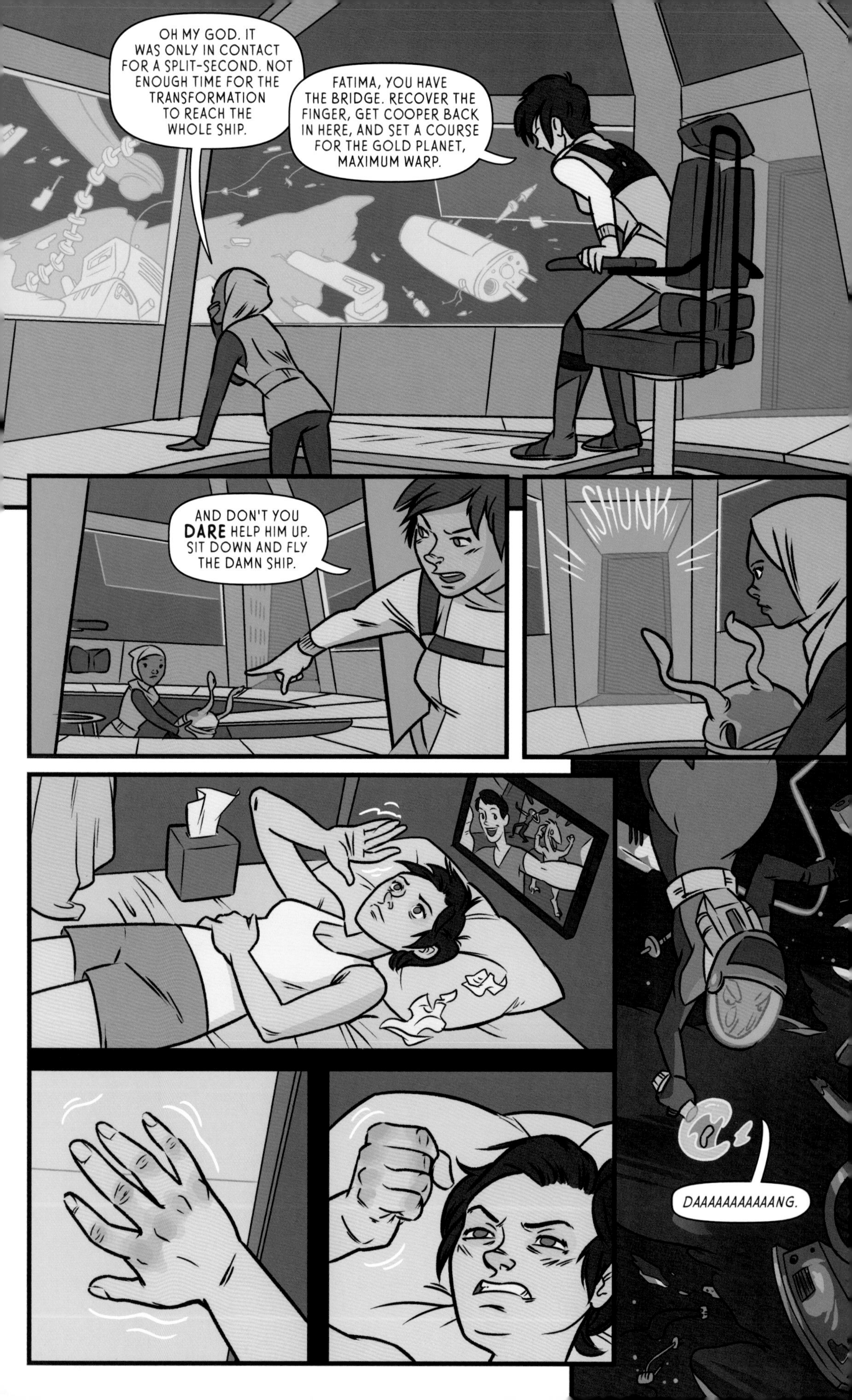
OH MY GOD. IT WAS ONLY IN CONTACT FOR A SPLIT-SECOND. NOT ENOUGH TIME FOR THE TRANSFORMATION TO REACH THE WHOLE SHIP.
FATIMA, YOU HAVE THE BRIDGE. RECOVER THE FINGER, GET COOPER BACK IN HERE, AND SET A COURSE FOR THE GOLD PLANET, MAXIMUM WARP.
AND DON'T YOU **DARE** HELP HIM UP. SIT DOWN AND FLY THE DAMN SHIP.
SHUNK
DAAAAAAAAAAAANG.

"SCREW IT AND SCREW THEM. **LET'S DO IT.** LET'S SAVE EVERYONE."

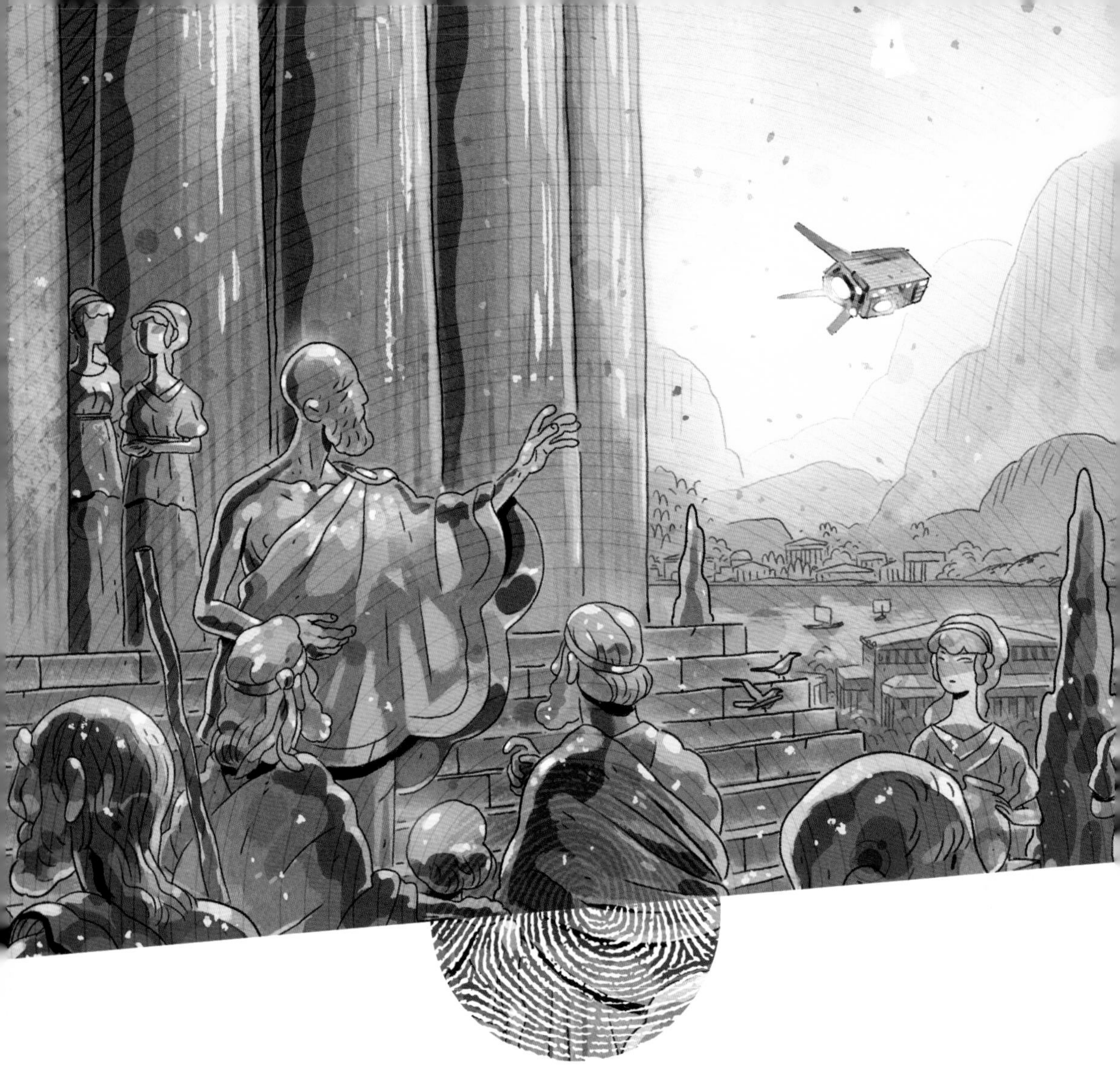

COVER
GALLERY

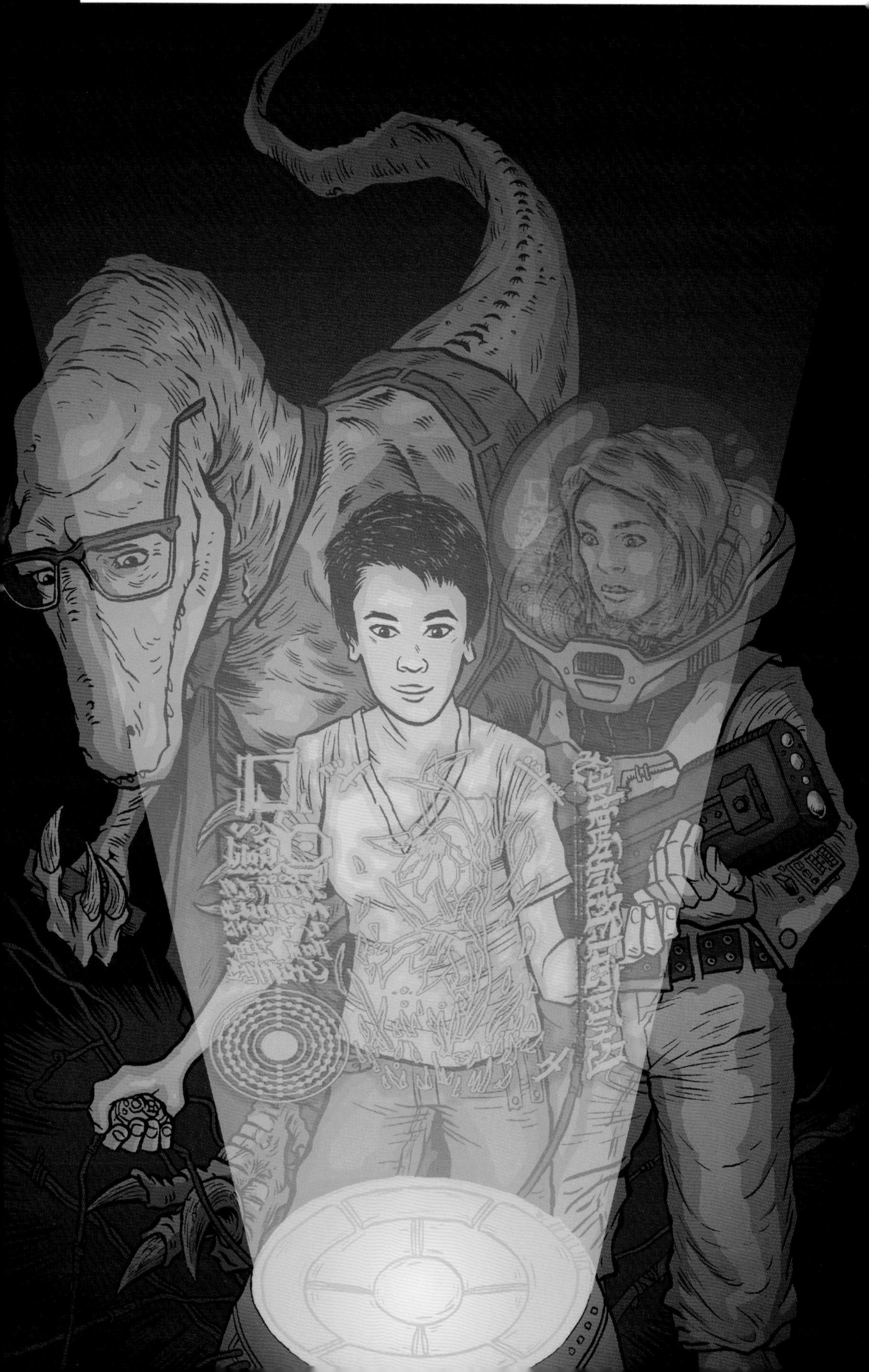

ISSUE ONE VARIANT **EMILY PARTRIDGE**

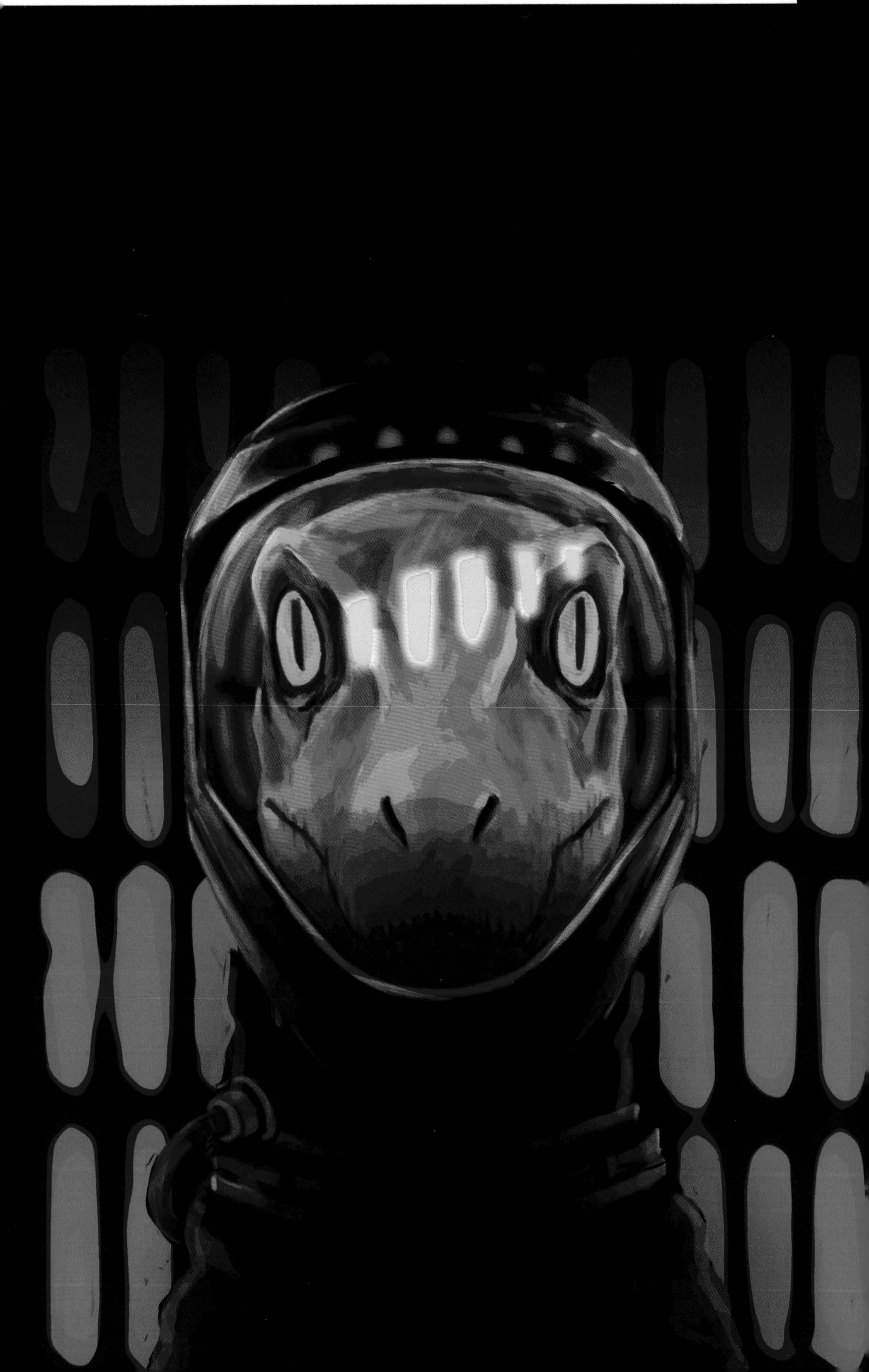

ISSUE ONE VARIANT **NOELLE STEVENSON**

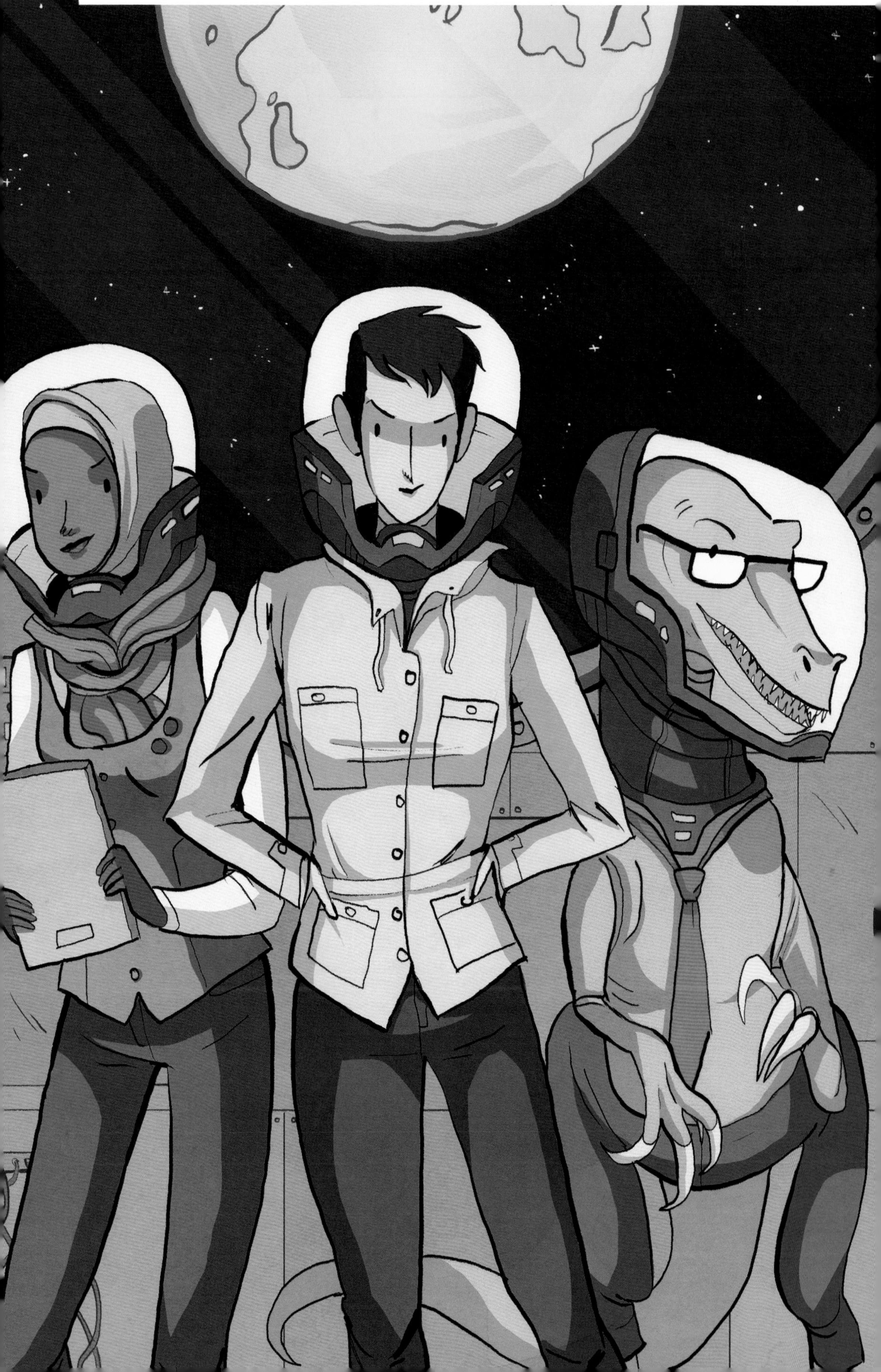

ISSUE ONE WRITER'S VARIANT **BROOKE A. ALLEN**

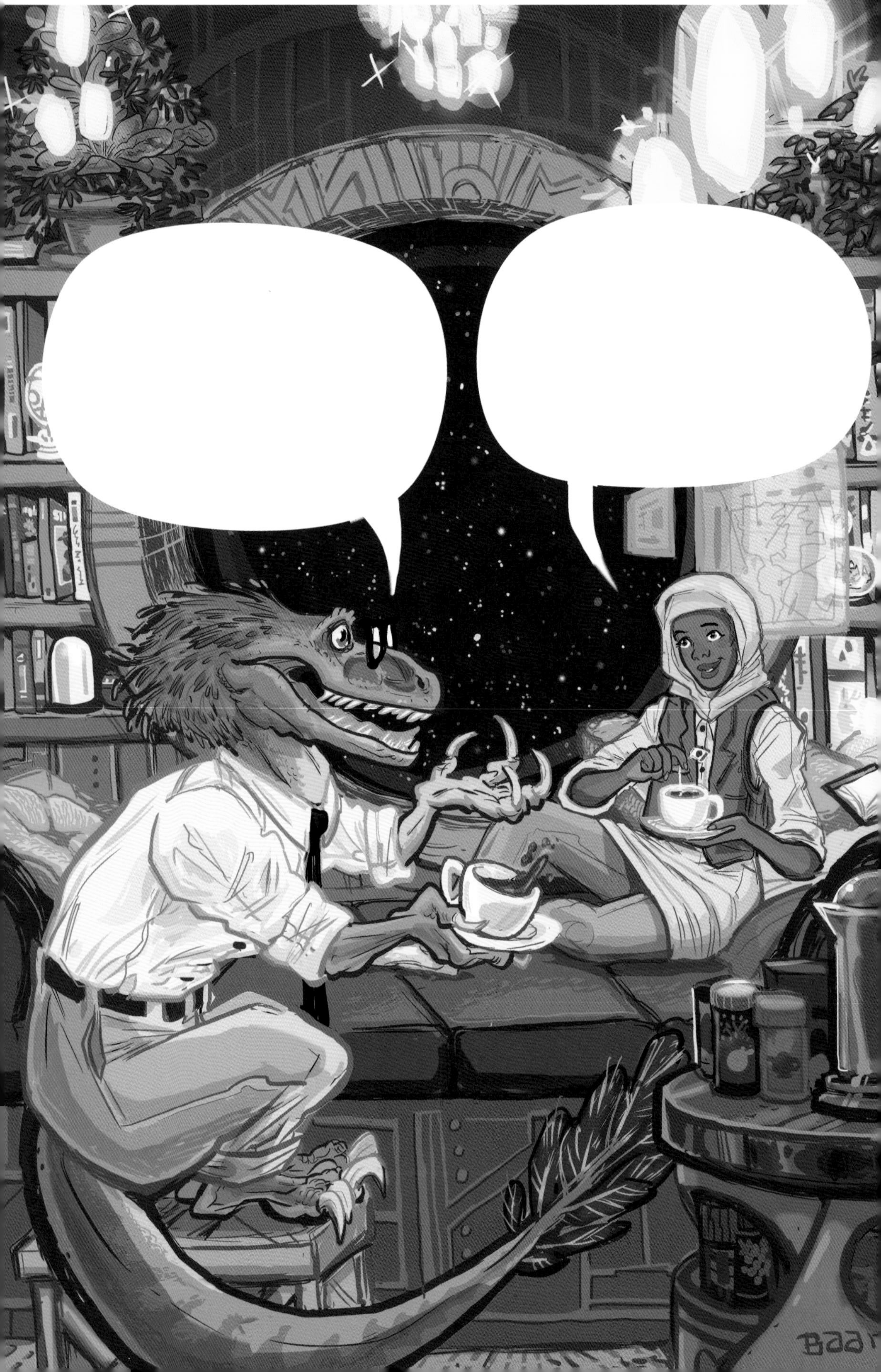

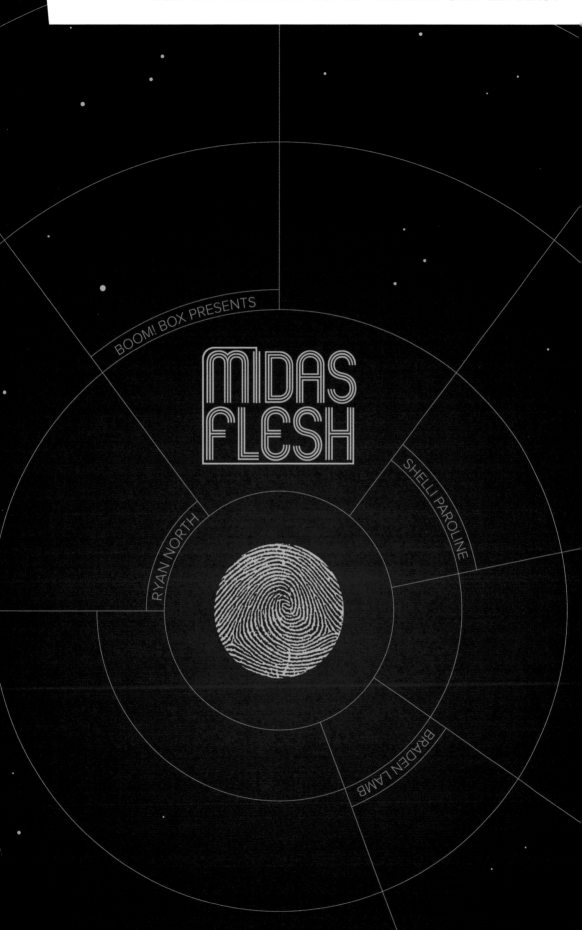

ISSUE ONE EMERALD CITY COMICON EXCLUSIVE **CHIP ZDARKSY**

BOOM! BOX PRESENTS

MIDAS FLESH

RYAN NORTH

SHELLI PAROLINE

BRADEN LAMB

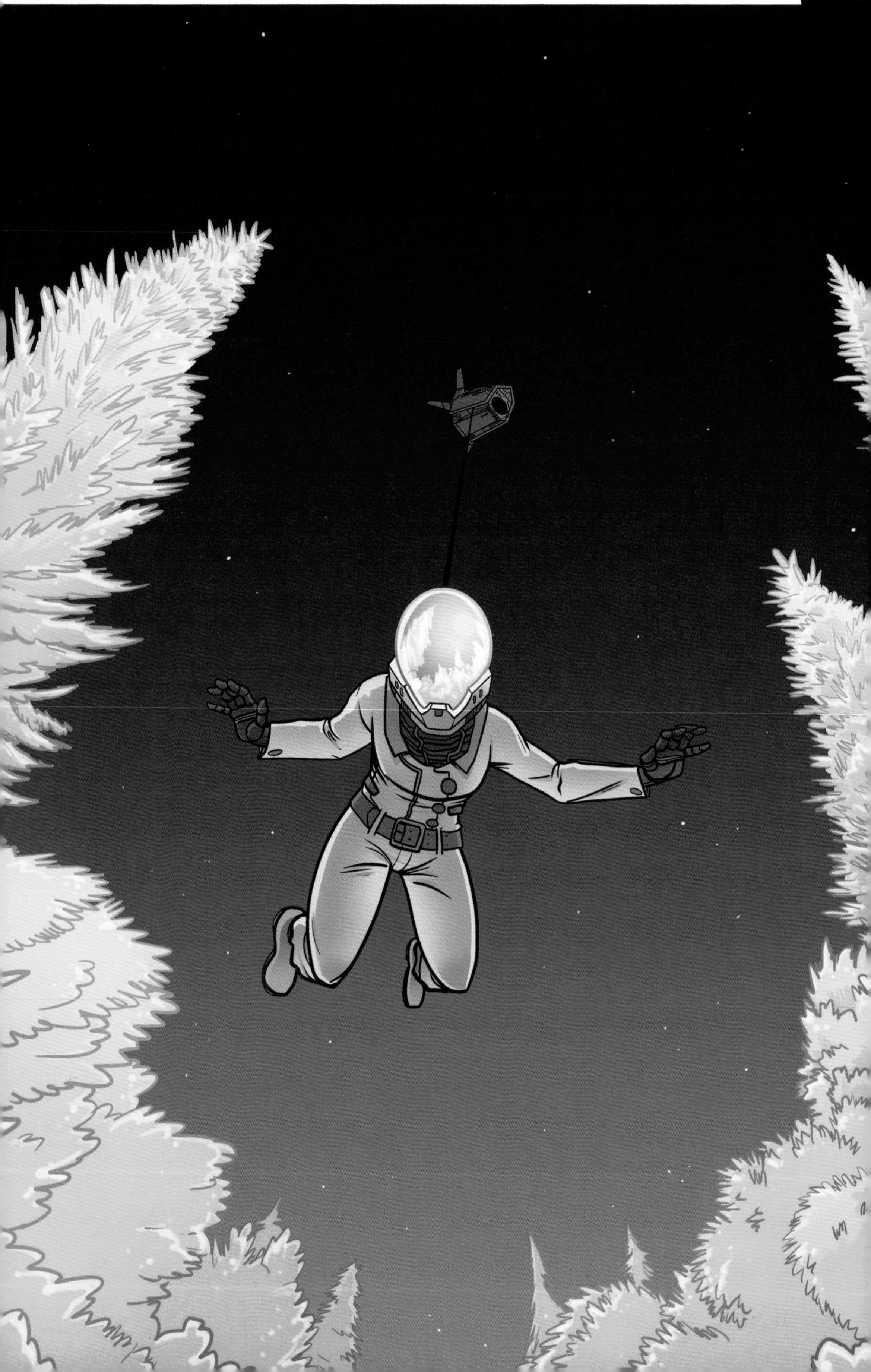

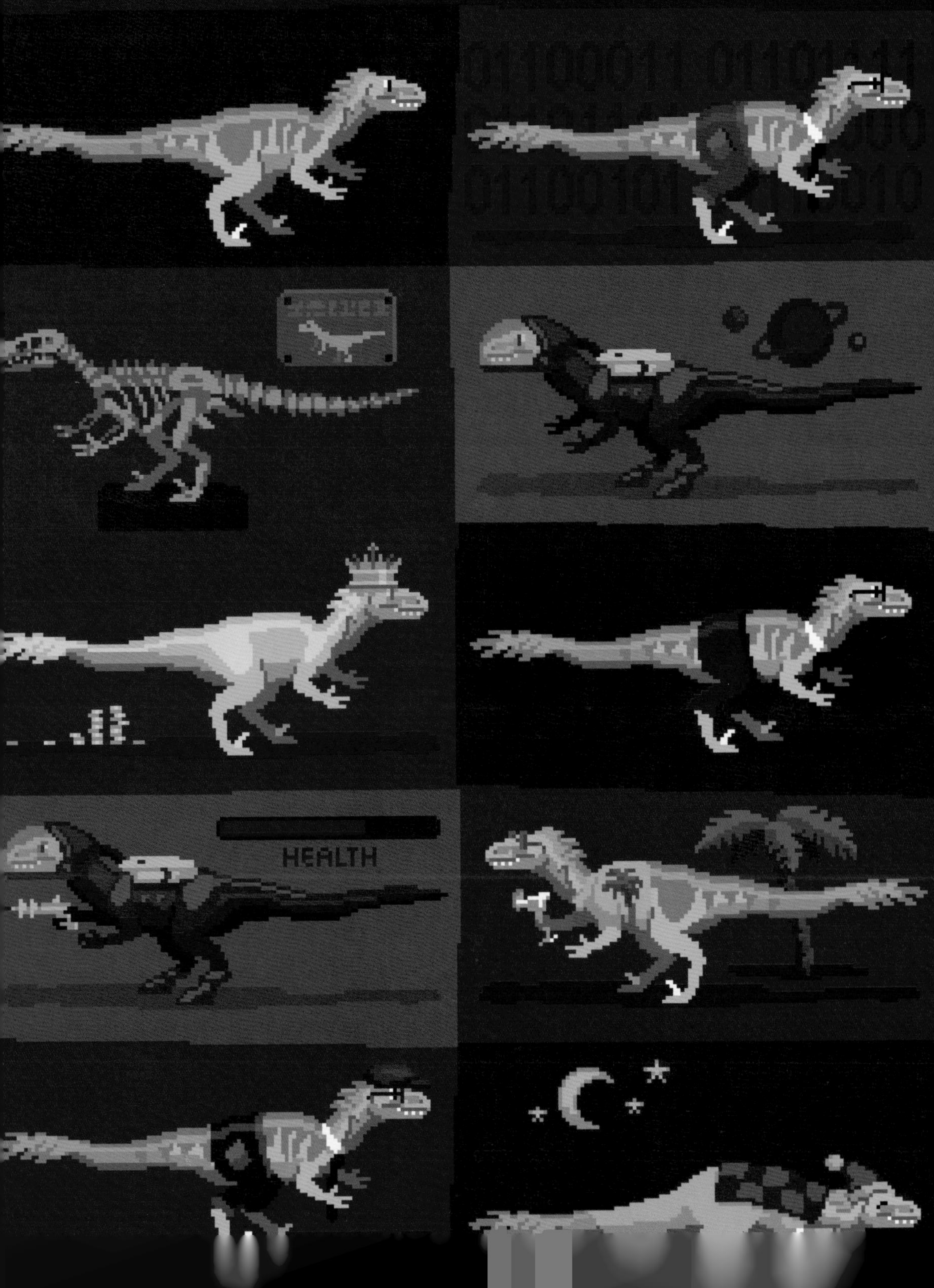
HEALTH

ISSUE ONE BOOM! EXCLUSIVE **STEPHANIE GONZAGA**

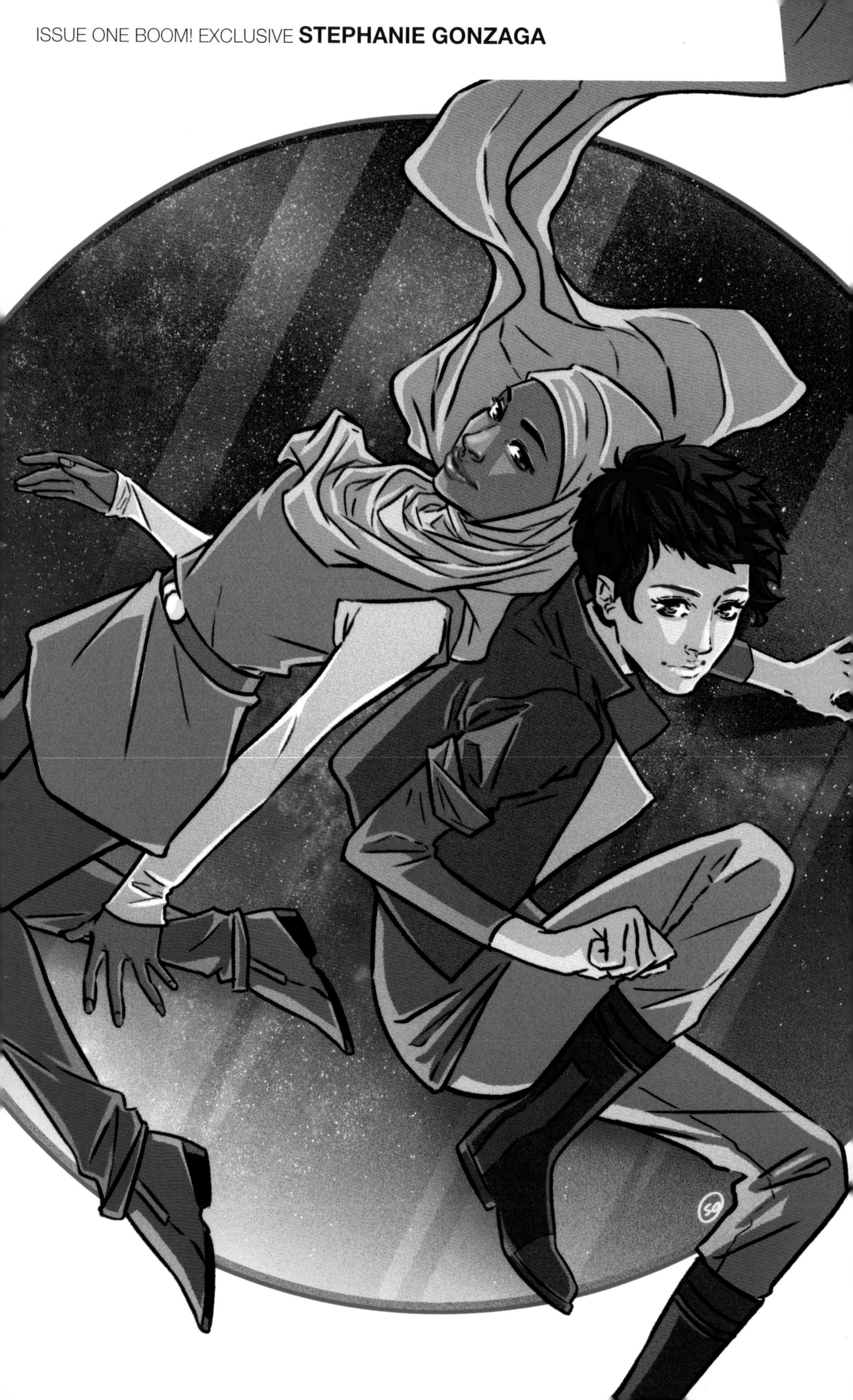

ISSUE ONE SECOND PRINT **JESS FINK**

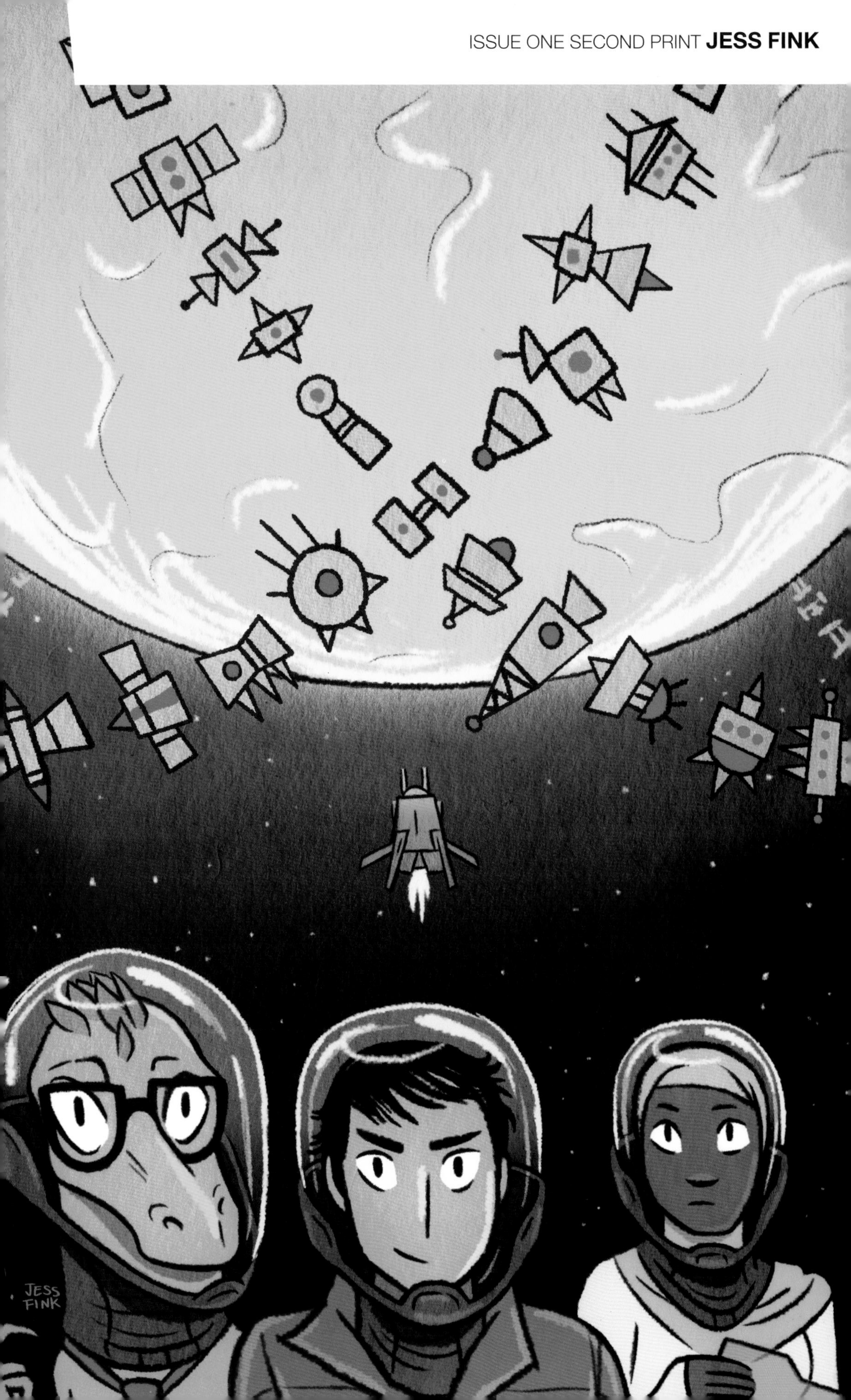
JESS FINK

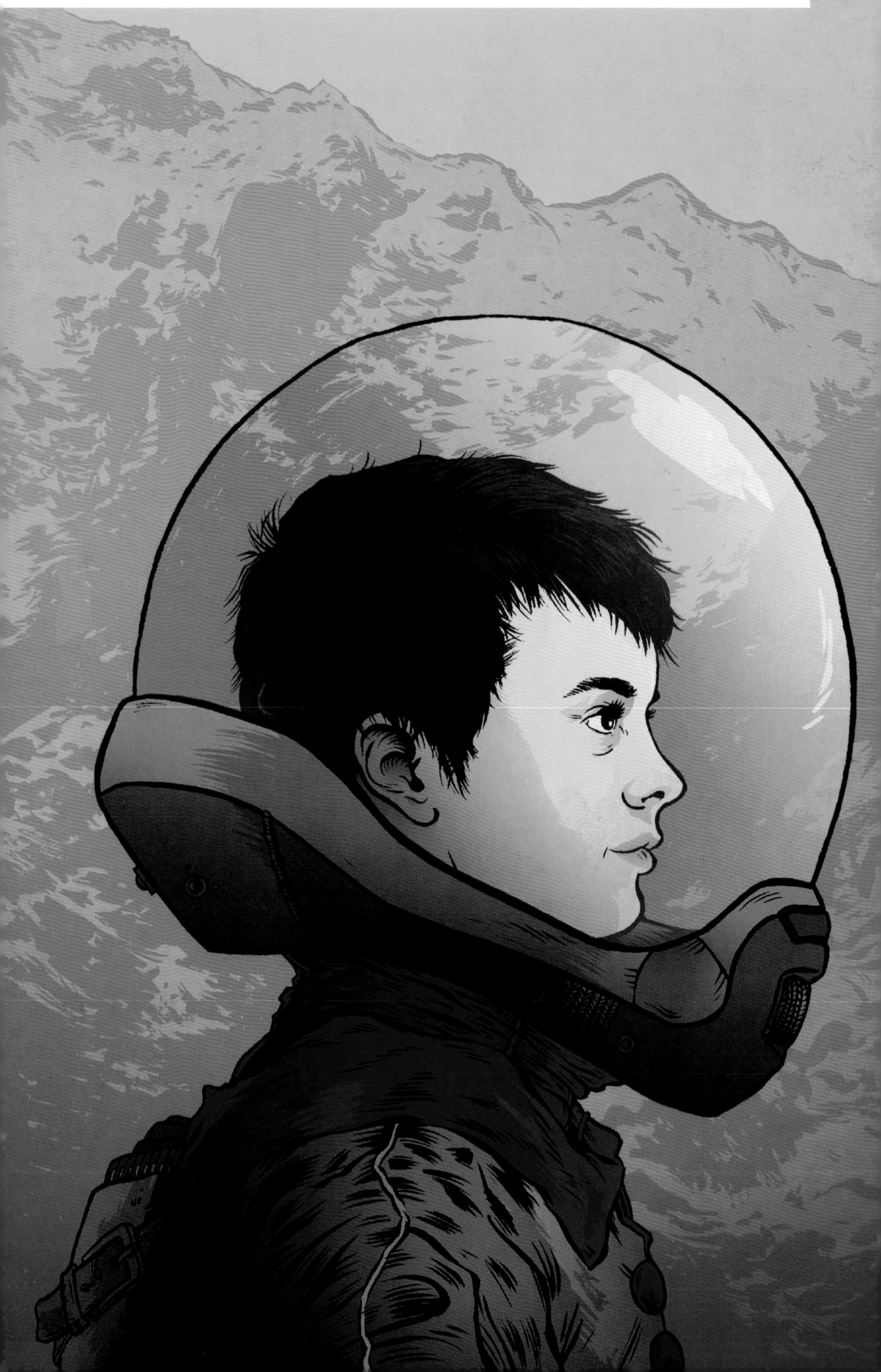

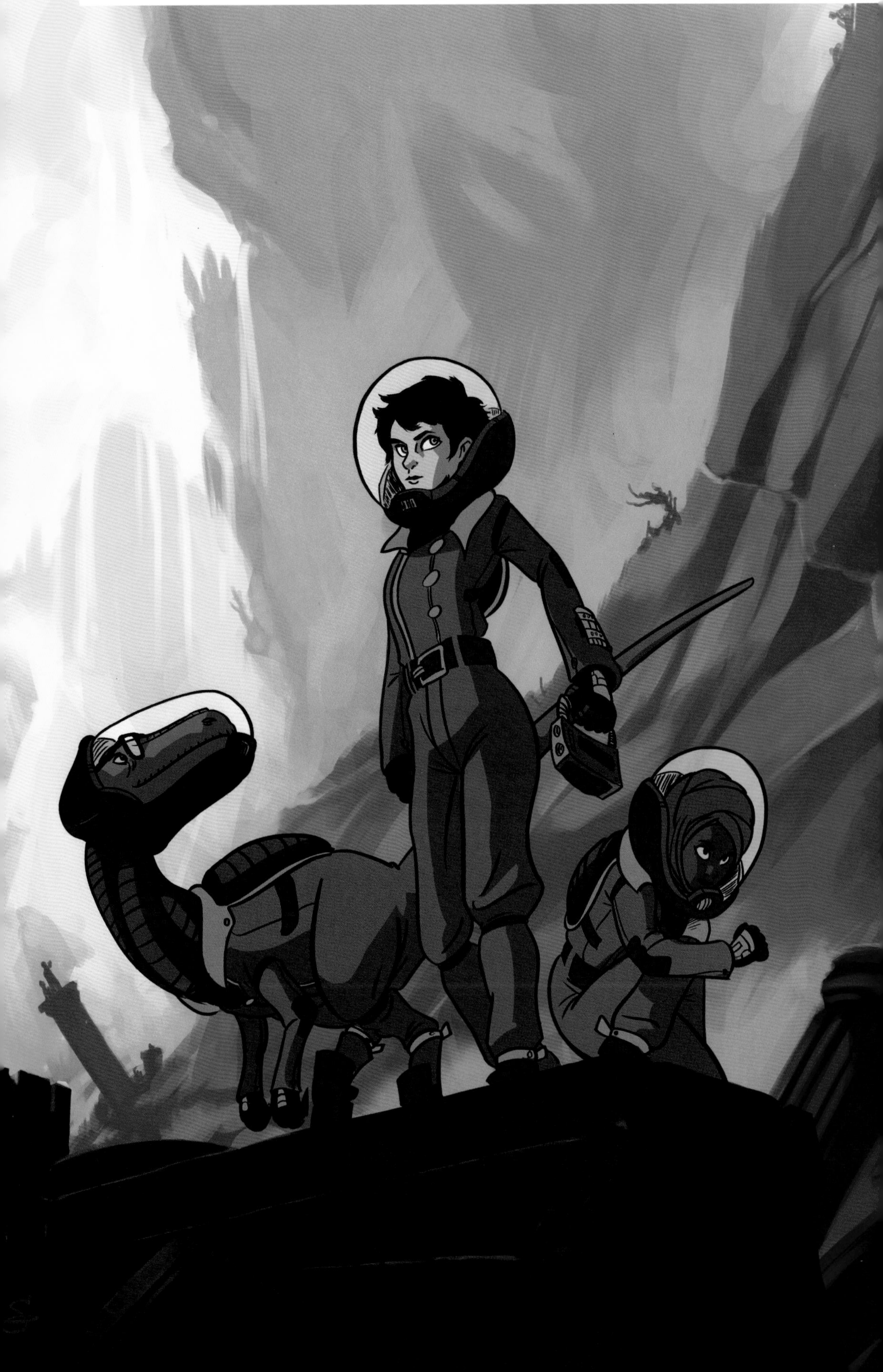

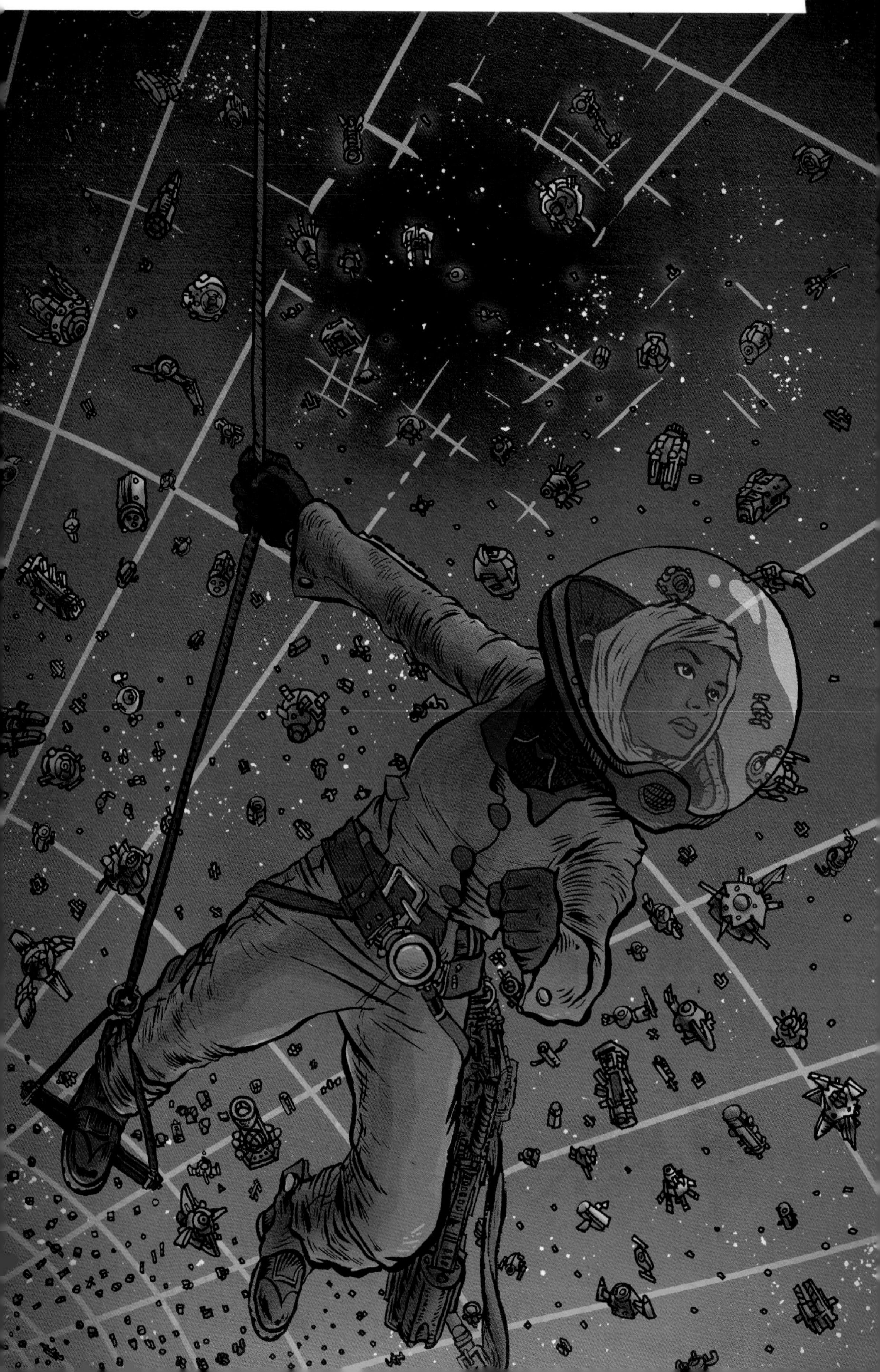

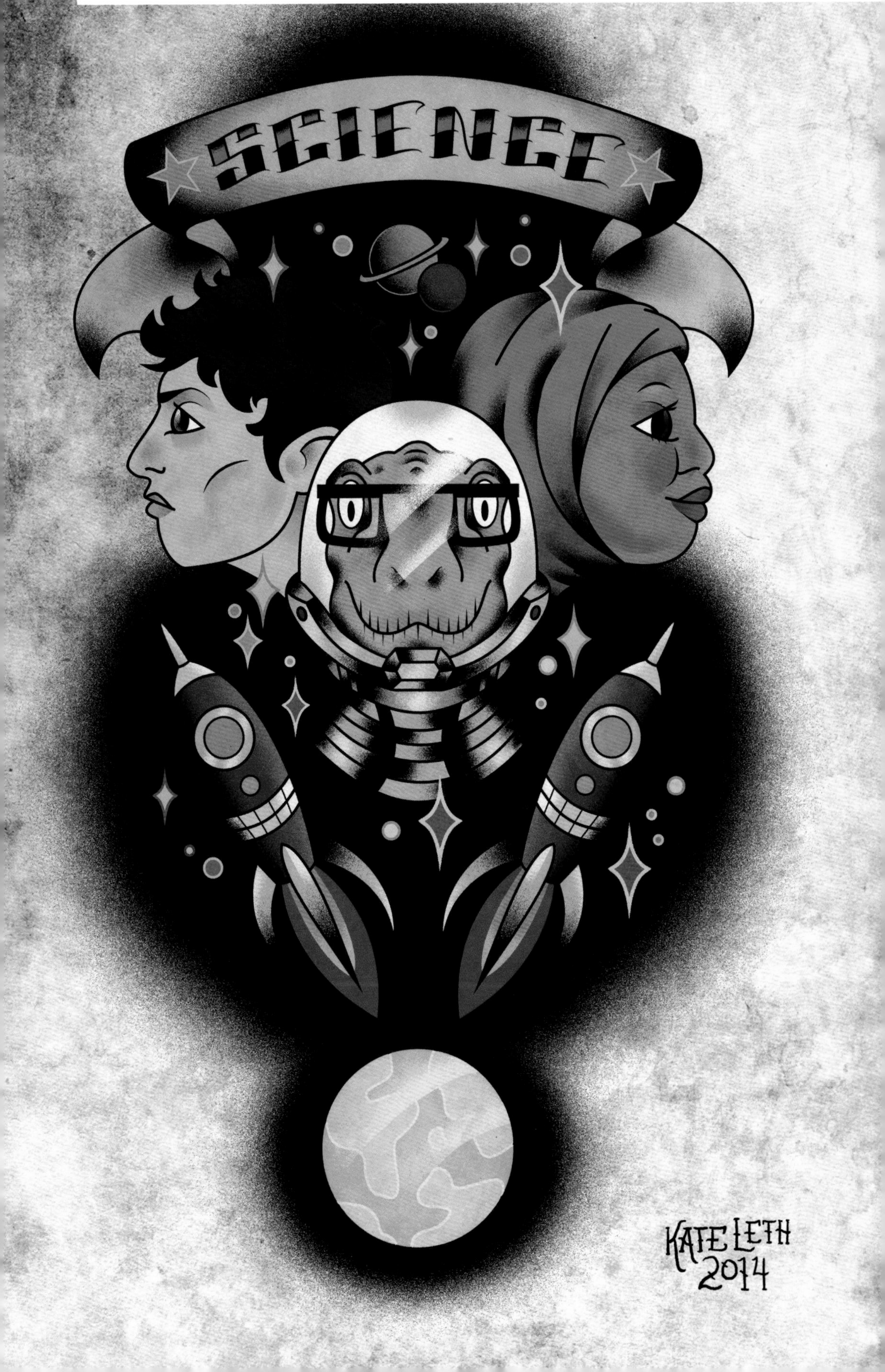
SCIENCE
KATE LETH
2014

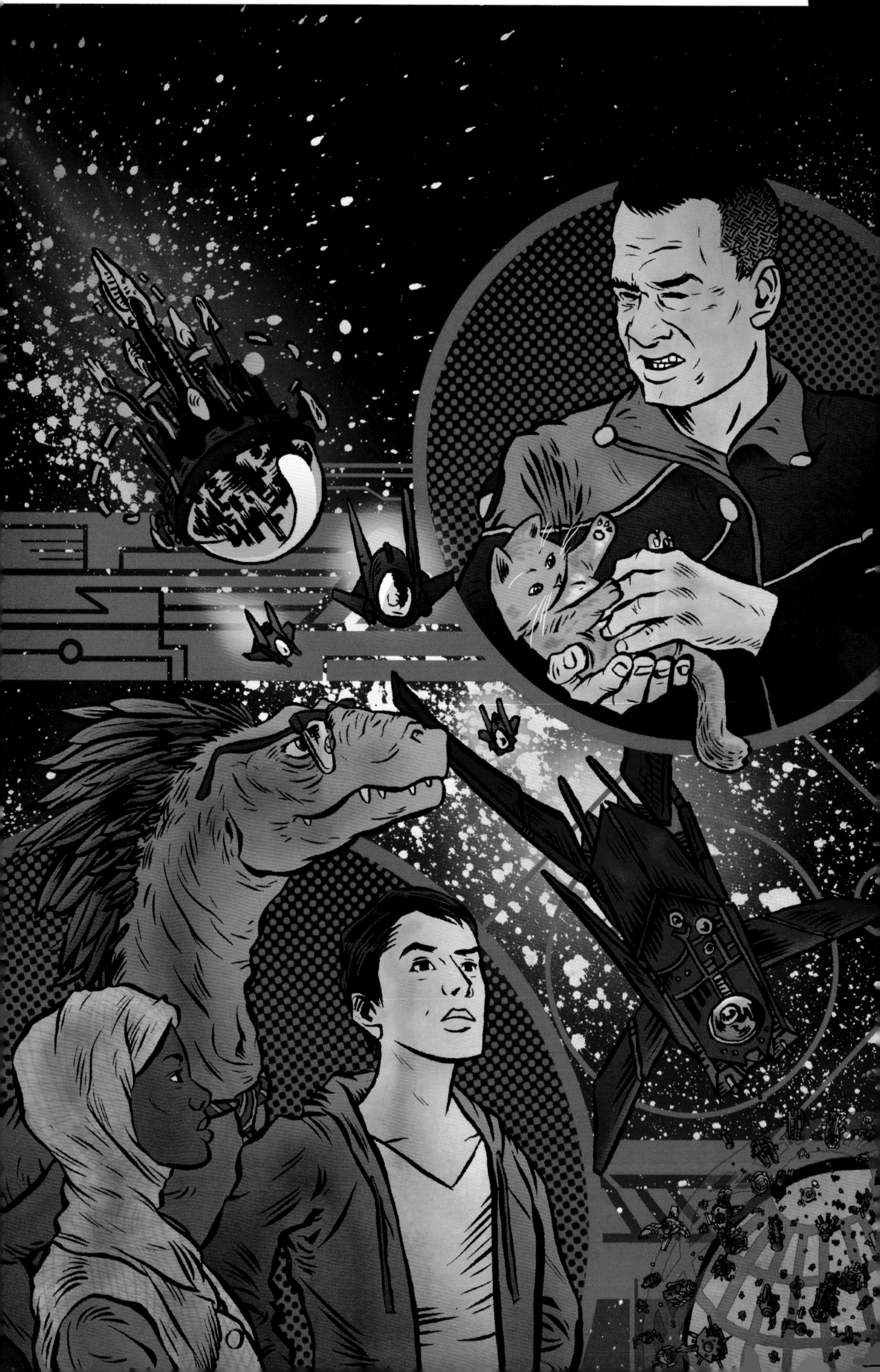

ISSUE FOUR VARIANT **SAM BOSMA**

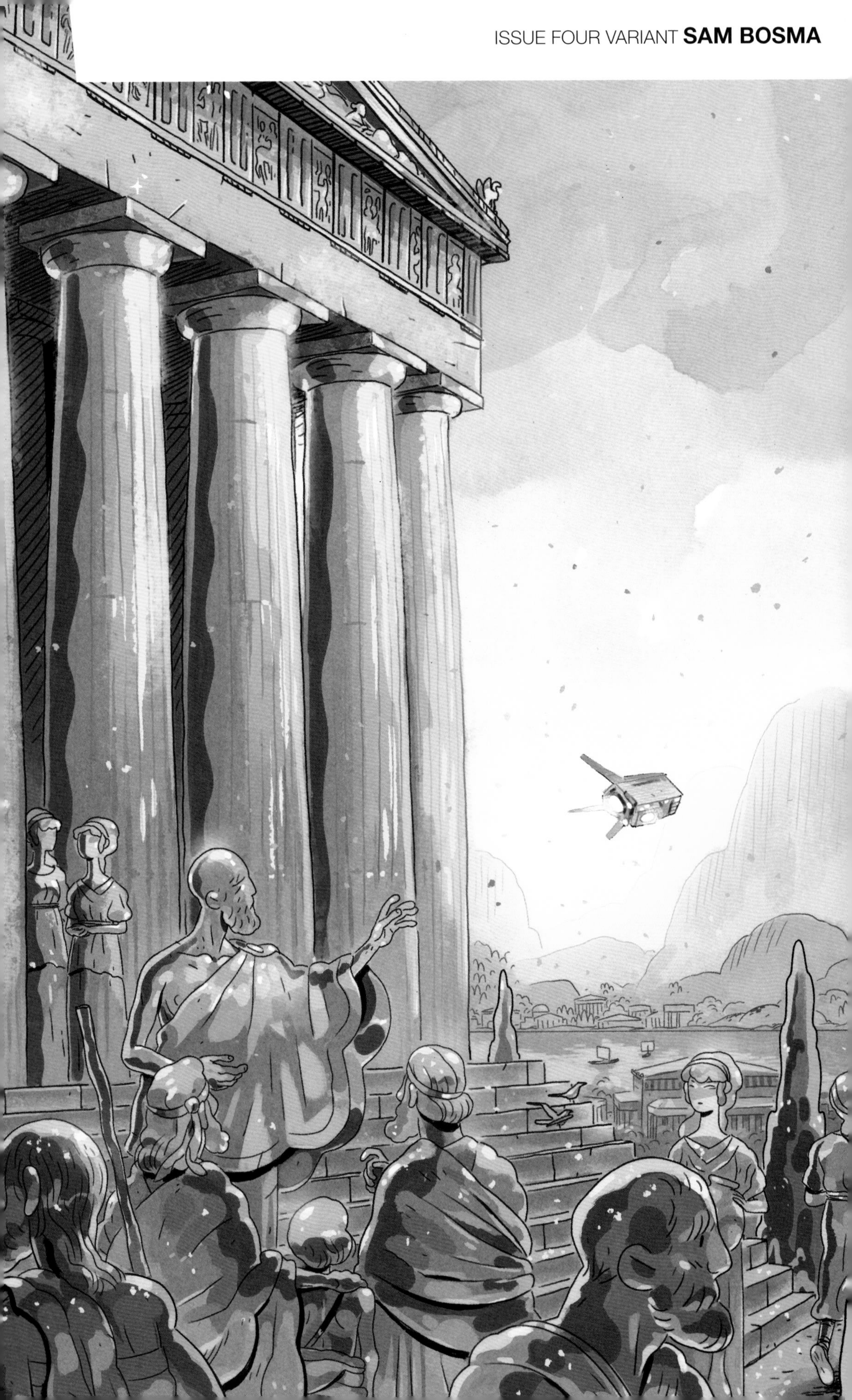

THE MIDAS FLESH
ORIGINS

WITH AN ESSAY FROM **RYAN NORTH**
AND CONCEPT ART FROM **SHELLI PAROLINE,
BRADEN LAMB, & JOHN KEOGH**

ORIGINAL COOPER, JOEY, AND FATTY CHARACTER DESIGNS BY JOHN KEOGH